Play Like You Mean It

Play Like You Mean It

Passion, Laughs, and Leadership in the World's Most Beautiful Game

REX RYAN

with Don Yaeger

DOUBLEDAY

NEW YORK LONDON TORONTO SYDNEY AUCKLAND

All rights reserved. Published in the United States by Doubleday,
a division of Random House, Inc., New York, and in Canada by
Random House of Canada Limited, Toronto.

www.doubleday.com

DOUBLEDAY and the portrayal of an anchor with a dolphin are
registered trademarks of Random House, Inc.

Book design by Tina Henderson

Cataloging-in-Publication Data is on file with the
Library of Congress.

ISBN 978-0-385-53444-4

PRINTED IN THE UNITED STATES OF AMERICA

10 9 8 7 6 5 4 3 2 1

First Edition

To my father, Buddy, who taught me so much about football . . . and taught me how important it was to love the game. I am where I am today because of you.

And to all the coaches and players who I've been so fortunate to work with so far in my career. Your combined talents have allowed me to enjoy a career that is greater than anything I could have imagined.

— RR

To Danny Jordan, a mentor in every sense of the word. Thank you for making me better every day.

— DY

Contents

1. 2010 . . . A Wild Ride

On January 24, 2010, I looked up from the sidelines at Lucas Oil Stadium and watched the clock tick down to 0:00. The hard realization set in: Our 2009 season, my rookie season as head coach of the New York Jets, was over. The Indianapolis Colts had won the AFC Championship. Losing is brutal—I don't think anyone can deny that. But some losses, well, they burn a little deeper. As 63,000 fans cheered for the Colts, and their players started putting on their championship hats and T-shirts, I jogged to the middle of the field to shake Jim Caldwell's hand with only two things on my mind: 1) Damn . . . Peyton beat me again; and 2) When do I get another shot at him?

Losing in the AFC Championship was tough enough, but having Peyton Manning take a second Super Bowl ring from me just pissed me off. In 2006, when I was the defensive coordinator with the Baltimore Ravens, we got beat by the Colts in the playoffs. The whole thing just haunts me. Wait, let me rephrase that. *Peyton Manning* haunts me. In my opinion, simply winning isn't enough. You have to win against the best, and Peyton Manning is the best. Now, don't get me wrong, we deserved to lose that 2009 AFC Championship Game. We were outmanned, injuries killing us all over the field during the second half. And no one knows how to abuse your weakness quite like Peyton. But to watch our season end on that note was frustrating, and the only way I knew how to deal with that frustration was to let it drive me. That's why my first instinct was to imagine how we were going to beat Peyton the next time around . . . and to envision the Jets, if only in my mind, playing the Colts in the playoffs again.

My moment to mourn was short and sweet, because the second my hand left Caldwell's, the 2010 season began and we were 0-0.

Setting the tone with my Jets in that postgame locker room speech was a huge step toward a new season. Fortunately, it took very little effort. I just went in, was true to myself, and told them exactly what I believed. I told them that the fastest way to kick ourselves in the ass was to go into 2010 with the assumption that we were going to make it to the AFC Championship Game. From that point on, every team was on a level playing field. There were no guarantees. We knew what it felt like to be right there and lose it. That would make us hungrier. We wanted to take it all. I told them to strive to get a home game in the 2010 playoffs. I said let's play for it again, let's win it, and let's do it in our city, at our stadium, in front of our fans. I wanted them to wear their Jets gear and be proud. We finished in the top four in the NFL, we turned an underdog team into an AFC title contender, and we earned the respect and support of the people in New York. I mean, they lit up the Empire State Building green and white the week of the AFC Championship Game. If that didn't make my players proud to be Jets, then they shouldn't be on this team.

The future, I told them right there in the belly of that stadium, came with a challenge. I told the coaches and the players that I was challenging each of them, and myself, to find a way for us to get better. I didn't know how it was going to happen, but we were going to find a way for each of us to get a little bit better. I knew as a team we were going to have to make some roster improvements. We had to get better in the corner and better in the back end. I also knew it was crucial for us to get a closer as a pass rusher. We needed someone who could close out guys so I wouldn't have to blitz every snap.

Coming out of that game and going into the off-season, we went right at those weaknesses to prepare for 2010. We signed Jason Taylor and Antonio Cromartie as free agents. We drafted Joe McKnight, who could help us in both the running and passing game; Kyle Wilson, who I know will be a dynamic player down the road; John Conner, who is an outstanding fullback; and Vladimir Ducasse, who is a dynamite player on the field. We also ended up getting LaDainian Tomlinson, Santonio Holmes, Nick Folk, and Trevor Pryce. We were determined to do everything we could to improve in every way possible. We even picked up Mark Brunell, an 18-year veteran quarterback, who has turned out to be a fantastic mentor to Mark Sanchez.

Unfortunately, this business is all about give-and-take. So, as excited as I was to get such amazing guys before our 2010 season, I was equally upset to have to let some go. We released Alan Faneca, Thomas Jones, and Marques Douglas, who was one of my guys from Baltimore, and traded Leon Washington to Seattle. That is, by far, the worst part of my job. These guys are truly amazing players and people. If I had it my way I would keep everyone, but that's just not how it works in the NFL. Every decision is for the betterment of the team.

With a week or two to go before our 2010 season opener, I was feeling good. We were back in Florham Park after spending training camp at SUNY Cortland, we had officially decided on our 53-man roster, and we had settled some lingering contract negotiations. If you watched us on HBO's *Hard Knocks* at the beginning of the season, then I'm sure you're well aware that two of the contract negotiations I'm talking about were with our cornerback, Darrelle Revis, and our center, Nick Mangold. I'll get into further detail about this later in the book, but for now, let me just say that compared to the Revis situation, Mangold's contract was a breeze. Both of these players are great guys, but the way their situations played out was far different. Our owner, Woody Johnson, and our general manager, Mike Tannenbaum, approached Nick about a lucrative seven-year extension, and he signed two weeks later, making him the highest-paid center in the league. On the day he signed, I actually held him out of practice. I mean, we're talking about a lot of money here! The last thing he needed was to walk out there and fall in a hole with that much on the table.

Revis, on the other hand, signed a big-time four-year deal after one of the most publicized holdouts in recent NFL history. The day he came back to practice might possibly have been one of the happiest days of my life. I have never wanted something to be over more than that whole ordeal.

From the very beginning of the season, it seemed like the New York Jets were the most talked-about team in the NFL. A large part of this was due to our appearance on *Hard Knocks*. Apparently, some people think I'm entertaining. The truth is, I don't really care what other people have to say about me, including an NFL blogger, a broadcaster, or even a former head coach. I knew *Hard Knocks* was going to generate interest. Not everyone was going to like it, and that's fine; that's what remote controls are for. I'd be lying if I said that I didn't like our name constantly in the press. People were talking about us, and that's really all that mattered. We were exactly where we wanted to be.

We put ourselves in a position where we had no other choice but to prove ourselves. I knew people looked at the Jets and me like, "Okay, Rex, we've been hearing about you guys all preseason. Now show us what you've got." I felt challenged by all the media attention, and I LOVE a challenge.

I also don't mind if the media's coverage of us isn't 100 percent positive, but I really don't like being portrayed as something we definitely are not. We had developed what the media called an "*Animal House*" image. At first, I think we got this image because people viewed my language on *Hard Knocks* as offensive, and when they watched the show they thought they saw a team that was all play and no work, a claim I had to defend a million times in the media.

It really escalated in September 2010 when Inez Sainz, a female reporter for Mexico's TV Azteca, accused some of the players and coaches, myself included, of acting inappropriately toward her during a visit to one of our practices. The story hit the media on Monday, September 13, and we were exactly one week from opening the season against the Ravens in our new stadium . . . and this is what I'm dealing with. Now, I could go on for pages and pages about what happened, and what definitely did not happen, but at this point the whole incident has been discussed and dissected, and I don't think anyone on either side found much to talk about.

The incident shook me up beyond belief, partially because my name was being dragged into a situation that I hadn't even witnessed, and partially because we already had the image of being goof-offs because of *Hard Knocks*, and now we were on the verge of developing a reputation for being jerks, too. It was, honestly, killing me. It was a poor reflection of our football team, and I knew we were just the opposite of that. We always said we wanted to have some real badasses on the field and gentlemen off the field—and that's what we had. That's why this whole thing made me madder than hell.

But in the end this was an example of the kind of distraction you have to expect from out of the blue—these things can either derail you and your team, or you can come together and learn from them.

The Sainz story began to fade after a few more days, and our full attention was on our home opener. Obviously, if I had to choose an opponent to face while opening up our new stadium and starting our season, I never would have chosen Baltimore. They are an outstanding team with a strong defense that plays with everything they've got each and every time they take the field. We are the exact same team. We knew going into it that this would be a competition to see who could play more physically. I thought we would kill them, I really did. We were opening up our new stadium, our fans were so into it, and it was supposed to be a special night; unfortunately, it just never turned out that way.

The effort we gave was tremendous, but mistakes killed us. It was tough to get beat 10-9, like taking a punch in the stomach. Offensively, we struggled. We were one for 11 on third-down conversions. When you compare that stat alone to Baltimore, who converted 58 percent on third downs, we should have been clobbered. Defensively, we played solid, but penalties cost us. We took pride in playing great, physical defense, but you can't have 14 penalties and win. You have to play smarter than that.

Coming out of that long rainy night, the thing we tried to remember is that it was going to be a long season and we could—and would—come back. I had confidence in myself and in our coaches. I knew we were going to get better; the team just had to believe in us.

I've always said that every time we play New England, they're going to think they are better at two positions: head coach and quarterback. Mark Sanchez and I like to laugh about it, because, honestly, we are matching up against Bill Belichick, one of the best coaches in NFL history and the coach I personally admire the most, and Tom Brady, a quarterback who solidified his spot in the Hall of Fame years ago. Well, that might be true, but it doesn't stop Mark and me from looking at each other before we play the Patriots and saying, "So what? We can take 'em." I've always said as long as the rest of our team can overcome me as a head coach, and Mark as a quarterback, we should be able to beat New England!

Turns out I was right in Week 2. A 28-14 victory over the Patriots was big for us, and I was so proud of the true team effort that we gave. This game definitely saved us from drowning in our loss the week before. It proved just how talented this team really is. The only negative coming out of the game was an injury to Darrelle Revis, but when he went down with a pulled hamstring on a touchdown to Randy Moss, we found a way to overcome it. We held Tom Brady to a 72.5 quarterback rating, forcing him to throw two interceptions and six incompletions in a row. Mark had a 124.3 quarterback rating and started what I would say was the beginning of a beautiful relationship with Dustin Keller. There were no individuals on the field that night. We played like a team. That's what I was most proud of. New England is a great team; everyone knows that. But this night, we were greater.

We couldn't make it to our third game of the season before our "*Animal House*" image was back. On September 22, at 6 A.M., I got a phone call from Mike Tannenbaum telling me that Braylon Edwards had been arrested near the Lincoln Tunnel for a DUI. Like anyone else would be, I was pissed. By that point, I was fed up. I told Braylon and the team that I was tired of dealing with these issues. It's embarrassing, not just to me, but to our owner. I told the guys that it's not just about them, that there can be no selfishness on a great football team. They represent a franchise. They wear the logo of that franchise, they wear the colors of that franchise, and every week millions of fans scream for them because they are part of that franchise.

To do something like get a DUI just blew my mind. We have a Player Protection Program available to these guys to prevent situations like this from happening. Not only did it look bad on the organization that Braylon either wasn't aware of or chose to ignore the program, but two veteran Jets, D'Brickashaw Ferguson and Vernon Gholston, were in the car with him. I was so tired of the Jets carrying around this stigma that we're just a group of thugs. I had worked long and hard since my first day on the job to improve what people thought about the Jets. I wasn't going to let the carelessness of a few guys ruin it, and I made sure they knew that.

Once time passed, I was able to calm down a little from the whole thing. I am able to see now that in the long run this may have been the best thing that could have happened to Braylon. He's really a good kid, and while it's disappointing what happened to him, sometimes you just have to take the consequences like a man.

I truly thought he had been embarrassed enough. My only punishment was choosing to sit him out for the first quarter against Miami. I heard every opinion possible about my decision. Some people criticized me by saying that being benched for one quarter isn't a punishment, that I don't know how to discipline or control my team. Most people said they would have suspended him from the team right then. I just don't work that way. I think we all mess up at some point in our lives. Now, I'm not going to let someone walk all over me, but I'm not going to turn my back on him either. Braylon was paying for his mistakes, whether the media knows it or not.

As we approached the next game, I decided to share my personal math formula with the team. Basically, I look at every divisional game as if it counts as a game and a half—which means our third game down in Miami could either put us up half a game or down two and a half. I know it's not everyday math, but it works for us. My point is that the game against the Dolphins in Miami was not just a normal regular-season game. For us, it was huge. There is a history there.

The fact that we were 0-2 against them in 2009 is still a burr in my saddle. And on top of that, you may have heard about a minor issue I had with a couple of fans at the Pro Bowl last year, which of course made front-page news in Miami and New York. I'll get back to that.

Needless to say, I wasn't exactly expecting the stadium to give me a standing ovation when I took the field in Miami. Given our past, I wanted to play so hard and so tough that we'd absolutely kill them. In the end it was a bittersweet victory. I was excited that we walked out with a 31-23 win, but I wanted more from my guys. Our defense allowed 463 yards. That stat alone killed me. This game was sort of personal for me because of the relationship I've built with Jason Taylor, who had an amazing career with the Dolphins. The truth is he never wanted to leave Miami; they let him go. Fortunately for us, their loss was our gain in 2010.

Jason's an unbelievable guy. He came to New York, into our building, and immediately became one of the guys. He had the best attitude and was so humble. Our victory over Miami was a memorable conquest for him. Knowing how special it was, at the end of the game I dumped the Gatorade jug on him. It was the first time a coach had ever done that to a player. It was my own tribute to him, and one that he fully deserved.

After returning to New York and before heading to Buffalo for our fourth game, we made some minor adjustments to our roster. We released veteran Howard Green and signed Trevor Pryce. In the time I was with Baltimore, Trevor averaged a quarterback hit for every 10 snaps taken—not 10 passes, 10 snaps. The minute we heard the Ravens had released him, we saw it as an opportunity for us. A lot of people questioned why I would "violate" some apparent unspoken rule in the NFL not to sign a player that another team releases with the intention that it plans to make him active again. I must have been sleeping in Transactions 101, because apparently I missed this rule. To me, that's part of the game. We released Howard Green and went after Trevor Pryce. That's the risk you take. In my opinion, you don't cut a guy as the Ravens did and roll the dice.

The matchup against Buffalo is what they call a classic trap game. We opened the season on *Monday Night Football* against the Ravens and got beat by a point. Then we had New England and then a huge Sunday-night game against Miami. So already we had three big games right out of the gate. In reality, they were probably the biggest games in the NFL at that stage of the season, and we were involved in all three of them. Now we are headed to play a team that we are physically and strategically better than, so people think it's an automatic win. That's a trap game.

We were in the same situation in 2009. We won our first three games against Houston, New England, and Tennessee and then played at New Orleans and ended up getting beaten. We threw six interceptions and lost. That's why I made it a point to never look past ANYONE. We can't assume we will get a victory, because it doesn't always work out the way you plan. Fortunately, in this case it did. The 38-14 win over Buffalo was another great divisional win for us.

The second of the five prime-time games we had scheduled for the season was against the Minnesota Vikings right here at home.

The hype surrounding this game was inevitable due simply to the fact that Brett Favre played here for a year in 2008. So here he was, back to take on his former team, and the media storm began. Of course, in the days before our game the focus had shifted from his return to New York to a new scandal involving Favre and one of our former employees. When the story broke, it was like a Tiger Woods media frenzy all over again. To add to the hype, the Patriots made an unexpected change to their roster and traded Randy Moss back to the Vikings. I thought to myself, "Why did Belichick have to trade him this week? Couldn't he have waited until after we played them?"

It made me laugh, but in all seriousness, if there is one person you don't want to have to face twice it's Randy Moss. He is a freak of an athlete, and we already had to prepare for him once that month. All I could think about was whether I was going to see another ridiculous one-handed catch like he made against us in Week 2.

Fortunately for us, the game went our way. We were dominating the game, yet not scoring touchdowns—just kicking field goals. Games like that you usually lose. Plus, you have Brett Favre on the other side and all you keep thinking is "Oh man, I know any second now this guy's going to get hot." We really seemed to drown everything out and focus on the goal, though. When we got an interception to wrap it up and the game was ours, I looked over at Matt Cavanaugh, one of our offensive assistant coaches, and he was smiling because I had predicted that exact ending. We ended up beating the Vikings 29-20 in one hell of a game.

Despite the off-field distractions—the hour-long delay of game, the brutal weather conditions, and a total change to our game plan because of Randy Moss—we still managed to beat what I considered, at that point in the season, to be one of the most talented football teams in the league. Brett Favre is as good as they get in terms of an experienced quarterback, and while he didn't have a 2010 season anything like he expected, there's still nothing more nerve-racking as a coach than watching him start to scramble.

Our next matchup was against the Broncos. Denver is a difficult place to play for us. Not only is it a long trip, but the conditions are not anything like we are used to in New York. I don't care what anyone says, it takes a while to get used to playing in high altitude like that. We left earlier than we usually would for this reason. To sum it up, we walked away with our fifth win of the season, beating the Broncos 24-20. We now had the best record in the league, at 5-1, and it sure felt good. Yes, we definitely made some mistakes against Denver, but I think Bill Parcells is right when he says, "The best record reflects that you are the best team." I have always agreed with that; I was just waiting for other people to see it, too.

Coming off our bye week, we played Green Bay at home on Halloween night. The Packers handed us our second loss of the season, embarrassing our offense in the process, shutting us out, 9-0. I have to give Green Bay all the credit. They were unbelievable on that day, far better than we were. On a positive note, I thought our defense was outstanding. We held them to only 14 percent on third-down conversions. Overall, we just couldn't pull it together as a team.

Mark Sanchez couldn't throw the ball for the first half of the game, and then once he found his rhythm in the second half our receivers couldn't catch the ball. Nick Folk missed field goals that he usually could make in his sleep. All the way around, we were a mess. It's frustrating to watch a team you know is so damn good just throw it away like that.

My immediate reaction after a loss is to want to get that moment back. Unfortunately, in this league there are no do-overs. I can spend all day going over the things we could have done differently. We just had a ton of errors, like Steve Weatherford calling for a fake punt when we were fourth and 18 on our own 20-yard line. I love Weatherford; he's an aggressive athlete, and by giving the guys an option to call their own plays on occasion, they can sometimes get too excited and act before they think.

All of those things contributed to our opening loss against Baltimore, and here they were again. What was disappointing was not only that we tarnished our record, it's that we lost on our own turf.

Losing at your place, that's never okay. It was the first time all year that we didn't play like Jets, and the worst part was that our fans had to see it live.

Going up to Detroit after that loss, I was glad to see how we handled the game mentally. Sometimes after teams suffer a loss, they can become mentally defeated, which takes a long time to overcome. Not us. We were still there to take it all. We came away with a 23-20 victory in overtime. I thought this was a huge turnaround for us. This game was all about mixing it up. We took a different approach and ran the ball a lot more, which is something Brian Schottenheimer, our offensive coordinator, and I had been talking about for some time.

I thought Mark did a great job, especially on the last three drives. He was calling two plays in the huddle and our guys were ready to go. We executed well and had so much confidence in our two-minute offense. Going into overtime, Sanchez came up to me and said, "Coach, if we get the ball back, can we stay in that two-minute mode?"

I said, "Heck, yeah, kid. Go for it! If that's what you want, you go ahead."

He was so confident, and I thought that was a great changeup for us. Mark proved more than once this year that he can lead this team to victory when we're behind in the fourth quarter. It was cool to watch him each game as he got better and better. I know people want to rip on us for barely beating a team like Detroit, saying that we didn't play well and we just got lucky. The way I look at it, we still won. We were 6-2 and felt like there was a lot more gas in the tank.

Sibling rivalry—there's nothing better. Playing Cleveland, I went head-to-head against my twin brother, Rob, the defensive coordinator for the Browns. Both of us had been looking forward to this match-up all season. It was do-or-die all the way. Rob wasn't our only connection to Cleveland, though; we were also going up against Browns head coach Eric Mangini, the head coach of the Jets just before me. The entire week leading up to this game, Rob and I did nothing but give each other hell. It was great. Rob and I are so competitive. We would call and rip on each other's coaches. We would put each other on speakerphone and just go at it. I even went as far as to dress up like Rob in a press conference. The media gave this a lot of attention, but to me, it was just a way to keep things light for my players and to have a little fun. As you'll see in this book, I think it's vitally important to have fun with what you do—especially if you're lucky, like me, to have a job you really love. That's why I put on that wig and stuffed my shirt with a pillow. If you need a good laugh, look for it on YouTube.

In all seriousness, though, I knew that Cleveland game was going to be a great game. Rob is among the most creative defensive minds in the league; he and Mike Pettine are about as creative as it gets. They are unbelievable in putting their players in positions where they can be most successful. Rob doesn't worry about what a player can't do. He focuses on what he can do.

Against the Browns, we were able to win our second overtime game of the season, this one 26-20. At the end of the day, I think it's remarkable that Cleveland pushed us into overtime. I thought we were in total control of that game, but the scoreboard didn't show what I was feeling. The game showed us that we couldn't keep relying on fourth-quarter points to pull us through. We had to find a way to score in the red zone. We had the opportunity in the first three quarters, but for some reason we couldn't make it happen. We had fallen into a bad habit of not scoring until the end of the game. Cleveland really exposed what a problem that was for us.

For the week after Cleveland, we worked in practice on becoming a more aggressive offensive team. It's a good thing, because when we faced the Texans the following Sunday we scored 30 points—but we gave up 27! Beating the Texans put us at 8-2, a terrific start. It's safe to say that the standout of that game was Santonio Holmes. He grabbed a six-yard scoring reception with 10 seconds left. He finished the game with seven receptions, 126 yards, and two touchdowns. He's a stud. There's not much more you can say.

The next week was Thanksgiving, and in the NFL nothing says "Thankful" better than a win on Thanksgiving Day in front of a massive TV audience. Cincinnati was a great win for us. That game was won because of our special teams and Brad Smith. Our defense did an awesome job, too. Although we rushed for 171 yards, our offense lagged behind a little, at least for our standards. We got off to a slow start, which like I said had been our routine those past couple weeks. But in this case, I felt during the second half that the momentum was shifting in our favor and we were about to take control of the game. Sure enough, that's what happened. We won 26-10 and felt like things were rolling in 2010 just as we had envisioned. We were confident.

We started into that following week with a laser focus on preparing for our biggest road game of the year—our second match-up against the New England Patriots. Both teams were 9-2, and this *Monday Night Football* game was being billed nationally as an epic battle. It felt like a critical point in our season.

I'm going to take a break here and come back to this moment. So much happened in 2010 and before. Stick with me—there are a lot of details and stories I need to fill in.

2. Blunt-Force Trauma

I've always said that one big hit can change the momentum of a game faster than anything else—faster than a turnover, faster than anything that happens on the football field. I've always believed that, and that's the way we've built our teams. I build them with the picture that big hits are part of our game plan.

I want 11 guys who will run to the football, bottom line. Actually, they better haul ass to the football. That's what I want on every single play, every single down. Make a statement. Knock the snot out of somebody. Not only do I want big hits, which set the tone, but I also want turnovers that are generated from those big hits. We know how to take advantage of turnovers, too. Not only will we get an interception or a fumble recovery, we want to score off our opponent's mistakes. I create plays off turnovers. Everyone looks at me like I am a dumbass: "Oh, how is this going to work?" It does work.

Midway into the 2010 season, we led the NFL with a plus-10 turnover differential. Our cornerback, Dwight Lowery, iced consecutive wins over Minnesota and Denver when he made good with turnovers. He returned a Brett Favre interception for a touchdown to foil a possible Minnesota Vikings comeback in Week 5 and recovered a bad Denver Broncos snap to stuff a potential game-winning drive in Week 6. We also had recovered nine fumbles at that point, tied for the league lead.

We've got players who know exactly what they are going to do with the football when turnovers happen. Take an interception, for example. There are a series of events that automatically happen. We block the intended receiver, and that guy becomes the trailer for the pitch. If you want to pitch the ball there needs to be a trailer, and the trailer needs to be four yards wider and behind the guy carrying the football. That way when you turn and pitch it, you know who you are pitching it to. You could pitch it blind, and that guy would still be there. That's a relationship you want to keep when you are trailing a play. Then we set edges as fast as we can to give more room for the returner. These are designed plays that we practice. Not a lot of defensive coaches approach the game this way. For us, it's not enough just to stop our opponent; we want to "traumatize" them from both ends. Ultimately, you have to score.

I remember we blocked a field goal while I was with Baltimore. Our cornerback Ed Reed picked it up and started to return it upfield, and then pitched it back to Chris McAlister. Ed probably could have scored if he hadn't pitched the football, but he turned and pitched it to Chris anyway. The officials ruled it a forward lateral, but it really wasn't. We had it schemed perfectly. The point is we will always want to score off a turnover. Our first objective on defense is not to let them score—to keep their points to a minimum. Our second one is to create turnovers off big hits. And our third objective is to score off those turnovers. When a defense scores off a turnover, it is extremely difficult for an opponent to overcome it. It can squeeze the life out of a team and demoralize it. You can see it in an opponent's body language. That's why it's so important for us to try to score when we create turnovers.

Each game we might also designate an opposing player with a

dot. Players don't want to be dotted by the New York Jets, because that means we want that dude knocked out of the game. Of course, it has to be legal and by the rule book. We don't play dirty, and no way will we intentionally hurt a player with an illegal, cheap shot. We dot players fair and square. There are players out there who think they are badasses, and you just might see two of our players knock the hell out of him. *Pow! Pow!* That's our mentality. Everything we do is aggressive and, hey, we may make a mistake, but we will go one hundred miles per hour and we will knock the hell out of you. Big hits create turnovers. You haven't been Punked—you've been Dotted!

I know when people read about dotting players that they will immediately think of my father. It has been written that where Buddy Ryan led, trouble often followed. He coached the Eagles in the so-called Bounty Bowl in 1989, when he was accused of offering a reward to any Philadelphia player who injured Cowboys kicker Luis Zendejas. "I wouldn't want to hurt him," my father told the media. "He couldn't kick. I wanted to be sure he was in there." (Zendejas left the game with a concussion after being tackled.)

Michael McCrary, a former Ravens defensive lineman, told *The New York Times Magazine*: "I loved that Buddy was strictly a defensive guy. I heard from some Cardinals that offensive players hated him. If defensive players got fines, he'd pay them. Offensive guys, he wouldn't even talk to them. Hated them. Rex used to be the same way. Don't let him fool you. But he wasn't as blatant as his father was. Now the whole team's going to love him; he's there for everybody."

That's right. I am there for everybody, and everybody knows how I want to play the game. We are going to try to intimidate opponents—and how do you intimidate them? You do it with big, vicious hits in your pursuit of the football. Again, that's part of our game plan. We want our guys and our opponents to know each Sunday will be a double-chinstrap game. Fifty percent of all NFL games are decided by eight points or fewer, which means big hits can change the game's momentum. That's an edge I want each week.

I think every team in the NFL preaches about running to the football. We talk about it one time and we don't talk about it again. We don't coach effort. If you don't play with effort on the New York Jets, we will not coach you for long. You might be good enough to play in this league, but it won't be for us. We run to the football as hard as anyone in the league. If a player doesn't run hard, he sticks out like a sore thumb when we review game film. We only have one speed— full speed. The Jets don't have "thud" drills in practice, where defensive players wrap up the offensive player with the ball. It's always at full speed. We always go at full speed. As far as I see it, there is no point in practicing at half speed. If you want to get better, the only way to do it is full out, every single time—so that's the way we work.

Big hits happen, but they are coached, too. My defensive coordinator, Mike Pettine, and I are like two peas in a pod. We know each other's thoughts at all times during a game. We don't dance around each other, either, because there's not enough time. If you ever heard us on the headsets during games and what was said to each other, it's stuff that might end friendships. Not ours. We are shoulder-to-shoulder after wins, smoking cigars, drinking a beer, laughing. We are like brothers. We both get it and see the same things on the football field. We might fill an entire white board in our office with schemes and formations, all great stuff, but the key is to condense it into a plan that makes sense to the players. Mike takes all that information, organizes it, and then we implement it into our game plans.

My defenses when I coached in Baltimore—and in New York, for that matter—were a force of relentless, unpredictable mayhem founded on my premise that "whatever you do best, we're going to take away from you." There are six basic defensive fronts in football, and teams usually play one of them. The two most popular are the 4-3, with four down linemen and three linebackers, and the 3-4, with three linemen and four linebackers. We might use all six, each packaged with dozens of variations. We might often line up the defense in one front and then shift to another before the snap. We are going to get to the player with the football and knock him silly.

Even so, we have stayed traditional in our approach. That means we won't ever get away from fundamentals and proper technique. We are extremely creative on defense, but it is never at the expense of fundamentals and technique. We always want to make sure our defensive players get into a good stance—let's make sure we get off the ball, let's make sure we can beat a block. Coaches can have the greatest playbook in the world, but if your technique and fundamentals are not very good, it won't work. My defensive coaches and I are both very old school in that approach. We constantly preach fundamentals and technique in team meetings and in our daily walk-through with players. We might have the most creative blitz package, but if a player takes a wrong step or he doesn't release from a block properly, we're all over it. We have so many schemes and formations that our cutting-edge stuff, our opponents will look at it and say, "My God, I would never do that with 11 guys at the same time." But it's important to us that we cover the basics. That will never change, because we have one goal: We need every one of our players to pull the rope in the same direction.

I always use myself as an example when it comes to teaching the proper technique. I can only bench 225 pounds. But this guy over here can bench 500 pounds. Yet I can teach the guy like myself who can bench-press 225 pounds that by just playing with proper technique, I can use a stronger guy's momentum against him. I teach players to release off blocks. There's no question it works. Maybe it's because I was a limited player during my playing days. But I functioned and was successful because my technique was better than most other guys'. Any little thing that I learned I have applied to my players. Even when you have great players, if you teach the proper technique, it's unbelievable how much better they can be.

Trevor Pryce is a perfect example. He's a 14-year veteran from Clemson—a great defensive end and a quick learner. One time against Pittburgh, we are lined up and I have him slide across the line and I tell him he has one shot at the quarterback, and this is the technique we will use to do it. It's a passing down and we expect a pass. Our defensive backs expect the ball to be thrown quickly. So Trevor has one shot and, sure as shit, he slides over, beats the offensive lineman like he was standing still, and sacks the quarterback before he can throw the football. It's little things like that that just make coaching great. It's a blast when you pull it off and you see somebody that you're coaching have success. It makes you feel like King Kong.

———————

There are two kinds of techniques in the NFL. There's the penetration system, much like what Tampa Bay employed all those years under Monte Kiffin, who is now the defensive coordinator at Southern Cal under his son, Lane. And there's the two-gap system, much like what Bill Belichick has installed at New England. We are probably somewhere in the middle. We are an aggressive, attacking team, but never from the outside edge—we want to go through our opponent. We call them knock 'em backs. That fits our team's personality. Most teams in the NFL also talk about fits. How are you going to fit a play? We don't use the f-word. Our linebackers, for instance, will be aggressive, they will run downhill, but it might not be from the same gap every time.

We put in a brand-new defense in Baltimore and the funny thing is Mike Nolan, the defensive coordinator at the time, couldn't tell me how to coach a D-line because he had never coached it. I was the D-line coach, but I had never coached these certain techniques that we used—head up on a guy—so I established what we still call the knock 'em backs. To get my point across to my players, I found this video of a guy who was branding a horse. As he is applying the iron, the horse lifts his leg and kicks this dude right in the chest and he goes flying. I thought the horse had killed him. It was an unbelievable hit, I mean the horse kicked the shit out of him. I thought, "That's exactly what I wanted to establish—the knock 'em back—and that's how we would play." I showed the video to our players and asked them, "You get the idea? We want to beat the offensive linemen to the punch. We want to knock them back." We spent hours on the practice field. We'd run our feet, and I wanted my defensive linemen to lock their eyes on the player across the line of scrimmage. I wanted my guy to look straight through him and I wanted my guy to bust his ass and make the tackle.

Bob Sutton, our linebackers coach, has coached football for nearly 40 years, including 17 seasons guiding officers at West Point. He told *The New York Times Magazine,* "Around the league, my friends who are coaches are studying what we do. But they can't see what Rex is doing." Sutton picked up our defensive playbook and said, "You could take this and give it to somebody else, and it wouldn't work. It's the other things he gives you besides phrases and diagrams in a playbook that make the playbook effective. Some say he's too brash. But he's just telling you what he really believes. This guy has some tremendous leadership skills. To me, he's the hard-charging general who doesn't do everything by the book but wins. He gets other people to buy in."

I think it's important not to do everything by the book—that's what makes it work. I still have a lot of little kid in me, but I also don't bullshit people. Never have, never will. I won't piss on you and tell you it's raining. I expect our players to be prepared, too, and we are fortunate with the Jets because we have a smart team. I am serious. Every one of our players has the responsibility to learn our defense. We give them a playbook over the summer to study and it might just be four or five of our basic installations. But if they don't open that playbook, they will be in trouble when training camp starts. They will be behind, because that first day of camp Mike Pettine sounds like an auctioneer. He will review nearly 30 defensive packages in rapid-fire succession. This is not the first grade. We don't ease into training camp. We want to fire bullets from our gun in that first meeting, and it's the players' responsibility to learn that defense. I give our owner, Woody Johnson, and general manager, Mike Tannenbaum, credit because they built a Jets team with intelligent players. Our guys are book smart and football smart, and we want them to be working at their full capacity intellectually.

Of course, a coach might have a roster filled with smart players, but you can't coach with a broad stroke of a brush. Each player is different. There's a psychology to motivating and teaching players, and it's the cornerstone of what we do. We have a saying that everyone is treated fairly but everybody's not going to be treated the same. Players who have been in the league and have played at the highest level and have put together a résumé of experience, they will be treated differently than a rookie or a player who is wet behind the ears and has been in the league just a few years. We do treat everyone fairly, but just not the same in every situation. I think our veteran players appreciate our approach.

Even with veterans, however, you still have to learn how they react to criticism. Everyone is different in that area, too. For instance, Bart Scott is a player I can dog-cuss up and down, all day Sunday, and it doesn't bother him a bit—goes right off his back. But a guy like Shaun Ellis, well, I might have to be more careful, because he reacts differently to criticism. I simply can't coach every player the same. Even from a teaching standpoint, there's a difference. Safety Jim Leonhard, from Wisconsin of all places, is a smart dude. Way smarter than me, but that's not saying much. He can flip through the playbooks and say, "Okay, I got it." And, bingo, he does. It's amazing. But not every player's Einstein. We implement a variety of teaching tools to help players learn our defense—video, meetings, PowerPoint presentations, walk-throughs before and after practice. We might have more walk-throughs than any team in the NFL, but that's okay. It's our job as coaches to understand how guys learn the best. This is a get-it-done business, and we want to get it done—and get it done correctly.

Our approach is different than most teams', too. We install our defense as a full group, which means every player on defense is in that room. It's the assistant coaches' job to separate into their respective segments and coach the individual parts. It's as if everyone is responsible for a piece of the puzzle, but everyone is responsible to know the entire puzzle. I want our defensive backs to know what the

D-line is doing; I want the D-line to know what the defensive backs are doing. I will stand in our defense meetings and ask the cornerbacks what the nose guards' responsibilities are in a certain package. I will ask the linebackers what the defensive ends' job is on a certain blitz formation. It makes sense to me, because that approach creates team chemistry. Nobody wants to be the weak link. My intention isn't to embarrass a player in meetings, but I want our guys to know they are held accountable. It's a different deal, because we watch game film as an entire defensive unit; players don't break into their respective position segments. Nobody can hide. If we repeatedly correct a player in front of his peers, one of two things is going to happen. He will get it right, or he will be gone.

When I was with Baltimore, Brian Billick said when a coach emphasized everything, he emphasized nothing. There are coaches in the NFL who overcoach, no question. I coached with a guy in Baltimore who each week passed out a huge packet of tips and reminders to his players. I mean, it was thick, 20 pages or so, and it had all the information he wanted his players to review about Sunday's opponent. That's overload. Each game when Mike Pettine passes out his tips and reminders, it's one or two pages, max. One side is on our defensive scheme; the other side is on our opponent's offense. We test the guys, because we want to get a feel and make sure our guys understand our plan. I am also not afraid to keep it simple, stupid.

When we play Tennessee, for example, we might want to remind our linebackers that they need to set the edge: No way can we let Tennessee running back Chris Johnson get to the outside—set the edge and turn him inside. I am a bullet-point coach, too. We are in the NFL and these players are the best of the best. I am not going to stand in front of them in a meeting and act like the Swing Doctor in golf: "Step here, wrap your thumb around the club, lock your hips, roll your hips, head down, follow through." That's not me. Sometimes I simply challenge my guys to line up and whip the other guy's ass across from them on the line of scrimmage. Fans might shit because we might make millions and millions of dollars as players and coaches, but sometimes it's that simple. Let's kick somebody's ass and make a big hit.

We give our players our game plan, give them the concept of how we want it run, and we let them fail or succeed. If they fail, we as coaches get it corrected. It's teamwork. Let them play and we will coach them on the big stuff. When I was with Baltimore, I had one guy raise his hand in a defensive meeting and ask me when I was going to collect the playbooks and check their notes. Check their notes, my ass. Class is on the practice field and in games. That's when all of us are graded.

With veterans, for example, it's difficult at times to break old habits. They get it done on the field, but it just might not be the way we draw it up on the board. Ray Lewis, one of the all-time great linebackers, sat in our defensive meetings in Baltimore and he prepared himself in his own way. He understood football. He was not one of those guys who look at the playbook and remember each detail. But he studied film, he understood angles, personnel groups, and what opponents would do on down-and-distance from the outside hash mark. Ed Reed was the same way. Those guys are special, but they prepared in their own way and I never had to worry about them. Nor did I micromanage them.

With the Jets, I told my defensive guys when we headed into the 2010 preseason, let's go graduate level. We installed our scheme in our first season in 2009. They understood the basic concepts, the finer points of our plan. Now let's take that next step mentally. Each week it's like we pull items from a menu. We might change our blitz package, we might tweak a formation, but it's also about remaining true to our fundamentals and technique. We reviewed three years of cutups from when I was with Baltimore, and, from a technique standpoint, we had the ability to shed blockers better than anyone in the NFL. The players may have changed over those three years, but our approach did not.

Of course, I always want the big hit. That hasn't changed either.

In 2009, I signed linebacker Bart Scott, who I had coached in

Baltimore. When we were with the Ravens, Scott had one of the best big hits I have seen, against Pittsburgh quarterback Ben Roethlisberger. I knew we could get to Ben if we could make him slide his pass protection a certain way at the line of scrimmage. When we watched film, we knew their center snapped the football to Ben the moment he put his head down after Ben said his cadence at the line. So Bart lined up in one spot, and the moment the center put his head down, Bart sprinted to the opposite side of the line. It was too late for Ben to audible his pass protection for the play, because the ball had been snapped. Ben thought he had backside protection, and, of course, he did not. Ben never saw Bart, who said he had hoped to God that Ben didn't have the time to unload the football. Bart said it was the cleanest hit he ever had on a quarterback. All I know is Bart's hit jacked up our entire defense and changed the game's complexion. It was like watching a baseball game and seeing a guy hit an over-and-out-of-the-stadium home run.

Even baseball has a place in our football game plan when it comes to big hits.

3. Son of Buddy

My dad, Buddy Ryan, began his young adult life in foxholes as a soldier. He ended up changing the way the NFL game is played, both defensively and offensively. He was brave, he was tough, he was a leader, and he left an indelible mark on the greatest game in the world.

Who wouldn't look up to a man like that? Who wouldn't want to grow up to be just like that, just like his old man? You hear about that all the time. Sons of lawyers grow up wanting to be lawyers. Sons of doctors grow up wanting to be doctors.

I grew up wanting to be Buddy Ryan.

Of course, that kind of goal isn't without some serious complications. My dad has all those great characteristics I just mentioned and, well, he was a little over the top from time to time. For instance, my dad got fired from his first job as a high school coach. He was in Gainesville, Texas, serving as both football coach and athletic director.

The only problem is that he thought he was athletic director of one sport, football. The school fired him when he spent all the money in the budget on the football team. Likewise, my dad has never been afraid to get in someone's face or to make a point, even a brutal one. As my older brother Jim once said: "There's no diplomacy to Buddy. If you don't want to hear the answer, don't ask the question."

As I said, my dad was that way from a very early point in his life. He grew up near a little town called Frederick, Oklahoma, as one of four brothers: my dad, Pat, D.A., and George. We're talking about the 1930s and 1940s, when rural kids would basically fight all the time to toughen each other up. D.A., who's real skinny, would get into a fight with George, the youngest one. George was well built, but D.A. would whip his ass, then Pat, who's a big man, would whip D.A.'s ass, and then my dad would whip Pat's ass like it was nothing. Then the old man, my grandfather, would whip my dad's ass for getting into it with the other brothers. That's just the way they all were, young, tough, hardheaded as hell. Hey, it's genetic, what do you want me to say?

It's like when Buddy and Pat went into the National Guard and they'd be out on these training hikes. They'd go 10 miles and my dad was right there along with him. My dad would end up carrying Pat's pack. That's just how tough my old man was. He would carry both his pack and his brother's pack.

When the United States got involved in Korea, my dad went over there as a teenager. When he was 18, Buddy was in the Korean War. When I was 18, I was trying to figure out where to buy beer in college. My dad was a master sergeant in the U.S. Army. His most important job was to get guys to fight at the moment of truth. He was barely a man himself, and he was leading men in battle. Not *into* battle, *in* battle. He would jump in that foxhole, and if a guy wasn't fighting, it was his job to get him to fight, one way or the other. If that meant he was going to have to slap the shit out of somebody, then that's what he'd do. He made it to where you would rather fight the enemy than him. His job was about life or death.

My dad really learned how to understand how to motivate each person. By the time I worked with him in Arizona, I think my dad could say four words to someone and that guy would be ready to lay it on the line for him. He was natural; he was himself. You talk about great motivators, you better be a great motivator if you're going to do that job in the Army. They'd have these missions in Korea and there'd be one guy who would ask for volunteers to go with him and he couldn't get anybody to volunteer. When my dad would ask for volunteers, every hand would go up. Everybody felt comfortable going with him. That was the way he was, he would get emotional like I do and you knew that he was going to lay it on the line for you, so you'd lay it on the line for him.

Just as important in that is that my dad was smart. He understood tactics, and that's what you saw with his defenses wherever he went: the Jets, the Bears, the Vikings, the Eagles, the Oilers, even the Cardinals. His defenses just dominated because he understood the tactics, not just the yelling and screaming. Don't get me wrong; my dad has redefined how to use four-letter words. My God, people talk about how I talked on *Hard Knocks*, but my dad talked like that in front of the Philadelphia Chamber of Commerce one time.

Swearing, ranting, and all that crap doesn't mean anything if you don't understand how to design plays and how to execute what you're doing. There's an old saying about coaches and players: A player only listens to a coach if the player thinks the coach can help him. If the player doesn't think the coach can help him, the coach is useless. That's just the way it is. Players will drift off, do their own thing, and completely tune out the coach, no matter how many times you drop an f-bomb.

I don't know if I can emphasize enough just how good my dad was at motivating people to get out there and do what was required of them. I always admired that about him.

You watch war movies and they don't show that stuff, the guys who are pissing down their leg, paralyzed by fear, scared to face the bullets because they're worried the next one is coming at them. I'm not making fun of those guys. Thank God I was never in that position, so who am I to tell somebody in a war what they should do when real bullets are flying? But my dad wasn't just facing those bullets, he had to tell guys what to do while they were facing them, too. He had to look at some guy who was scared out of his mind, wanting to run away, and get that guy to fight.

Not that my dad ever bragged about that. I only know this stuff because my dad's friends from the war have told me. At 18, Buddy Ryan was a fully formed man ready to defend his country and the guys he was in that foxhole with.

Understanding that, now maybe you can understand why he took that swing at Kevin Gilbride, a guy he was working with not in the foxholes of Korea, but years later on the sidelines in Houston.

I hate to bring up the story, but it's one a lot of people talk about with my dad. Heck, I remember it vividly because I thought everybody would think I'd do the same thing someday. I thought my brother Rob and I were never going to get NFL jobs again because of it.

My dad was defensive coordinator of the Houston Oilers in 1993. It was an incredibly talented team. Just loaded. But the team started 1-4, capped by a 35-7 loss to Buffalo. So my dad, and everybody else, was taking a lot of crap from the fans and the media. That's the way it goes. But the defense came together and had only one game the rest of the regular season in which it allowed more than 17 points. It was an amazing run and the Oilers won all 11 games. Man, what I wouldn't give to win 11 straight sometime. That's not easy.

The problem for my dad was that he hated the Oilers' offense, which was a version of the run-and-shoot, a four-receiver base offense that called for minimal blocking for the quarterback on virtually every play. It left the quarterback so vulnerable that my dad called it the "chuck-and-duck," because he knew how defenses would attack it. Warren Moon, a future Hall of Famer, was the quarterback and Gilbride was the offensive coordinator. Moon used to take some vicious shots. The problem my dad had with Gilbride was that Gilbride often left the defense hanging out to dry. Instead of running out the clock when our team was ahead, Gilbride would often call pass plays. When they failed, the defense would have to go back on the field. My dad's opinion was that he lost two starting defensive backs during the season because of Gilbride's play calling. (The funny part is that my dad is sort of to blame for the use of the run-and-shoot—and all the other different types of three-, four-, and five-receiver sets used around the NFL—because those schemes were basically an answer to his heavy-blitz schemes.) I've met Gilbride, who's now the offensive coordinator of the New York Giants and was when they won the Super Bowl in the 2007 season. He's a pretty good guy and he's certainly turned out to be a great coach. But you get on my dad's bad side and that's it.

So it's in the final game of the regular season, on January 2, 1994, and Gilbride calls a pass play at the end of the first half with the Oilers winning. Backup quarterback Cody Carlson fumbles the ball and the defense has to go back out there. My dad starts yelling at Gilbride, who starts yelling back and walking toward my dad. So what does my dad do? He punches Gilbride in the jaw and the players have to break them up.

Now, that's not normal, I'll admit. But you have to know my dad. The really sad thing about the Gilbride story is that sometimes it overshadows the important contributions by my dad, like how he and Walt Michaels came up with the defensive plan that stopped the Baltimore Colts in Super Bowl III and led the Jets to victory in the greatest upset in NFL history. That's the game that led to the merger of the AFL and the NFL.

They forget about how my dad invented the 46 defense, the scheme that made the Chicago Bears champions in 1985 and made them the greatest defense in the history of the game. They forget that the 46 defense forced unreal changes in how the game is played today. You know those pretty spread formations and all that cutesy wide-open offense that everybody loves? (Well, everybody except defensive guys like me, of course.) So much of that is an answer to the schemes my dad developed with the 46 defense.

People also forget about his time with the Minnesota Vikings, when he helped develop the Purple People Eaters defense. They forget that he helped three different teams (the Jets, the Bears, and the Vikings) get to the Super Bowl, that he was part of two historic teams and was a head coach for two different teams. Sure, my dad had some interesting moments, like the whole Gilbride thing and the "Bounty Bowl." He wasn't much for Jimmy Johnson, Tom Landry, or Don Shula, and they weren't real big fans of him. Heck, my dad couldn't even get along with Mike Ditka . . . and they won a Super Bowl together. That's my dad; he wasn't going to BS anybody.

But when they use the old expression for defensive linemen, "Let's meet at the quarterback," that's my dad talking. He came up with that. He really was one of the great innovators in the history of the NFL. Two different times, my dad came up with strategies where the league had to hold emergency rules meetings in the middle of the season to adjust for things he did. He came up with the idea of guys faking injuries to get extra time-outs. He tweaked the competition with what he used to call the Polish Punt Team, putting 13 guys on the field at the end of games to prevent returns and burn clock time even if he got caught. Yeah, my dad never found a rule or fellow coach he didn't want to challenge.

My dad is nearing 80. Now, if you look up his biography online, it will say he was born in 1934. Not exactly. My dad was born in 1931, but when he was breaking into the NFL, he kind of had to change the numbers a little. Even back in 1968, age was a factor. The NFL was already becoming known as a young man's game, even for coaches. So my dad put down that he was 34 instead of 37. My brother Jim once gave my dad a hard time about it, pointing out that my dad's real age was listed on Jim's birth certificate. My dad just grumbled something at him in response.

Not that it much matters. Even at his age, Buddy Ryan could still be a defensive coordinator in the league and be one of the best. No question, he could still dominate. Not just that, he could still lead. My dad was tough: His personality, his language, the way he coached—everything about him was tough. I've always wanted to be just like him.

When people say, "Oh, Rex Ryan is just like his dad," I'm proud of that. In Ron "Jaws" Jaworski's book *The Games That Changed the Game* (which, by the way, is great for people who want to learn something about the game), a couple of people paid me some really nice compliments at the end of a chapter about my dad's 46. (I told you it was that important!)

Doug Plank, the guy who wore 46 and inspired the name for the 46 defense in Chicago, told Jaws: "Rex has taken his father's ideas and improved on them. . . . He's created more new looks, more opportunities for his defenders to make plays. It's still all about creating confusion in the quarterback's mind, not just hitting people hard. Rex looks for favorable matchups. He'll give players multiple responsibilities on each play, so when he moves people around, he has the capability of making it look like a totally different defense. The number of men he uses up front is constantly changing. He'll get more movement from hybrid players rushing from a variety of different angles. Rex's schemes rely on the *threat* of pressure coming, but that pressure isn't always geared to overpowering the opponent each play."

Then Jaws himself wrote: "I think Rex has expanded the scope of the 46 in ways his father could not have envisioned. Rex will take a linebacker from one side of the field and move him to cover a wide receiver—and rotate his down linemen in unconventional ways—with coverage concepts I've never seen before. Rex is vigorously responding to the many new looks he sees from offenses, figuring that he needs to be aggressive in order to stay ahead. In that respect, he's a chip off the old block."

Or as Mike Singletary, the Hall of Fame linebacker who worked with my dad and learned to love him after some early tribulations, told Jaws: "It's obvious Rex is carrying on his father's legacy. He's so much like Buddy, it's frightening."

Gentlemen, you don't know how much that means to me. I'm not nearly as tough as my dad. I didn't have to grow up like him. Thank God I never had to grow up that way. But he is who he is and I'm who I am. Am I a gentler version of Buddy Ryan? I would say so. But everything I am as a coach is based on watching him, learning from him, wanting to be like him. My mom, Doris, is a tough lady. Trust me, she'd be a nasty defensive coordinator, too. There'd be a lot of hurt quarterbacks if she was the one calling plays for the defense. However, when I was growing up, my twin brother Rob and I wanted to be coaches like my dad.

My mom and dad got divorced when my brother and I were two. They tried to reconcile one time, but it didn't work out. My mom will tell you that she just wasn't much for the coach's life as my dad worked his way up from the high school ranks to the University of Buffalo. They met at Oklahoma A&M (now Oklahoma State) after my dad got out of the service. One of my mom's sorority sisters at the Kappa Delta House introduced them and my mom was "enamored with football people," as she likes to say. Like my dad, she grew up in Oklahoma, just north of the Texas-Oklahoma border. Everybody loves football in that part of the world, and my mom still loves it. She'll watch three college games on Saturday and then my games and my brother's on Sunday. Like I said, she'd be a heck of a coach herself.

Anyway, my folks were married for about 10 years before they divorced, but the funny thing is that they get along great now. My dad calls my mom at 7:30 some mornings just to talk, forgetting she's an hour behind him. They had some great times together. My dad loved to dance, and he made her laugh with all his snappy one-liners. He loved her enough that he converted to being a Southern Baptist and he even got baptized in the church before they got married. They tithed 10 percent of what they were making to the church even when they were making nothing. They didn't allow liquor in the house.

But the coaching life wears on the wives, particularly if you have kids. I thank God for my wife, Michelle, and how supportive she has been, especially raising our sons. Like I've said, there are two types of wives in the NFL: ex-ones and great ones. I know firsthand. This business is about long hours, and that means not much support for the wife. Plus, when you're a coach like my dad was, like I am now, life is pure joy for you. You're doing what you love. Next to actually playing football, coaching is the greatest job in the world. You're as happy as Tony Siragusa at an Italian meat market. But that's not necessarily true for your spouse.

Here's a story that will put it in perspective: My dad didn't even know we'd been born until we were three days old. Seriously. Now, it's not because he didn't care. First off, you have to remember that cell phones weren't around in 1962 and communication wasn't quite as easy. My mom had gone back to Ardmore, Oklahoma, where she grew up, to have us so she could have more help, since my dad was traveling for work. Her mom, Alabama "Bamma" Ward, still lived there, as did most of the rest of Mom's family. Because she was carrying twins, the doctor sent her there about eight weeks before her due date, since twins usually come early.

And that's just what Rob and I did. We were born about six weeks early on December 13, 1962, while my dad was on the road trying to recruit players. My mom tried to get a message through, but he was traveling around and the message didn't reach him right away, plus he wasn't expecting us to be born that soon.

Eventually, my mom realized she just couldn't do the coaching life. I don't blame her. She had some goals of her own and she fulfilled them. Plus, she had double trouble when my brother Rob and I were born. She already had Jim, who was six, and then came the Ryan twins. Talk about wearing a mom out. I can only imagine. She likes to tell this story about one time when a friend of hers came over while she was giving us a bath. We were both screaming our heads off and my mom's friend asked, "How can you stand it?" My mom looked at her a little confused and said, "What do you mean?" She had learned to tune out the noise.

At that point, my dad was coaching at what's now known as the University of Buffalo. It was his first big break at the college level. He was the defensive coordinator there and he was working some extremely long hours. In fact, the other coaches were complaining about how much my dad worked and he just mocked them.

Buffalo was already the fourth or fifth place my mom and dad had moved to. After he got fired at Gainesville High, he went to Marshall High in Marshall, Texas. Then he got a college assistant job at Pacific (all the way in Stockton, California), then Buffalo. He had another stop at Vanderbilt down in Tennessee. That is part of the stress the coaching life puts on a family. When coaches get hired, it's not like they do a lot of the packing. As a coach, you're expected to drop everything and go to the next place because there's always work to do. The place that's hiring you is replacing some guy who probably left and they need you immediately.

That leaves the wives to do the packing and all the other details that go with moving. The wife of a coach better be a saint. And even if she is, it's tough. We were in Buffalo when my mom had enough. She's a smart woman and she wanted to do more with her gifts than follow my dad around the country each time he got fired and hired somewhere else. She got her degree from Oklahoma A&M and taught high school wherever my dad's job took us. When we got to Buffalo, she finished her master's degree in education. After she and my dad split up, she went to the University of Chicago and got her PhD in education administration in two years. Along the way, she was Phi Beta Kappa.

While my mom was at Chicago getting her doctorate, the three Ryan brothers went to Ardmore to live with Grandma Ward. Bamma Ward was great—tough, but great. How can you not love football if your grandmother is named Alabama? Seriously.

After my mom graduated, she got a job at the University of Toronto, working for the Ontario Institute for Studies in Education. She taught and conducted some research there on the education of children from remote areas. Ontario is this huge territory in Canada, as big as Texas, Oklahoma, and Arkansas combined, and she was looking into the educational opportunities and performance by kids who spent hours each day just getting to school, like taking snowmobiles just to get to where the bus would pick them up.

Like I said, my mom has lived a great life herself. She was in

Toronto for 19 years, then spent seven years as the vice president of the University of New Brunswick in Saint John, Canada. She's worked for the World Bank and traveled the world to places like Indonesia, Australia, France, Germany, and Singapore—all in all, I think she's had a really interesting life.

But I'm getting ahead of myself. The three of us boys moved up to Toronto with her once she accepted the position there. Toronto was a great place to grow up—clean, safe, and fun. When we were young, Rob and I would jump on a bus to get to the train and take it into town to go watch hockey games or do whatever we felt like doing. I remember when we were 14 and the Toronto Blue Jays started up in 1977, we went to the first game. We didn't have to have Mom cart us around or watch over us.

The only thing is that Canada isn't really too big on football. They like it enough; you've got the CFL, after all. But as they like to say up there, they play both sports: ice hockey and road hockey. It was ice hockey in the winter and road hockey in the summer. When we were growing up, the biggest show on TV was *Hockey Night in Canada*. That was every Wednesday and Saturday night (it was before cable TV got big), and that was religion in Canada. It was either the Maple Leafs or the Canadiens on TV, and the whole country would watch. In fact, that's why for all those years either the Leafs or the Canadiens would always play at home on Wednesday or Saturday night. You had to have the screaming crowd in the background to add to the excitement. We all learned to play hockey. My big brother Jim still plays to this day, more than 40 seasons in the books. He's proud to tell you he plays in an adult league in St. Louis.

Football was a little different matter, though. Like I said, they play up there, but it's not exactly the same thing. You can be pretty physical in hockey and everybody expects that. As graceful as you have to be to skate and play a sport, it's still a rough game. When my brother and I played football with that kind of aggression, the refs didn't quite understand it. They once kicked us out of a game for hitting too hard. Of course, part of the problem was that we hit the coach's son too hard, but my mom was standing there after they kicked us out, yelling at the officials, "It's football!"

While we were in Toronto, my mom was great about my dad, too. We kept in close contact with him all the time. We even went down to Miami with her to be around my dad at Super Bowl III, between the Jets and Colts, back in January 1969. There Rob and I were, all of six years old, playing in the sand on the beach while Joe Namath was guaranteeing a victory even when he's this huge underdog. Then we watched him and the Jets back it up.

And you wonder why I like bravado so much.

By the time we were 14 or 15, we were going back and forth a lot to my dad's, and my mom realized the sports up in Toronto weren't very well organized. We went to live with my dad so that we could take advantage of developing our skills, since athletics was really where our interests lay. I imagine my brother and I were probably a pretty good handful, too. Actually, I don't imagine it; I know it. We gave the schools some fits. We hung out every minute together. I mean, every minute. We did everything together.

One year before we moved in with my dad, the principal of the school we were going to in Toronto called my mom and said, "We're going to split the boys up in different classes." My mom said to herself, "Well, that's not going to work." It didn't. Rob and I are not identical twins, but we were pretty darn close back then and we looked an awful lot alike. We'd switch classes half the time, particularly if one of us had a test that we weren't ready for and the other one could do it. We drove the teachers crazy pretty quickly. Finally, the principal called my mom back and says, "Well, this isn't working, either."

Not long after that, Rob and I went to live with our dad. Jim was already in college at the University of Minnesota, and our dad was on the Vikings' coaching staff as defensive line coach. Jim is smart, too, like my mom. He's an academic. He got his degree from Minnesota, got his MBA from Notre Dame, and his law degree from the University of St. Louis. He's a lawyer in St. Louis now. He wanted to be a sportswriter for a while, then he went into the ad business before becoming a lawyer. He's just a sharp, sharp guy.

Let me say one thing about Minnesota. For my dad, it was a great place because he got a chance to work with Bud Grant, a guy he really looked up to in a lot of ways. People don't really know this, but Grant was one of probably the three most influential people in my dad's career: Grant, former Jets coach Weeb Ewbank, and the great George Halas. Obviously, Ewbank gave my dad his first pro job and was a special person. He's still the only coach in NFL history to win championships with two different teams. He won two NFL titles in the 1950s with Baltimore, including the 1958 title game still known as The Greatest Game Ever Played. Then he won Super Bowl III and put the AFL on the map.

Talk about putting a stamp on history. Ewbank really knew how to relate to players. Ewbank also had a huge influence on my dad's thinking about how to attack the quarterback. Ewbank used to spend a lot of time devising ways to protect Namath. Namath was the meal ticket, as Ewbank used to say. Namath already had bad knees, so keeping him protected was a must. What my dad realized, like so many others, is that the defense had to attack the quarterback, the nerve center of the offense. That had to be the primary goal, whether it was physically or mentally. The quarterback has to be pressured somehow. And Halas is Halas. You're talking about one of the fathers of the game. He also meant a lot to my dad because he stood by him.

But Grant was special from another perspective: his sideline approach. Bud Grant was stoic, unflappable, and didn't put up with any BS. You couldn't rattle Bud Grant, and he wanted to make sure you couldn't be rattled. At least that's how my dad understood Grant, and he understood it right away. My dad still tells the story of interviewing with Grant for the assistant's job.

He sat down in Grant's office and then Grant walked in and sat down. Grant didn't say anything at first and the silence went on and on. Finally, after about five minutes, Grant asked, "You got any dogs?" My dad said yes. Another five minutes went by and Grant didn't say anything. Finally, he asked, "You hunt with them?" My dad said no. Another five minutes went by and Grant said, "Okay, you got the job." To this day, my dad thinks Grant just wanted to see if he would get nervous.

As much as people may not believe it, my dad styled himself on the sideline like Grant. He remained calm. Now, people don't believe that because of the Gilbride thing; they think he was a crazy man, but he was just the opposite. Of course, he would swear in a game and he might give you the kind of answer that would melt you to your kneecaps, but he wasn't losing his cool. He was just getting to the point.

My dad also met Alan Page, the Hall of Fame defensive tackle, when he was in Minnesota. Page wasn't just a great player; he was a serious scholar and a gentleman. In fact, he was elected to the Minnesota Supreme Court as a judge in 1992. Page played the first 12 years of his career with Minnesota before finishing up his last three years with the Bears after my dad went to Chicago with coach Neill Armstrong, another Vikings assistant the Bears hired. That association with Page proved vital for my dad.

For Rob and me, moving to Minnesota wasn't so great. We lived in Edina, a pretty affluent community near where the team trained. It was a nice enough area, but everybody was kind of stuck up and clique-ish. You had the jocks on one side, the druggies over on the other side, and then other little groups. That's not what my brother and I were about. We wanted to hang out with everybody. It's like later, when we were in college at Southwest Oklahoma. We played football and then we hung out with all these regular guys. We were both 6-foot-2, 225 pounds at the time. We'd be at the bar on a Saturday night and some guy would look to start something with one of our smaller buddies, and the next thing you know he's looking at Rob and me. We liked that.

But we weren't in Edina too long, because at the beginning of 1978, my dad went with Armstrong when Armstrong was hired by Halas and the Chicago Bears. That's when my dad ran the defense himself for the first time. My brother and I went with him, too, and we all lived in Prairie View, Illinois, which was a lot better for us. We loved it there and we ended up going to Adlai Stevenson High School.

More important for my dad—and eventually me and my brother—that's when he started coming up with the schemes for the 46 defense, which really changed the game.

Now, remember that and think about this: In 1981, the Bears were about to fire Armstrong and his staff after four seasons. The team wasn't very good. They'd gone 30-35 over the four seasons, making the playoffs once and getting bounced after the first game.

Rob and I were freshmen at Southwest Oklahoma at the time. My dad had a friend down there who helped us get going with the football team. Really, I should have probably been playing baseball by that point. I could really pound the ball in high school. But my senior season was bad, because I lost one of my contact lenses and I was afraid to bug my dad to get a new one. I remember just not being able to see the ball at the plate. I know it sounds kind of dumb as I look back on it, but my dad was having a rough time. The 1980 season, which was the first half of my senior year of high school, hadn't gone so well and then my dad found out he was going to have to get a big section of soft tissue on his back sliced off because he had some kind of growth on it. I just didn't think the contact lens was that big a deal, comparatively.

Then came the 1981 season, and Armstrong was done after that. I was wondering what was going to happen to my dad. What happened is that he ended up with more leverage than ever before. Here's how it went: All of the Bears' defensive players got together and signed a letter asking Halas to keep my dad. Every single one of them. It was Page, the guy my dad had begun coaching back in Minnesota, who wrote the letter and the rest of the guys signed it. So old man Halas (he was 86 by that time) did it. He kept my dad and the entire defensive staff, which really pissed Mike Ditka off when they hired Ditka to replace Armstrong. Here's Ditka, a Bears legend himself and the first tight end ever elected to the Pro Football Hall of Fame, having to let my dad run the defense. Ditka tried talking to my dad a bunch of times and my dad never listened. Well, he listened, but his response was usually "Fuck you. I run the defense."

The simple fact of the matter is that the players believed in my dad. They knew he had ideas that were going to work. Besides all the brilliant concepts that were developed for the 46, the philosophy of the scheme was basically pure aggression. This is what defensive players want. My dad knew it then. I know it now. My brother Jim put it this way: "Dad was always tapped into the mind of the defensive player. Defensive players understand the concept of bend-but-don't-break and read-and-react, but it's not what they're about. The whole basis of a defensive football player is to be aggressive and destroy. My dad epitomized that philosophy when he designed the 46 in Chicago."

Better yet, the Bears were starting to get the players who could make those ideas work.

Now, before I get to that, let me backtrack a little. The chapter in Jaworski's book about the 46 does a great job of describing how the defense worked and its impact. I would love to give you a full breakdown on the defense, but I could go on forever. I could write a whole book about the 46 and what it's done for football, but I'll just say that if you want to learn more, Jaworski does a nice job of describing not just the technique but also my dad, even if they didn't get along too well during their one season together in Philadelphia.

By 1981, my dad realized he didn't have enough good pass rushers on the Chicago roster. Sure, he had a young Dan Hampton and the Bears had just picked up Steve McMichael that year, but McMichael was an offensive lineman when Chicago first got him. Linebacker Otis Wilson was a great athlete and middle linebacker Mike Singletary was a rookie, but it was more a bunch of parts that my dad was trying to figure out how to fit together. From a traditional sense, the fit wasn't great.

So what did my dad do? Blitz. If you don't have guys in the front four who can get to the quarterback on their own, you better find other guys who can get there. At the time, my dad also had Doug Plank, a punishing safety who was the prototypical hitter. Like I said, the defense was named the 46 because of Plank, not because of the formation, like the way the 3-4 and the 4-3 defenses got their names.

What my dad created was a system that required really smart players who could react to all the different offensive sets thrown at them. This took time and there were bumps along the way. At the end of the 1982 season, Vince Ferragamo lit up the Bears for 509 yards, what was then the second-highest total in league history. It was the end of the season and it didn't go over too well, but the players understood that what my dad was trying to do was going to take some time.

Eventually, the Bears got Richard Dent, an amazing pass rusher the team somehow found with an eighth-round pick, and linebacker Wilber Marshall, a truly great, dynamic athlete out of the University of Florida.

Along the way, Singletary and my dad started to figure things out. It was rough. What most players loved about my dad is that he didn't BS around. He didn't just play guys because they were supposed to be good. You had to earn it. Rookies were called "assholes," and most of the time my dad's critique of their play was limited to the word "horseshit." My dad was a man of few words, but they were choice words. Even once you got to be a veteran, the best you'd get from my dad was him calling you by your number, like, "Hey, 51, get your ass in gear." Once you started making some plays, then he'd learn your name.

Just look at how he treated Singletary. Here's a prototypical middle linebacker, a guy who went to the Hall of Fame, a 10-time All-Pro and a two-time Defensive Player of the Year. It took Singletary nearly two years to get off the bench and start full-time with my dad. Singletary started most of his rookie season in 1981 and was an All-Rookie player, but my dad was still jerking him back and forth between the bench and the starting lineup until 1983.

My dad spent those two years pushing every button in Singletary's psyche, needling Singletary again and again so that he'd get every ounce of talent out of himself and become the brains of what was going to be a complicated defense. I know Singletary hated hearing that stuff and he didn't get along with my dad for a long time. I think he thought my dad hated him, which wasn't true at all. My dad just liked to challenge him. In Singletary's rookie year, he was in the game early and made a bad call at the time. My dad pulled him and Singletary spent the rest of the series on the bench. The next time the defense was supposed to go back out there, Singletary went up to my dad and said he was ready to go back in the game.

My dad just looked at him and said, "Son, we're trying to win this game." Could you imagine the nerve my old man had? You're telling a guy as intense as Mike Singletary that he's not ready to help the team win? Talk about some big stones. But that's what happens when you grow up in a foxhole. You don't have time to waste worrying about somebody's ego. You just have to survive.

Once you earned his respect, he loved you.

Of course, the guy who never loved my dad under any circumstances was Ditka, as I mentioned before. It's funny, because so many people will tell you to this day that my dad and Ditka are basically cut from the same cloth. Singletary, who ended up being very close to Ditka, used to say how much alike they were. Still, they couldn't see eye-to-eye. Ditka ran the offense and my dad ran the defense. Ditka always had the basics under control because he had "Sweetness" in the backfield. Walter Payton, probably the greatest running back and guy you'll ever meet, was Chicago's running back. My brother and I loved Walter Payton. We studied all the great players. Heck, we knew who Cookie Gilchrist was before we said our first words. In a press conference one time, I said, "Lookie, lookie, here comes Cookie" in front of the New York media and they looked at me like I was from another planet. Then again, they kind of always look at me that way.

Walter was funny. When we were at training camp and I was a ball boy, I used to work with the offense. I was a teenager and he'd joke with me. He'd pull my pants down out on the practice field and tackle me, but he would also show up when we got older at our baseball games. You'd see my dad and a couple of other parents out there in the stands—and then Walter Payton might show up. That's a pretty neat childhood.

Anyway, back to Ditka. He and my dad just went around and around. It never stopped for the entire four years they were together in Chicago. In November 1985, the championship year, the Bears' defense was starting to hit its stride when the Bears went to Dallas and just annihilated the Cowboys 44-0. I made the four-hour drive down from Southwest Oklahoma to Dallas to see the game. That was my senior year in college. You know, in college, you see some lopsided games from time to time. Usually that's where one is from some big school and can recruit and the other team is just picking up a check playing the game, like maybe Oklahoma against McNeese State.

Well, that day in Texas Stadium was as close as you get to Oklahoma–McNeese State at the NFL level. (Unfortunately, so was the ass-whupping we took from New England in the 45-3 Monday Night Massacre.) It was brutal. Dad's defense was at its best. By midway through the second quarter, the Chicago defense had scored two touchdowns before the offense got in the end zone. The Bears knocked Cowboys quarterback Danny White out of the game twice and rattled backup Gary Hogeboom so bad that he looked like a nervous high school kid. Really, it was almost scary to watch, wondering which Cowboy was going to get hurt next.

The truth is, my dad didn't like the Cowboys very much. (How ironic is it that my brother is now their defensive coordinator?) It wasn't so much Tom Landry; it was the whole image of Dallas as America's team, how squeaky clean they pretended to be and how much they thought they were better than every other team. For a long time, the Cowboys were good; you have to respect that. It's just like what I said about Bill Belichick and New England the first year I got to New York: I respect them, but I'm not kissing Belichick's rings. I'm not bowing down to him.

My dad took it a step further. It seemed like he wanted to take a lifetime of frustration out on the Cowboys in that one game, and he pretty much did. By the second half, Ditka was asking my dad to call off the dogs. Enough was enough. After starting his career with Chicago, Ditka had played for Landry and the Cowboys and even got his start in coaching with Dallas. He didn't like crushing Landry that way, but even when Ditka asked, my dad told him to fuck off.

That wasn't even the worst moment between those two. After the Dallas shutout, the Bears shut out Atlanta 36-0. Then came the famous *Monday Night Football* game at the Orange Bowl against Miami. The Bears were 12-0 and going up against the Dolphins and Don Shula, the only team and coach to ever go undefeated, back in 1972. Of course, my dad and Shula already had a pretty good history going by this time. Back in the famous New York Jets Super Bowl win over Baltimore, Shula was the coach of the Colts. Beyond that, my dad was good friends with Ewbank and it was Shula who had taken Ewbank's job in the early 1960s in Baltimore.

Beyond that, my dad resented Shula more and more because Shula was on the NFL's Competition Committee at the time. This was just after he had drafted the great Dan Marino, a future Hall of Fame quarterback who was in the early stages of breaking every passing record. In 1984, Marino's second season in the league, he set a league record with 48 touchdown passes. At the time, that was staggering. Most quarterbacks were lucky to throw half that many back in those days. Marino was in the midst of taking the passing game where my dad was taking defense. Marino and the Dolphins also made the Super Bowl in the 1984 season, eventually losing to San Francisco.

The problem, at least the way my dad saw it, was that Shula was making it easier to take advantage of Marino's talent. In 1984, the NFL started enforcing the bump rules against cornerbacks and safeties even more strictly, allowing Marino to have more open receivers. My dad saw right through that and used to tweak Shula publicly every time he could.

Now, in this huge game, here they were again. The atmosphere was unreal. The Dolphins again looked like the class of the AFC going up against the Bears, who were clearly the class of the NFC by this time in the season. This game is not just about the history of the undefeated season (a bunch of the 1972 Dolphins showed up on the sideline to cheer the current Dolphins on). It wasn't just about the rivalry between my dad and Shula. This was a realistic Super Bowl preview with four weeks left in the season.

I have to give Shula credit, because he came up with a good plan of attack against my dad. More important, it was an idea that is not a part of standard offense to this day. That's where I say that my dad helped change the way offense was played in the NFL, even though he never coached offense (and didn't like it much, either). Shula had Marino and the Dolphins come out in a base three-receiver set most of the game, spreading out the Bears' defense. Until that point, the conventional wisdom of most teams that played the Bears was to keep extra blockers in to handle the vast array of blitzes the 46 defense employed. The problem is that my dad always knew that he could bring one more guy than the offense could block. The other problem is that if the Bears didn't blitz, the offense had too many guys back in to block.

Shula went the other way, putting veteran wide receiver Nat Moore in the slot with Mark Clayton and Mark Duper split wide. While Marino's final numbers aren't that awesome (14 of 27 for 270 yards, three touchdowns, and an interception), he hit a bunch of big throws along the way. I mean, you average 19 yards a pass in any game, you're having a good day. You do that against the greatest defense of all time and you're having a phenomenal day. By late in the first half, the Bears were down 24-10 and then they got a punt blocked just before the half. The Dolphins cashed that in for another touchdown and it was 31-10.

That's where Ditka lost his patience with my dad. You see, my dad refused to play nickel defense when the Dolphins put Moore in the slot. They ended up with linebacker Wilber Marshall or safety Gary Fencik covering Moore a bunch of times, and that was a mismatch. Moore was just too quick. What can I say; sometimes Ryan men are stubborn. At halftime, Ditka screamed at my dad to put in the nickel defense and my dad gave him the usual f-bomb greeting. They started pushing and shoving, and eventually the players had to break them up. The whole thing got into the press eventually after Chicago lost 38-24, but it ended up not mattering.

The fact is, like most of those "Super Bowl previews" that the media likes to sell the fans on every year, it didn't happen. The Dolphins were good, but they lost to New England in the playoffs that year, getting upset at home. Chicago rolled the rest of the season and the playoffs were like a coronation. My dad's defense posted back-to-back shutouts in the NFC playoffs before facing New England in the Super Bowl in New Orleans. It was another massacre. Appropriately, the Bears won 46-10. If that wasn't enough of an affirmation of what my dad did, the players provided the rest. While a bunch of the players carried Ditka off the field, a bunch of the defensive players carried my dad off the field. It was the first time an assistant coach was ever carried off the field like that. Later on, Ditka finally got the divorce he wanted from my dad when Philadelphia hired my dad as its next head coach.

The funny part, in retrospect, is that the Bears' defense was actually statistically better the next season in a lot of ways. But it wasn't the same. The Bears went 14-2 in the regular season, but lost in the first round of the playoffs to Washington. In fact, the game against the Redskins really humbled them, and Ditka even complained about the play of the defense after the game.

You think Ditka might have wanted my dad in the foxhole, so to speak, with him and the rest of the Bears that day? Complicated question. The good news is that Ditka and my dad were recently together at a Bears reunion and they really seemed to bury the hatchet. They acknowledged how good they were for each other and the team. And they have championship rings to prove it.

4. Joining the Family Business

Near the end of my first season coaching the Jets, after we beat Cincinnati in the AFC playoffs in the 2009 season, I gave my dad a game ball. This game was obviously special for a whole lot of reasons—most important, for the team. It showed that all the stuff we talked about during the regular season actually meant something. This put us on the way to the AFC Championship Game. It was the first time the Jets had been there since 1998 and only the third time in team history that the Jets won two playoff games in a season (the 1968 Super Bowl season was the first and 1982 was the other).

For me, sure, it was personally satisfying. I think the reason it meant so much to me is mainly because I felt like I was representing my family, my brother Rob, and most important, my dad. You see, this was our family's first playoff victory with one of us being the head coach of the team. It's ironic when you think about it. As great as my dad's career was, as important as he was to the development of the

NFL, and as long and hard as Rob and I have worked in this league, this was it: our first postseason win with a Ryan man in charge.

See, this was part of the knock. So many people have said for years that the Ryans were great coaches, but they weren't *head* coaches. The three of us have been part of four teams that combined to win five Super Bowls. All three of us have a Super Bowl ring. In fact, I only have one, while my dad and my brother each have two. Still, my dad had to wait until he was 54 to get a head coaching job. I had to wait until I was 46, and my brother, whose defense was so good with Cleveland last season that they hammered the defending Super Bowl champion New Orleans Saints in the Superdome last season, is still waiting.

I get it. There are reasons people questioned our ability to lead. My dad had some moments that made people wonder about him, like getting into it with Kevin Gilbride or not getting along with Mike Ditka. But the worst reason I ever heard about my dad's leadership was this one: He never won a playoff game when he was a head coach. Really, you're going to hold that one against him? Ridiculous.

My dad went from Chicago to Philadelphia after he got his first head coaching job in 1986 and proceeded to build another truly great defense. After two losing seasons, the Eagles made the playoffs three straight years under my dad starting in 1988. They won 10 games each season, too. Now, some people might say that's no big deal, but remember that they're playing in the NFC East, which had the Washington Redskins and Joe Gibbs and the New York Giants and Bill Parcells. Dallas still had Tom Landry, but the Cowboys were on the decline. Still, the Cowboys were only a few years away from hiring Jimmy Johnson and drafting Troy Aikman.

Between Gibbs and Parcells, there are five Super Bowl rings. Johnson came in and created a team that won three more in the 1990s. When I tell you the NFC East was the best division in football, I mean it might be the best division in football ever. That depth was unreal. The team my dad created ended up winning 10 games or more five straight years. That's tied for the longest streak the team has ever had winning 10 or more. They had Reggie White and Randall Cunningham already, and then my dad drafted Jerome Brown, Keith Jackson, Seth Joyner, Eric Allen, Byron Evans, Keith Byars, and Clyde Simmons, and signed Mike Golic as a free agent.

I mean, Jackson and Byars are offensive guys and everybody said my dad didn't know offense. I know he pushed quarterback Ron Jaworski out of there and made Cunningham the starter. Everybody loved Jaworski, and why shouldn't they? He's a great guy and he really knows the game. But it's not like Cunningham wasn't incredibly talented. He made the Pro Bowl, too, and the plan for the organization, even before my dad got there (Cunningham was drafted in the second round in 1985, the year before my dad came to the Eagles), was to make Cunningham the man. My dad just pushed it faster because he didn't want to waste time building his team.

From there he went to Arizona as the head coach in 1994. My dad was 63 by this point and he went to one of the worst franchises in NFL history and led them to an 8-8 finish his first year there. That may not sound like much, but the Cardinals had nine straight losing seasons before that year. The following season they slipped down to 4-12 and my dad got the blame, even though the defense was great. It's easy around the NFL to draw conclusions about a coach's record, but it's important to take a step back and really look at the situation. That's why I took a moment after the win over the Bengals in the playoffs and gave my dad that ball.

I realize that my dad wasn't perfect as a head coach. Even though he's a great leader of players, a great leader of men, and a great strategist, you can't deny that he had his faults. My brother Jim talked about it after my dad's first chance as a head coach with Philadelphia, remarking: "I think Rex learned a lot from watching how my dad handled the front office in Philadelphia. My dad was abrasive. As I said before, my dad wasn't a diplomat. He was always getting on people if they didn't see it his way, and that wore down the front office of the Eagles after a while. It sounds funny coming out of Buddy's mouth, but then you have to work with people you've just made fools out of." Jim then added: "I think the most important lesson Rex learned from watching my dad in Philadelphia was that you have to have everybody working together. It has to be united, the players, the coaches, the owner, the front office, everybody on the same page."

The best example about how it went wrong for my dad, as Jim pointed out, was the whole Jim Lachey situation. People probably don't remember a lot about Lachey, but he was a great left tackle who was drafted No. 12 overall in 1985 by San Diego. He made the Pro Bowl three times and was a first-team All-Pro. He was the whole deal. He played three years for the Chargers and then he wanted out. He said he was tired of the organization and wouldn't play for them anymore. It was 1988 at that point and my dad was in his third season with the Eagles. The left tackle situation was a mess, just awful, and my dad knew it. Again, everybody thought my dad didn't know offense, but he knew.

So my dad told the Eagles' front office to go get Lachey. I don't know how hard they tried, but partway through the season, Lachey first got dealt to the Raiders and then he got sent to Washington. Not only did the Eagles not get Lachey, but one of their fiercest rivals in the NFC East got him instead. In the 1989 playoffs, the Eagles lost to the Los Angeles Rams 21-7. Why? The Rams outside linebacker Kevin Greene just went crazy that day putting pressure on Cunningham. Greene was so good that the Rams didn't blitz one time. NOT ONE SINGLE TIME. They played zone defense the entire game, bottling up the Eagles' passing game. Philly didn't score until the fourth quarter.

If that's not bad enough, here's the topper: My dad got fired the next year after losing his first playoff game again. Who did he lose to? The Washington Redskins, with Lachey at tackle. The Redskins went on to win the Super Bowl that year.

I'm not trying to rehash a bunch of history. There's a point here and I learned it. I'm not happy I learned it through watching my dad suffer, but I'm not going to ignore it either. My brother Jim said it best: You have to work together. The organization has to be united.

That's what we have with the Jets. We have a great coaching staff—
the kind of guys who are willing to put in the time and the effort.
We have owner Woody Johnson, who cooperated with the Giants
to build a new stadium that's a palace. He moved the team to a new
facility in Florham Park, New Jersey, where we have everything we
could possibly need. He helped in the effort to bring a Super Bowl to
New York for 2014, which is the first time the league is bringing the
game to a cold-weather, outdoor venue. We have General Manager
Mike Tannenbaum and his front-office staff, and we have players
working hard to be ready.

You have to have everybody pulling the same direction in this
game. It's just too hard to have it any other way. There are a thousand things that go into winning a Super Bowl—literally, a thousand
things. You can have great players, but if they don't work, it's not
going to happen. You can have great coaches, but if one guy isn't
doing everything he can, you can fall short. If you don't have people
handling the finance side, whether you have a salary cap or not, the
whole thing can get out of control. Then, on top of all that, you've
got to be a little lucky. I believe in the saying that you create your
own luck, but you still have to have some things bounce your way,
whether it's the ball or being lucky enough to stay healthy.

What my dad did was aggravate the people above him too much.
It got to the point that it was unhealthy. My dad is not one to toler-
ate fools, or at least the people he thinks are fools. He expects results
when he asks for something. Sometimes you have to massage people
and work with them to keep them with you. You can't be ripping
into them, pretending like you know their job better than they do.
It's like with the negotiations we had with cornerback Darrelle Revis
when he was holding out. I don't understand that stuff. I poked my
head into it at one point, but I wasn't telling anybody how to do what
they do. More on that later.

Anyway, while all this was going on with my dad in Philadelphia,
I was just getting started in the business. My brother and I graduated from Southwest Oklahoma in 1986. We graduated *summa cum*

laude, too. Okay, not really, but here's a good one: My brother and I had a little fun with our graduation cards and typed in "*summa cum laude*" at the bottom. We ended up being called on stage with all the graduates who made high honors. We were standing up there with all the brains, smiling these big, shit-eating grins, and my dad was in the audience laughing along with a bunch of people. It was a pretty good joke. Both Rob and I planned to get through college and land in the family business of football.

Now, obviously, we weren't the Ryan & Sons Coaching Firm. It doesn't really work that way. There are some sons who have followed their dads into coaching and have gotten a pretty good boost in the process. David and Mike Shula both got to be head coaches pretty fast at the NFL and college levels because they were Don's sons. David didn't last, but Mike is still working in the business, and he's a good quarterback coach from what I've seen. Brian Schottenheimer works for me and I'm sure it helped him being Marty Schotten-heimer's son, but Brian is a damn good coach in his own right. The fact is, he's an offense guy and his dad was more of a defense guy, so whatever Brian learned for his specialty wasn't just from watch-ing his dad work. I think Brian is going to make a great head coach someday, and I hope he will be with me until that day comes. Kyle Shanahan is working for his dad, Mike, in Washington. I can tell you that Kyle is a terrific offensive coordinator, just like his dad is a great offensive coach. Those guys know how to call plays.

There's no question for my brother and me, too: It helps more than it hurts to be Buddy Ryan's son. First of all, we fell in love with this job from the time we knew what our dad did. By age six, we were hooked. Then there's the stuff we learned just by watching our dad. I remember seeing him with a pad of paper, watching the TV or the tapes and drawing up schemes. Sometimes he'd draw up formations on napkins at the dinner table. He was always doing all sorts of stuff like that.

It was a little different for our older brother, Jim. He's six years older than us and he took our parents' divorce a lot harder than

Rob and I did. I think he saw what coaching did to the relationship between Mom and Dad, and as a result, he's a little more resentful about what the coaching job did to the family. He still loved sports. In fact, he studied journalism in college and wanted to be a sportswriter. He was a ball boy for the New York Jets in 1968, the Super Bowl season, and he got really close to Joe Namath. After he went to law school, he tried to be a sports agent, but that job is almost as hard as being a coach. Chasing college guys around all the time and trying to get them as clients—there's nothing easy about that.

The fact is that our dad told us time and again that he didn't want us to go into coaching. He kept telling us to do something else, that coaching is a hard life. Sure, it looks glamorous, but the truth is, it's not an easy way of life. Don't get me wrong—it's fun to be on the sideline during an NFL game. I mean, that's as great as it gets. You're competing at the highest level of a sport. Everybody is watching you. Everybody is talking about what you do, talking about the players and talking about the team. Then there's the Super Bowl; trust me, that's an awesome experience. When I went to the Super Bowl with Baltimore in 2000, when we beat the snot out of the New York Giants in Tampa, my brother Rob was in the stands. He hadn't been in one yet (he won two after he joined New England and Bill Belichick), and he told me after the game about how he started getting all choked up, all emotional that I was out there. Believe me, Rob isn't the kind of guy to get all emotional and open about his feelings. I might do that from time to time, but that's where these twins start to go our own directions.

But what makes coaching such a tough profession is what you don't see on TV. What you have to understand is that no matter who you are in this profession, you have to pay your dues. You have to prove yourself at a lot of levels before you get a chance to play with the big boys. My dad wasn't giving us a free pass into the game. He wasn't hiring us straight out of college. He understood the importance of having to suffer to prove yourself. Even after he broke into the NFL in 1968 with the Jets, it wasn't so glamorous then. He was living at the YMCA for a while, splitting a room with another coach. Here he was in his thirties, and he had to do that to chase his dream.

Sure, we were ball boys with the Bears when we were kids and that was a blast. In fact, we probably deserve credit for a forced fumble in one game against the Seahawks. It was a rainy day and we had this one ball that was still all soaked. As the Seahawks were getting ready to score again, we threw this sopping wet ball to the ref and he puts it down. The snap goes through the quarterback's hands and the Bears recovered. One of their guys started chasing us down the sideline. Man, that was great. That kind of thing doesn't really happen today.

My brother and I did have real jobs in high school and college. By real, I mean actual work. It's not like we just showed up at the Bears' offices and our dad handed us a bunch of money to go out all of the time. When we were kids, we had a paper route. Later, we worked at a Pepsi factory in Chicago, and one summer we worked with hot tar as roofers. Man, that stuff was hot and sticky. We used to get it all over us. We'd get up at 3 A.M. and drive all the way down to some part of south Illinois to tar a school roof or something. We got to the point we could run up the ladders and slide down them.

Whatever job I did, I loved it. I worked as hard as I could to be the best at it. My brother was the same way. When we were working as roofers, the company laid everybody off at one point, but the guy who ran the company ended up calling us and said he wanted to hire us back because we were the best guys he had.

When we started coaching, it wasn't going to be that cushy. There was no such thing as being a special defensive breakdown assistant for an NFL team. Our dad helped us find positions where we could start, but it was getting graduate assistant jobs. I got one at Eastern Kentucky and Rob got one at Western Kentucky, both NCAA Division I-AA schools. Rob almost got a job at Kentucky State, a "real job," as we used to say, but that fell through at the last minute. In fact, during spring break of our senior year in college is when we went out to start working on our careers. Most kids take spring break to go somewhere fun, like to the beach to stare at girls and drink beer. We went to some smaller college to be around sweaty guys.

At least we got to drink some beer.

Let me explain what a graduate assistant does, particularly at a small college: everything. You break down the film, you make copies of the game plan, you make sure the players aren't getting in trouble, you pick guys up at the airport and you drop them off. You make sure the head coach has gas in his car. You don't sleep. And you live on about $1,500, maybe, so you sneak every free meal you can possibly get. By the way, there's next to zero chance of this turning into a long-term job. Unless somebody dies in the middle of the season, it's a long shot. Still, when you're just getting started, you're cheap labor and you're just there to prove to others (and to yourself) that you like the job and you can do it well. Every school has a line of guys waiting to break into coaching, so you can get replaced in about 10 seconds.

You have to love it and you have to want to be the best at what you're doing in order to make it in the field. I went from Eastern Kentucky to New Mexico Highlands, a Division II school, for a year and got to be a defensive coordinator and assistant head coach at age 26. Then I went back to Kentucky and coached at Morehead State for four years.

Each time I took a new position, I loved it and I was getting more and more experience. When I went to New Mexico, it was a chance to run the defense. I was so excited until I got there and realized I had the all-midget team. Seriously, I didn't have a single player over six feet tall. But I told those guys that it didn't matter how big we were, we were going to lead the league in turnovers if we bought into what I was teaching them. Sure as hell, we did it.

Now, was I a great coach when I first started out? There's no way in hell, because I didn't have the experience. But that didn't matter. The only thing that mattered is that if I thought I was great, then I could be convincing to the players. I knew I was passionate about it, and I'm sure the players saw that and knew my heart was in the right place. How much did they learn from me? I was just starting, so I don't know, but they knew I would give them an honest effort and an honest opinion.

It wasn't any different for Rob. After his one year at Western Kentucky, he got another grad assistant job at Ohio State. To make some extra money on the side, Rob worked unloading trucks at a Burger King. Then he spent five years at Tennessee State, where at different times he coached running backs, wide receivers, and the defensive line. I kind of get a chuckle out of one of us coaching wide receivers. Yeah, the Ryan brothers working with graceful, elegant wide receivers; I can't really picture that one.

The big break for us came in 1994. By this time, our dad had gotten back in the league. He took a break from the NFL for a couple years after the whole Philadelphia thing and in 1993 got back into it as a coach for the Houston Oilers. The Oilers won 11 in a row during the 1993 season but ended up getting beat in their first playoff game. Immediately after, my dad was hired by Arizona. By this time, we had paid enough dues in his mind for him to give us assistant coaching jobs. We were making about $80,000 and we were on top of the world. Now, I wasn't making anything close to what I make now, but man, life was good. It's crazy that way. When you're doing something you love this much and you start to make decent money—it's a dream. You don't feel like you're working at all. On top of that, Rob and I got to work with our dad every minute of every day. We saw how he worked with players, the way he was with other coaches, and how he designed game plans. We got to see our dad do the whole deal, live and in action.

I got to work with the linebackers and the defensive line. Rob worked with the defensive backs, which was great for him because we had the great Aeneas Williams, a really great cornerback who went to the Pro Bowl both years that Rob worked with him. Our first year, Williams led the league in interceptions with nine, and let me tell you, the overall defense was really good. We ranked second in the league in total defense, second against the run, and third against the pass. If we'd had any offense, we would have done a hell of a lot better. We scored only 235 points the whole season. That's less than 15 points a game. But to show how strong the defense was, we lost four games by four points or less. Over the final nine games, we didn't allow a single team to score 20 points in any game against us. Going 8-8 was pretty damn respectable.

The next year, we had quarterback Dave Krieg, who threw 21 picks, and we end up with 41 fumbles (a Krieg specialty). It was just a parade of guys hanging on at the end of their careers, picking up checks. The wide receivers were terrible. Running back Garrison Hearst was okay in 1995, but he was hardly special. On top of that, we were in the same division with Dallas, the New York Giants, Philadelphia, and Washington. The defense, however, was still terrific. We led the NFL with 32 interceptions and 42 total takeaways.

It was the Cardinals, so you just do the best you can on teams like that. The entire defensive staff got cleared out after that season. We still didn't have a lot of contacts in the NFL and we didn't have enough of a résumé to catch on anywhere else in the league just yet. I was lucky and caught on with the University of Cincinnati as the defensive coordinator for the next two years. Rob wasn't quite as lucky right away, but he was still successful. He went on to Hutchinson Community College in Kansas. He was the defensive coordinator and watched over the dorms, or something like that. For all that, he made $20,000. It was worth it for him. He was a stud. Hutchinson led the nation in total defense, allowing 228 yards per game, led in sacks with 56, and set a national record by forcing 49 turnovers.

After that, Rob hit it big and was hired by Oklahoma State, Mom and Dad's alma mater, as the defensive coordinator. He spent three years there and was even named Coordinator of the Year by *The Sporting News* during his first season. That's because not only did Oklahoma State break a streak of eight straight years with a losing record (going back to the days of Barry Sanders) by going 8-4 that year, but they also beat Texas in one of the greatest turnarounds in college history. In 1996, the year before Rob got there, Texas just crushed Oklahoma State 71-14. In Rob's first year, Oklahoma State won 42-16. It was the biggest reversal of scores in NCAA history.

Of course, Rob got a little help on that one. He and Dad sat down and looked at the cutups of Texas and came up with a plan. I'll let Rob tell it in his own words, because he explains it best:

> We're playing Texas after I got hired and I came home and told my dad, "Shit, it's going to be tough." After what they did to us the year before, I was racking my brain trying to come up with ideas. Dad goes, "Well, bring home all the cutups." So I brought all the cutups to his farm in Kentucky. Every night we'd watch a little bit more of them, and he's like, "Well, hell, boy, maybe you ought to try and run that wide tackle 6." I say, "Yeah, I don't know." I'm looking at it and he has something doodled on a napkin, but it wasn't a wide tackle 6, I don't know what it was. But we run it and beat the shit out of Texas with it. We made the greatest comeback, the biggest lopsided score in the history of college football from one season to the next, Oklahoma State beating Texas. It was a defensive front that they had never seen before. Really it was a napkin at our farm in Lawrenceburg, Kentucky. Dad was drawing up the wide tackle 6, but it had never been a wide tackle 6 the way I had seen it. It had the same linebacker in our side, and I looked at it and took it. I'm like, "That's not the wide tackle 6, Dad, but that looks pretty good," against every one of their plays that they had. We ran it and beat the hell out of them.

By 1998, I had landed at Oklahoma as the defensive coordinator, so a few months later, Rob and I faced off. I'd love to tell you this was a beauty, but it sucked. My team lost 41-26. They must have cheated us somehow. That's the only way they could have won. Either that or my brother gave them a hell of a lot better scouting report on me than I gave our guys on him. As badly as we played that game, we did finish sixth in the nation in total defense that season.

I lasted only that one year at Oklahoma before I got my biggest break of all. I was hired by Baltimore, and started what would end up being a decade with the Ravens. My brother lasted one more year at Oklahoma State before getting hired by Bill Belichick in 2000 to join the New England staff. It was pretty good timing for both of us. Within one year, I was in the Super Bowl. Within one year of his return to the NFL, Rob was in the first of two Super Bowls. Then he went on to Oakland to coach for the Raiders for five years. I'm sure he could write a book about that experience, but I'll leave that to him. After Oakland, he moved to Cleveland to work with his old buddy Eric Mangini, coincidentally the guy I replaced with the New York Jets. Hey, that's the way it goes. We all understand that in this profession, and Eric didn't hold it against Rob.

See, we all love this job. If you coach in the NFL, it's pure joy because you've worked your ass off to get here. It's brutal hours, it's mentally exhausting, and it's physically draining, but you love it. You love to compete at that level and you love the challenge of putting your best out there every week. For my dad, my brother, and me it runs in our blood. It's the family business, just as if my dad had opened some store or business back in Oklahoma many years ago and asked us to come on board.

The best part is that the next generation of Ryan coaches is coming. My son Seth loves the game and is already talking about coaching. He's talking about baseball, too, and either one is fine by me. He's a smart kid and you can see it in how he plays. He really knows the game and knows what he's doing. In school, he's doing great in math already. He really has a mind for it and looks at the game in such a different way. If he keeps going and he really wants to get into coaching, if he has that ability, maybe I'll try to get him in a lot faster than my dad did. At least I know he's going to go to a Division I as a graduate assistant, not I-AA as I did. The thing about going I-AA was that I got to coach a position, I literally got to coach. My dad thought that was going to be great, giving me that practical experience. What you don't realize is how Division I snubs their nose at I-AA. It's all crap, because there's plenty of great coaches at all levels of football, but that's the politics of it.

Then there's my older brother Jim's son (and only child), James David Ryan III (my dad is James David Ryan, Sr., and my brother Jim is junior), who wants to become a hockey coach. James is a great kid, a tough kid. He went through this brutal form of cancer when he was 14. It's called rhabdomyosarcoma. It developed behind his eye and it's really aggressive. The tumor doubles in size every day, so he went from having what looked like a swollen eye to having this huge growth there in just a day or two. It was really scary. They had to operate right away, and then James had to go through a year of chemotherapy and radiation treatments. My brother still has the treatment schedule on the refrigerator door as a reminder of what they went through and how every day with his son is a blessing.

James is really close to both my sons. As soon as we found out James was sick back in 2007, we went there right away. James comes to visit us all the time now. James was playing hockey at the time, and he's still on the Lafayette High School team, but he can't really play as well. You put that kind of poison in your body for a year with chemo and radiation and you just don't ever recover right. But despite everything he's been through, he still loves the game and he wants to coach it. I think my brother Jim, even though he never got the coaching bug, understands the passion. He told James, "Don't go into coaching because you see your uncles in the NFL and think this is how you're going to make it to the NHL. You'll have about one-tenth of one percent of a chance to make it and you'll always be unhappy. If you do it because that's what you love, then go for it."

I can't say it any better.

5. Father of My Own

Growing up with as much love and passion for my father as I did, one of the things I looked forward to most was being a father. And I couldn't have asked for two better children.

My wife, Michelle, and I have two sons, Payton and Seth. They are both in high school—Payton's a senior and Seth's a sophomore. They're great kids, the best, and so much fun to be around. Even though I've been involved in football for their entire lives, spending so much time away from home—the practice, the preparation, the travel, the games—I've always had a strong connection with Payton and Seth. They are gifts, and Michelle and I are so fortunate.

Having children of my own, I marvel at how different they each can be, too.

Payton is the oldest, a senior in high school this year. He's quiet, as good-looking as they come, with long hair, lively eyes, and a great smile; but he is the more introverted of the two. He's not into athletics, either. Payton follows the Jets and wants us to win, but he's not the guy in the front row leading the cheers. He prefers a more disciplined approach to things, but only as long as it is something he truly cares about. He's a black belt in karate, for instance, and was doing phenomenal training and was close to earning a second-degree black belt. Yet one day he decided he had enough and moved on to something else. Payton prefers to be anonymous and fly under the radar, and it's an approach that works great for him.

My younger son, Seth, a sophomore in high school, is the complete opposite. He loves the crowd, is naturally very athletic, and is much more outgoing. I wouldn't be surprised if he ended up coaching football when he gets older, because he just loves the game that much. The kid is fearless. He comes to Jets practices and runs routes against my guys—it's pretty fun to watch a Pro Bowl cornerback knock him on his ass after the catch, but Seth bounces right up with a big smile. He might even talk some smack—imagine where he acquired that quality. When I was with Baltimore, Seth routinely disappeared down the hall and sat in the general manager's office with Ozzie Newsome. What kid at that age has that kind of courage? One might think the general manager of an NFL team wouldn't want to be bothered, but Ozzie always had time for Seth. Seth just wanted to talk shop.

When Payton was born, I told my mother-in-law that he would never have to fight a day in his life. I meant it. I was that emotional over my child's birth and that protective of him from the moment he took his first breath. I was going to be there for Payton, and to this day I am. It's the same with Seth. When I was a child, because I was a twin, I didn't know what it was like not to have someone always with you, always looking out for you. But as a parent, I have discovered the rules have changed. I have learned that you can't fight all of your children's battles. I am still there for them, and that won't ever change. Ever. They grow up, they make mistakes, they experience life, they make their own friends, and they find their way.

You think time goes by quickly? Have children. I can't believe they are teenagers already.

I try to spend as much time with Payton and Seth as I can, but it's difficult, especially during the football season. In July 2010, we spent a week on the Outer Banks in North Carolina and had so much fun. I rented a huge beach house for my coaches and their families before the start of training camp. It was just a great way to relax and connect before we returned to the 24/7 grind of football. It was so neat to watch Payton and Seth interact with everyone, playing and goofing off. From dawn to dusk, we always had something to do. We played golf, football, putt-putt, a game where you toss beanbags in a hole cut out in a wooden plank, and Boogieboarded in the Atlantic Ocean. One day we had a tripleheader: golf in the morning, putt-putt in the afternoon, and pizza on the way back to the beach house. Each night a different family was in charge of dinner. One night it was Mexican, the next night steak, the next night BBQ. The kids disappeared into the downstairs bedrooms and played video games; the parents sat around the table and talked and laughed, usually into the early morning. It was just an amazing week . . . the kind of family time you can't get very often when you're coaching.

Being a parent is tough enough, and the only way it works in the Ryan home is because of Michelle. I knew when we first met that I could fall in love with her. We were married in 1987. She's smart, she's talented, she's sweet, and she's loyal as hell.

Family means a lot to Michelle, too. Her family lives in a small home in southwestern Oklahoma. Well, shortly after I'd been promoted to defensive coordinator in Baltimore, Michelle and I were out visiting her parents and we looked at Seth and Payton and said, "We think we ought to buy Grandma and Grandpa a new home." They were excited and said, "Yeah! Let's go get one!" So we left the boys to occupy Michelle's parents, and she and I cruised around for a few hours until we found a house we really liked. When we got back that evening we told her parents about it. It was an absolutely great moment.

Last summer was Michelle's parents' fiftieth wedding anniversary and we went to Europe and cruised the Baltic Sea with them. Of course, the boys and I weren't real excited about it, but we pretended that we couldn't wait. I am here to tell you we had a great time. I couldn't keep track of the boys on the ship, but it was relaxing and a wonderful way not only for the boys to spend time with their grandparents, but for me to get away from football, too. I couldn't tell you who we signed or what had happened back in New York. It was actually a lot of fun to have that break and enjoy some unique family time.

Football has always been a mainstay in my life, but at first, Michelle didn't know much about it. She soon realized what it meant to me, and we have been a team ever since. Our support for each other has never wavered. There was one time when I was at Morehead State in the early 1990s and we were struggling badly. I bitched and moaned in the car on the ride home after one game, and Michelle stared at me and asked point-blank if I had given any thought to changing careers. We didn't have a house payment, we didn't have any children, and she pointed out that this was the best time to make a change. I looked at her and said no way. It was football or bust, and I knew I wouldn't bust.

Football is my domain, and everything else is Michelle's. She has helped me become a successful coach and a successful parent. I worry about the Jets during the season, and Michelle worries about everything else: our house, the cars, the bills, the schoolwork, Payton and Seth, and anything from A to Z that relates to our home. All I need to worry about is making sure my house key opens the door each night. The only thing Michelle asks me to do around the house is maybe move something that's too heavy for her. She takes care of everything else. She has to be the disciplinarian, she has to be the mom, she has to be the dad at times—she has to be the one who does everything. Of course, the boys love me because I want to do things with them when I am around. I am not the disciplinarian. When it comes down to good cop, bad cop—I am the good cop.

Michelle's sacrifices and determination have given me the freedom to concentrate on football and work the long hours I need to work to make the Jets successful. Some coaches' wives might not agree with that arrangement; they may want their husbands home at a certain time so they can catch dinner and a movie. Michelle, however, has never complained about my hours away from home and from the kids. She wants to take care of everything on the home front so I can focus on football. If I am successful, our family is successful. When you get to this level and you put in the time that my wife has (and several of the other wives with their husbands), they are really the unsung heroes of the coaching profession. It's the wives and the families who don't get to see their husbands and fathers for six months out of the year who make the real sacrifices.

What more can I ask for? I am so fortunate to be in a career that I love and I am successful at, and I have a great wife and two great sons. Michelle is so understanding and accommodating. She knows when I am down and tired, and she can see the stress in my face or maybe in my actions when things don't go well. I get quiet, and maybe even a little snappy after a loss. I may not say much on the drive home from the field, but Michelle understands. Even when we win games, I still might be pissed with the way we played. Those are the nights I need to go to bed; but one time I was so pissed at how we played defensively after a win that I went back to the office that night instead of going home. It doesn't have to be like that, and it's wrong, but Michelle never complained. Usually after games, I want to read the newspaper and watch television so I can see what the media has said about our team and me. That way I'm not surprised when I meet with the media at our daily news conference the following day. Michelle is the complete opposite. She doesn't read the papers or watch television when it relates to our games. She believes the media distorts winning and losing. She can't control the games, she can't control the press, but she can—and she does—control our home. Our home is my sanctuary away from football, and she's the one who makes it work. I can relax the few hours I am at home each night during the season because of Michelle. She makes it easy on me.

Take our games—Michelle knows my routine better than I do. When I break down film on Monday after a loss, that's when I usually start to feel better. I usually see that we played better than I had thought, that maybe one or two plays were the difference in the game. We may have lost, but I'll see some good things and I always believe we are going to win the next game. By Tuesday, I already start to game-plan for Sunday's opponent, so the previous week's game and loss are behind us. I need a short memory in this business. I don't forget how we lost or why we lost, but I can't dwell on it for too long because we always have another game in a few short days. Michelle and my kids know that. They understand me, just like I understood my father.

Michelle also understands that all my bravado, though genuine, is not always about me. I have confidence in everyone involved with the Jets, top to bottom. I know I have a great team and I have great coaches, so why shouldn't I be confident in myself? I tell my children to be confident. Why not? If you set your standards low, what are the odds you're going to achieve at a high level? If there's no pressure to win, why coach? Who wants to hear a coach say, "Hey, let's be average this year. Great! We're on course to win half of our games, so let's take it easy the rest of the way"? If a head coach, the leader on the football field, doesn't believe in himself, who is going to follow? That's why leadership, confidence, and bravado are an important part of the equation, in the NFL and, I really think, anywhere. If you believe in yourself, then you can often overcome a flawed plan or a negative circumstance just by willpower.

This is why I work so well under pressure and under the gun. There are a lot of people in the world, even in the coaching profession, who don't want the pressure on them. I want that pressure. I am confident in what I can do. I want our children to be confident and believe in themselves and each other, too. Michelle gets it, and that's why our family is such a great team.

Michelle and I really didn't have a chance to relish the moment I was hired in New York until a few weeks later after the initial press conference. I was so tired from the NFL season that had just ended, and after a few weeks we finally had the opportunity to enjoy it all and look at each other and say, "We made it." I had reached my goal to be a head coach in the NFL—and it was in New York City, of all places.

We absolutely love New York, too. We like to take the train into the city and walk around or eat at a restaurant that somebody recommended. I actually have tried to play more golf, too, during the last off-season since the boys enjoy it. There's a par-3 course near our home, and Seth and I will get out for a quick, 90-minute round. When at home, Michelle and I like to watch a good movie, or I might sit in my chair and work on a Sudoku puzzle.

People always see me smiling, laughing, and in a good mood, and they wonder if Michelle and I ever fight. That's what is so great about our relationship—even our disagreements end up in laughter. There are times when Michelle is determined to stay mad at me. She might slam the cabinet door or throw a pan down on the counter to get my attention when she is set on making me suffer. I get that look all wives probably give their husbands when they are mad. Of course, I pop off and say something smart-alecky or funny and Michelle, bless her soul, can't keep a straight face. She tries, but she can't.

I am also the kind of guy who always tries to make a game out of anything. The Ryan family has long made up rules as we go. Like when the kids were younger and I was on the couch watching football and wanted a drink of water. Now, how in the world are you going to get one of your children to walk into the kitchen, fill up a water bottle, and bring it to you? Not likely. I told the boys, "Okay, let's see who can get me the water bottle the quickest," and I'd time them. It worked every time, and the Road Runner didn't have a chance against Payton and Seth.

The two boys are close and pull for each other even though they have different interests. Payton is not comfortable in the spotlight. He loves the Jets and hates it when I lose. I think that's one reason why he elected to stay in Baltimore and finish high school, even after the Jets hired me. He lives with my brother-in-law. In Baltimore, he is removed from the highs and lows of our wins and losses. But he can tell you exactly what happened in our game, remember nearly every play, his memory is that good. He knows where we are in the standings. Payton might act nonchalant about our season, but it means a lot more to him than he might want you to think. I am so proud of Payton. He's a great kid.

As I said, Seth is the son who absolutely loves football. Of course, his favorite player is our quarterback, Mark Sanchez. Sanchez loves Seth; Seth is like his little brother. They text-message each other all the time. Mark went to every one of Seth's freshman football games, home and away. I told him to stop because I thought it would interfere with his preparation for our games, but he insisted, "No, no, this is part of my routine." Once people started to figure out Mark would be at the game, a lot of fans started to show for Seth's freshman football games. Mark didn't cut Seth—or even Michelle—any slack either. Seth had lost his game uniform pants before one game and the replacement pants Michelle had for him were huge and just about swallowed him whole. Mark busted Seth and Michelle and said there was no way Seth could show for his game in those pants. "You don't look good, you don't play good," Mark repeated about a thousand times. I was like, "Nah, he's fine. It's not a big deal." But it was a big deal to Mark. He absolutely killed Seth and Michelle about those pants.

I mentioned before that Seth attends practice with me and runs routes against our cornerbacks. A guy like Darrelle Revis won't give Seth any slack either. He has knocked Seth to the ground on a completion. One time, Darrelle stepped on Seth's shoe while Seth ran a route and the kid still caught the ball in front of Revis. Revis was pissed. So Seth has that on his résumé: "Caught a ball in front of All-Pro cornerback Darrelle Revis." When Seth's at practice, I let him run round and have fun. Even though he's my son, when he has run routes, our players think, "Hey, I don't care if he's the coach's kid, we don't want him catching the ball on our watch." They go after him pretty good. Seth is fearless, and it's kind of hilarious to watch. I don't know if that's going to be a good thing, but I just want him to have fun and play. I do know one thing, though. He's going to be a third-generation coach in the Ryan family, that's for sure.

But until Seth is coaching a team of his own, he's pretty possessive of mine, and everything that goes with it, including the little rituals. Of course, my wife and I and the kids have our own superstitions when it comes to our games. Each Friday night, we eat out at our favorite local Mexican restaurant. Michelle even has a lucky outfit she wears for the home games against New England.

Everyone is anxious and excited, and it's neat that my family has been involved in this journey. I am so blessed, so thankful, and so appreciative to have such a wonderful wife and a wonderful family. I am also hopeful that Payton and Seth look up to me the same way I look up to my father to this very day. There's nothing better than being a father of my own.

6. Tackling Dyslexia

When I said publicly in 2009 that I had dyslexia, my family was a little upset about it. My brother Rob said, "Why are you telling people about that? What's it their business?" We're twins, but lucky for him, he doesn't have that problem. I understand why my family reacted that way to me talking about it—they were trying to protect me. Some people get embarrassed about this stuff and, trust me, when I was a kid and I didn't know what was wrong, it made me embarrassed, too. I wanted to lash out when kids made fun of me for struggling with reading. And I really did struggle.

These days, I couldn't care less. I've come to realize that one of the reasons I am where I am in my life is that I found a way to deal with dyslexia, even when I didn't know I had it. In other words, in its own way, having to deal with it forced me to become who I am. I was unaware of being dyslexic for so long, that having this disability drove me to work harder, to use my strengths—and that led me down this path. It's my own personal kind of meeting with Darwin, I suppose. Either you sink or you swim.

I've heard that somewhere between 5 and 17 percent of people have some form of dyslexia, which basically means that letters look jumbled as you read them and there's kind of a disconnect between being able to read them and being able to pronounce them. It really screws up your ability to learn. A lot of dyslexic people will flunk out of school, even though they are intelligent. Doctors say there is absolutely no relationship between IQ and dyslexia. I'm not telling you I'm a genius, but the point is that just because I have dyslexia doesn't mean I'm dumb. What it means, according to one doctor I met with, is that the people who actually find a way to make it have learned to adapt—and it's unbelievable how high they can go.

As a kid I remember not having any problem with vision, which was why it seemed strange that I had problems seeing things on the page. Actually, I had great hand-eye coordination. I was a really good hitter when I played baseball in high school. Even as an adult, I could always hit. My brother Jim loves to tell the story about one time when we were in Mobile, Alabama, at the Senior Bowl. This was when Rob and I were just getting started as coaches, and Jim was pretty fresh out of law school and wanted to be an agent representing players. So we were all at the Senior Bowl at one of the little schools where the players used to practice (they practice at the stadium in town these days). We were leaving practice and we walked past the baseball field, where there was a kid pitching, working with the catcher. We chatted with him, trying to be friendly, but the pitcher started bragging on himself about how great he was and how he was getting ready for the draft, expecting to make it big. I was thinking to myself, "He's not really that tough." So I grabbed a bat, walked up to the plate, and said, "Okay, show me what you got." I was standing there in cowboy boots and jeans, just looking ridiculous going up to bat. The kid was so cocky as he wound up. He threw me a fastball, and I just crushed it. Jim guessed I hit the thing like 400 feet. On the first pitch, not even looking one over—that was sweet. I just dropped the bat and said, "Oh yeah, kid, you're going far." We all just walked away laughing. The kid was probably shell-shocked.

Anyway, the point is that I never thought there was something physically wrong with me, so it took me a long time to address the problem. Now that I know I'm dyslexic, I don't hide anymore from the things that might be wrong with me. I don't hide from the fact that I'm overweight or that I don't read that well. This kind of stuff basically tells who I am, about some of the struggles I have or have had; I'm man enough to admit it. If I can help somebody realize that I was able to accomplish what I've done so far despite what I had to overcome, it'll make me very happy. This wasn't a fun thing to deal with.

It's the same way with my players. If I'm willing to put myself out there with them, they're going to feel the same way about talking to me. They're going to open up as people, maybe telling me something that I can do to help them, motivate them, or make them better players. If I've got nothing to hide from my guys, they won't hide from me.

The one person who I think struggled most with my public announcement was my mom, and her problem wasn't that I talked about it. I think it's more about guilt. Like I wrote before, my mom has a doctorate in education administration. Think about it: She's incredibly smart; my dad was an Academic All-American; my older brother Jim has three degrees, including a law degree; and my twin brother Rob has his degree and never had any problems.

Then there's me, and my mom didn't ever figure it out. She explains it this way:

When Rex was a kid and he was getting started in school, we were living in Toronto. The people at the school thought maybe Rex was a little slow, but I knew that wasn't the case. He was very intelligent. It would just take him a long time to read things. Looking back, I thought they never really taught him to read. So I had him tested in Ontario and they told me they thought he was a little slow. Truly, I don't think they knew what they were looking for. He was such an outgoing, confident kid. He didn't show signs of being slow in picking things up, but here I am an educator and I didn't figure it out. When Rex finally found out all those years later, it all made sense to me and I felt so embarrassed. I felt so bad, and I asked him one time if there was anything I could do and he just said, "Mom, it's okay, I've gotten this far, I can deal with it," but as a parent, you feel so guilty.

I understand where she's coming from. I'm a parent now and I want to make sure I do everything I can for my boys, but I really want my mom to understand that she didn't fail me in any way. I mean, really: Is my life bad? I do what I love, and when you think about it, what might have happened if I had actually learned to read more effectively? Would I have ended up as a coach or would I have gone into another career? I know that my disability made me stronger in other ways that have helped me as a coach. When I say I'm doing exactly what I need to be doing, I mean it. I want to be a coach and I *need* to be a coach. I can't do anything else. This is where I can succeed.

I found out I had dyslexia around 2007. I was visiting a doctor for a completely unrelated reason and we got to chatting. I told her I'd always been a very slow reader. Well, she started asking me a few specific questions and a few minutes later she told me I was almost certainly dyslexic. I was pretty flabbergasted. I thought, "That's crazy! I would have known it by now." But then she gave me a test with a list of 100 words that I was supposed to read. It seemed to take me at least 15 minutes to get through it, because I was looking at those words and they were just a jumble of black letters on white paper. When I got done, they called my younger son, Seth, in and gave him the list of words to read. He rattled them off in about 30 seconds, right down the list like it was nothing. I was floored, finally realizing what was wrong with me for all those years. Then I remember just laughing about it, thinking about all the stuff I did trying to accommodate my problem without even knowing what it was.

Oddly enough, I wasn't embarrassed. In fact, I took some other tests related to reasoning and brain function and the doctors evaluating those said that I had the highest percent of problem solving and creativity they'd ever seen. That's how I compensated for what I couldn't do. You see what I mean about developing other strengths? More important, those problem-solving and creative abilities are crucial for coaching, especially in football. When you play in a game that has 22 moving parts at one time, you constantly have problems to solve and you're constantly looking for creative ways to attack the opponent. Problem solving and creativity work everywhere in this business.

Let me give you an example of how I dealt with dyslexia without even knowing it. Somewhere along the line, I figured out that I could read more effectively if things were printed on colored paper. I don't know where or how I figured that out, but it's true. So I developed a color-coding system for how to organize the plays I wanted to call. I might have had some on blue paper, some on green, some on yellow, whatever worked. If you'd ever see my call sheet for a game, it looks like a freakin' rainbow. Anyway, then I'd have Mike Pettine, who was one of our staff assistants in Baltimore and is now the defensive coordinator with me on the Jets, print the stuff on different-colored paper. Again, this was before I ever knew I had the disability. It would drive Pettine crazy. He'd say to me: "How can you read that better?" He didn't understand it. Heck, I couldn't explain it at the time; it just worked.

The other way that I would compensate is I'd listen very carefully. Again, it's not that I ever really thought about it, I just did it. I listened to what people were telling me. That's how I picked up stuff. With the TV and radio commercials that I do now, I have people read the copy to me and I repeat it back to them before we do the taping. It's just a lot easier for me to get the information that way. If you talk to me, I can pick things up better than I can by just trying to read them off a white piece of paper with black letters.

That's why I decided to tell people about my dyslexia when I got the job with the New York Jets. I also never hid it from the Jets when I interviewed. You can't hide stuff like that as you get further up the line in this business—really, in any business. It's one thing to be an assistant coach, where you're not out in the public all the time or expected to be the face of the organization. You're talking to players a lot, but you're not in front of them every day doing a speech or some presentation. Being an assistant coach, especially a position coach, you can be a little anonymous (which is good sometimes . . . like after a loss).

When you're a head coach, everything is on the table. Your life is an open book. That's why I figured this was the right time to talk about it. Of course, you may be thinking, "Okay, Rex, it's great that you admit you're dyslexic, but how exactly did you get a college degree from Southwestern Oklahoma State, and a master's in physical education while you were a graduate assistant at Eastern Kentucky? How did you even get through grade school?"

That's a good question. When I first got started in school—first and second grade—they'd give us little spelling tests. I would get maybe one or two right, and sometimes none at all. It got to the point that if I got the first letter and the last letter right, then that was like me getting the one correct answer. As I went along in school, things got to be more and more embarrassing. I knew I wasn't stupid, but when you keep failing tests, frustration mounts. So what I did to cope was skip school all the time. We were living in Toronto and my mom would be off working. I had a morning paper route and an afternoon paper route, so my brother and I would be out the door early. Then I'd go to school. If there was going to be softball or floor hockey or something fun during the day, then I would stay. If there wasn't, I would go home and my mom never really knew. I would never get away with that today, because they're checking all the time now, but back then it was easy.

The funny thing is, I really liked school, but I didn't want to be there if I knew I was getting a test back. That was part of the embarrassment. The other way I dealt with it was that if somebody made fun of me, I'd just beat their ass. I was big, so people never really said much. I was still embarrassed, but I was strong enough to keep people from really hurting my feelings. I'm not saying ass-kicking is a great coping mechanism, but I can only imagine how hard it would be for a kid to feel helpless and not be able to stick up for himself. Quitting school might feel like a better option. When kids would be reading in class, I would just sit there kind of looking at the pictures, turning the pages to make it look like I was keeping up, hoping the teacher didn't ask me any questions. If the teacher did, I'd make some joke or smart-aleck comment to get around giving the answer, because I didn't know what I was talking about. At least I stayed in school enough that I could get through to graduate, and I had enough athletic talent to play ball in college. I was lucky.

These days, kids with dyslexia are given a bunch of different ways to learn or read books or take tests, which is great news. But that's not how it was for me. Once I got to college, I remember how much reading there was and how much I struggled. I would try to learn the material as best I could. I tried to read and write my papers as well as I could manage, but I couldn't actually make it all come together. There would be so many misspelled words, the papers would make no sense. If I had been allowed to do the tests verbally, I feel like they would have been a snap. I could explain all the material by talking to you. But writing it down or talking about what I'd read? Then, I was stuck.

At one point, I finally dropped out and came back to live with my mom. Rob stayed in school because he was doing fine. He could handle the reading and paper-writing, but I couldn't. While I was with my mom, I took an English class at a local college. We were supposed to read 10 books, and I couldn't read one of them. So we tried something. My mom read the books out loud and we would talk about the plot and the material in a lot of detail. When I had papers due, I told her what I wanted to say and she'd type them up for me. When I would go take a test, I would think about all the different questions the teacher might ask, and I'd write down notes on what answers I might use if I got these questions. Whatever the questions ended up being, I'd think about those notes and figure out a way to use them on the tests. The professor would sometimes say, "Rex, you had a different take on it than I had." Well, I sure did—because I had memorized the first sentence or two of my notes and then I'd just try to make it work from there. That way I could BS my way through the test but still show I knew the basics. Now, the written tests never looked anything like my papers because my mom would help make the papers look good. My written tests, on the other hand, looked atrocious and were filled with mistakes because my spelling was so awful. But in the end, I was able to squirm by, and I figured out how to pass the course.

I'll say it again: It makes me feel really good to know there are productive ways to teach dyslexic kids now. Back at Southwestern and into graduate school, I still felt like I was always struggling to get around the system, but today it's all out in the open and kids are given a variety of ways to learn and be evaluated. Like I said, I was lucky. I had help and I took advantage of it the best I could. My mom didn't know what was wrong with me, but I went to her to help me get through college. There are a lot of people out there who don't have that kind of help. Either their parents aren't around, or maybe their parents just don't have the ability to help the way my mom did. That's why it's so important for people to figure out if they have dyslexia, or any other problem, and to get help with these things. It's hard to rely on being lucky.

The funny part is that I ended up marrying an English teacher. She's sharp, just like my mom. She can read a book in two hours, and I couldn't do it in two years. Funny how that works. Hey, I got a master's in marriage—I married the right one and I did that without any help at all!

7. Eat, Pray, Football

During the 2010 off-season I did a motivational video for a group called Victorprime.com. I along with four other coaches, Sean Payton, Mike Ditka, Mike Singletary, and Bobby Bowden, each picked one subject to talk about and then we broke it down in detail. The title of my section was "Give It All You Got." This was right up my alley, because that's what I've always done. Every job I've ever had, I've given it my all. I don't think, what's my next job? How long am I going to be here? When I'm in, I'm all in, and I'm completely devoted. It could be tarring roofs or coaching a bunch of midgets in New Mexico, regardless—I give it everything.

When my family moved to Baltimore, we bought a house right away, and we bought it in the best neighborhood we could find, with the best public schools we could find for the kids, because I wasn't thinking we were just stopping over. I was all in with that job. I thought I was going to be in Baltimore the rest of my career. That's what I wanted. It's like that movie *Eat Pray Love* with Julia Roberts. Now, I know that it is a chick flick, but I get what it is about. A woman gets divorced and understands that her life isn't what she wanted because she is not really putting herself out there. She's not giving it all she's got, so she gets out there and discovers her passion and finds happiness. That's me. I put myself out there in my job and in my life. It might be something that some people find embarrassing, like dyslexia or my weight, but I'm going to embrace whatever I'm doing.

Now, sometimes when you love your job as much as I do, when you're in deep with football the way I am, you can get yourself in trouble before you realize what you're doing. Yeah, this was a good one: the time I decided to write a letter to Baltimore owner Steve Bisciotti. Now, before we get too far along with this story, you have to know that Bisciotti is one great guy. He's a self-made billionaire. He's good to people, smart, good-looking, snazzy dresser—the whole package. The best part is that Steve isn't one of these owners looking for all the attention. He's like Woody Johnson, looking to help the team, not looking to take the spotlight. You don't see Bisciotti very much, because that's not the way he does business. He's not ignoring the team, not by a long shot. He's around, he knows what's going on, and he has a great feel for what they're doing.

He also has a really interesting, crystallized way of looking at life. He says: "Ninety percent of wealth is good and 10 percent of it is bad. However, 60 percent of fame is good and 40 percent of it is bad." In other words, if you're playing the percentages of what's going to be good for your life, fame is not the percentage play. That's why he stays out of the limelight a lot more than other owners. I think he believes in hiring good people and letting them do the job without all this interference.

So anyway, we opened the 2007 season on a Monday night at Cincinnati, which most people probably think should be a gimme. The Bengals traditionally aren't very good, but what people don't understand is that for a number of reasons, they're a tough matchup for us. They've got a good quarterback in Carson Palmer and they have Chad Ochocinco, who's a pain in the ass to cover and just drives you nuts with all his talk and antics when he gets going. I love it, but you do want to shut him up. He definitely gets the juices going. At the time, they had T. J. Houshmandzadeh, who is a terrific possession guy, tough route runner, just an all-around good football player. So we went in there and lost 27-20.

This was a tough game. We gave up nine points in the first quarter on a touchdown and a field goal. The first one ticked me off. We fumbled the ball and Ochocinco, Johnson, whatever you call him, went deep over the top of our defense for a 39-yard touchdown. Then they get a field goal. We got a touchdown in the second quarter and then we traded field goals just before the half to put the Bengals up 12-10. No biggie. Their longest drive in the first half was 48 yards. Aside from the one throw to Ochocinco, they were just dinking and dunking against us.

We made some adjustments at halftime and we were just stoning them on defense. I mean, defensively we were on the fire. They ran 25 plays in the second half and gained a total of 50 yards. Yeah, 25 plays, 50 yards—that's two yards a freakin' play. We were ridiculously good. The only problem was that our offense was ridiculously bad that day. Hey, it happens, but unfortunately it's true. We had six turnovers, four fumbles, and two interceptions. As a defense, you have to pick up the offense on days like that. When Baltimore won the Super Bowl in my second year there, the defense didn't make excuses when we couldn't score. Never happened. We just put our heads down and battled. That's the way it has to be.

The other thing is that we had Steve McNair at quarterback, and I give Steve a lot of credit. Unfortunately, we got him at the end of his career, but he was one tough guy. McNair took more hard shots than any quarterback I have ever seen and still managed to get back up. He was like a linebacker at quarterback. In his prime, he was one scary dude. RIP Air McNair.

The turnovers hurt us in the second half of that Cincinnati game, there's no question about that. On our first possession of the second half, McNair got sacked, fumbled the ball, and the Bengals returned it for a touchdown to get up 19-10. Finally, we got going in the beginning of the fourth quarter with a field goal, and we caught a break of our own when Ed Reed returned a punt 63 yards for a touchdown with about 12 minutes to go and we were up 20-19. The way our defense was rolling, all we had to do was avoid making another mistake.

We couldn't. In fact, the last 12 minutes of the game were like a nightmare. McNair got a pass intercepted at midfield and the Bengals returned it to our 22-yard line. They caught us with a 15-yard run and then a 7-yard touchdown to Houshmandzadeh, who's great in the red zone. They got a two-point conversion and went up 27-20 with 8:48 remaining. For the game, they'd scored 14 points on three plays where they gained 61 yards.

Still, we had time remaining and our defense even came up with a play. Haloti Ngata, our great defensive tackle, forced a fumble and Reed recovered it at the Cincy 24. Kyle Boller went in at quarterback when McNair got hurt and we eventually got down to fourth-and-goal at the 1-yard line. We just had to punch it in and we would be tied. Boller threw a touchdown pass to tight end Todd Heap, but Heap got called for offensive pass interference.

Then the Bengals got called for a penalty that gave us a first down again at the Bengals' 6. We got back down to the 2 on second down and threw an incomplete pass. Then, on third down, Boller got intercepted when the ball deflected off Heap and a Bengals defensive guy. Talk about frustrating. This was one of those ridiculous gut-wrenchers. Worse, our last three plays from the 2 or closer were all passes that went wrong. This is the kind of stuff that drives you crazy because you're second-guessing yourself. Whether you're a fan, a coach, or even an owner, you second-guess yourself like crazy.

After the game, head coach Brian Billick, both coordinators, and one coach from each side of the ball were going to ride back with Bisciotti on his jet. The idea was that we were going to get back faster because we didn't have to load the plane or do all the TSA check stuff (not that it took a long time, because we had our own special gate, but it was still about a hundred people to get boarded and a lot of stuff to get handled). As a coaching staff, we figured it was best to get a jump on the whole process. We were pissed and we wanted to break down the film. It was a short week already because we had to play the next Sunday, so we were not sleeping on that flight.

Well, the trip got off to a crappy start when the driver took us to the wrong airport. We finally got to the right place and we were sitting on the tarmac with Bisciotti. We were talking about the game, the controversial calls, the turnovers, the plays at the goal line. Then finally Bisciotti says: "Rex, what the hell? We should have run the ball. We should have done all this kind of stuff." Now, that was tough. Here's the owner talking, so you don't want to argue, but you have to be loyal to your head coach. Brian Billick was our coach, and he had Jim Fassel as the offensive coordinator calling the plays. I was not about to throw those guys under the bus. I just said: "Well, you know I'm not an expert in that type of situation. Our guys study film and always do what's in the best interest of the team. You know I've got to get people stops, so I can't concern myself with that, I've got to stop people." I just handled it the best I can, and then Bisciotti shrugged and said, "So you're just along for the ride."

Just along for the ride? What, are you freakin' kidding me? I'm *just along for the ride*? I was shocked, stunned, and pretty soon I was pissed, thinking: "I sleep at the office three days a week. I've been loyal to Brian. Some of the stuff I put a stop to could have really bit our team in the ass." I didn't know what to say, but I was not happy. So the first thing I did after we landed was to write Steve a letter and put it under his door. In that letter I told him, "I'm not even watching my kids growing up. Nobody is committed to this team as much as I am. Nobody. Along for the ride? That's friggin' bullshit."

I told Mike Pettine, the Ravens' linebackers coach and one of the guys I brought with me to the Jets when I got hired (he's our defensive coordinator), about it and he said, "Oh, Rex, don't do it, just go get the letter."

I said, "Hell no, I'm not going to go get the letter. That's how I feel." I knew that Bisciotti got it, because the next day his secretary came running down to my office. Steve wasn't in yet, but she had read the letter to him over the phone when he called in. And when Bisciotti arrived, he came in to see me and he said, "Rex, I said, 'Are you along for the ride?' Like, are you going home with us on the jet?"

Oh. Well, that's a little different. My head was spinning as I thought, "Oh my God, I just told off the owner of the team because I didn't understand what he was saying." I was pretty much a dumbass on that one, so all I could do was laugh at myself. I said, "Oh, sorry, Steve." What do you say after something like that? We still laugh every time we think about that one. I don't know if he was laughing at the time, because it kind of challenged him a little, but I did what I felt at the time was right.

Was I too emotional about what Bisciotti said? Sure, I could have taken a step back, but that's not what you get with a Ryan. Like I said, I love what I do. I loved doing every job I've ever done. I truly mean that. You have to have a joy with everything you do in life. You can't half-ass it and expect to get the most out of it. When I was growing up, my dad couldn't wait to go to work. He loved his job and you could feel his passion for the job. My mom loved her job. Think about it: She was taking trips all over Ontario to these little towns in the middle of nowhere to find out how to teach kids. You don't do that to get rich. You do that because you love it.

It's like my brother Rob said: "If you hire a Ryan, we're going to have emotion. We're going to have fire. It's not political and maybe it's not the most politically right thing to do, but we care. Every once in a while you get a screwup, but it's like I tell my players, 'Look, guys, you've got to have my back on this, you've got to play your ass off, you're going to have to do it.'"

This is why people connect with us. It's over the top sometimes, it's emotional, but it's totally honest. You want to know something really great about how we do business? After everything Mike Ditka went through with my dad in Chicago—the fights, the screaming, the pushing—he tried to hire my brother at one point in time. Man, you have to respect Ditka for that. Ditka was in New Orleans in the late 1990s and he had my brother come in for a talk. He told Rob, "I want an aggressive, kick-ass defense just like I had with your dad." You see, Ditka knew that my dad wasn't just a self-promoter, some guy just trying to make a name for himself. My brother and I aren't, either.

Players see that what we're talking about is totally honest. We're putting it on the line. Players know the difference. They figure it out pretty fast if you're not giving it everything you can. The other important thing about our approach is it gets everybody on the same page. That's not easy in sports. Think about it this way: When you're a head coach, you're always going to have about half your team that isn't exactly happy with you. It's just reality. It's the guys who aren't starting. Every guy thinks he should be starting. Yeah, some of them get the logic of how it works, especially the veterans who have been around long enough to understand a role, but in their heart of hearts, every guy thinks he should be a starting player. You wouldn't want a guy who didn't want to be starting, who didn't want to be out there trying to make a play. These guys have been starting forever. When they were in high school, they were the big stars. In college, they were either stars or they were certainly playing a lot. There aren't too many guys who have made it to the NFL without being pretty prominent players along the way.

As a coach, you have to overcome that. Now, when you're a defensive coordinator or a position coach, it's a little easier. You can always be the good cop and the head coach is almost always the bad cop. It's not that you're selling the head coach out, but everybody knows the buck stops with him, so the coordinator doesn't take all the heat. When you're the head coach, it's all on you—every eye is on you and every decision is on you. You're not going to keep everybody happy in that situation. You can't and you shouldn't expect to. If you want everybody to like you, you're not ready to be a head coach.

It's like what Tennessee coach Jeff Fisher said in the 2010 season after he benched Vince Young in a game early in the season. Everybody asked Fisher if he expected Young to be happy with the decision. Fisher said no, of course not. You don't pull a guy out of a game because you want him to be happy. Geez, what do you think is going to happen? The key is not trying to keep everybody happy, but to keep everybody respecting you. If the players think you are being 100 percent honest and 100 percent committed, they can't question your intention.

Let me jump to 2010 for a minute to illustrate a point. When we were chasing Jason Taylor last off-season and trying to bring him to the Jets, I knew with certainty that Jason Taylor wasn't interested in playing for the New York Jets. Are you kidding me? Do you know the history of Taylor and Jets fans? It's hysterical. Taylor has always been talking trash to Jets fans. He talks to them in New York; he made fun of them in Miami. I mean, the Jets were probably the last team he could have ever imagined playing for.

And I knew he really didn't want to do it. He wanted to go back to Miami and finish his career with the Dolphins. Back in 2008, when Parcells came in, they had problems right from the start. Parcells is big on the off-season program, and he's right about that. You need to build your team in the off-season, guys have to get in shape, and the players have to buy into what you're doing right from the start.

That off-season, though, Taylor was scheduled to be on *Dancing with the Stars*. Okay, I've never had to deal with this kind of thing. We did *Hard Knocks* in 2001 when I was in Baltimore and then again this last season with the Jets, but it's a little different. You're in training camp, so you're working anyway. I don't know how I'd deal with that, but I know this: Jason Taylor did it the right way with the Dolphins. Even before Bill Parcells was hired, Taylor told the team he was going to do that show. Plus, you're talking about a 10-year veteran. You know what Taylor is by this time in his career, and a guy like that has a lot of pride in what he does. Just look at him, you can see the pride just by his appearance. I mean, the guy looks like a movie star. He's tall, he's handsome, he's a thoroughbred athlete, he's smart, he's well-spoken—I mean, come on, how can you deny this guy a chance to do something special, to take a shot at fame like that? He's not going to fake it and not be in shape.

But Parcells hates that stuff. He wasn't the coach, but that didn't matter. He still hated it, and it made their relationship just horrible. On top of that, the team was coming off a couple of horrible seasons. They were 1-15 in 2007. Taylor wanted a trade as things got worse, and Parcells just got more and more pissed. The Dolphins were telling him they won't trade him. Taylor wanted out. We all knew it. Heck, if we didn't have Terrell Suggs over there, I would have been begging Ozzie Newsome to go get that guy. This was Jason-Freakin'-Taylor, one of the best pass rushers in the game. He was the 2006 Defensive Player of the Year. The Dolphins finally dealt him to Washington just before the season, but that didn't go well. In fact, it kind of backfired, because the Redskins ended up being bad and the Dolphins went 11-5. Hey, you can never tell in this league.

Taylor did one year in Washington and then they parted company when the Redskins wanted to redo his contract. By this time I was with the Jets, but Taylor wanted to go back to Miami. I knew what was going on because I was friends with Taylor's agent, Gary Wichard. Bill Belichick up in New England was calling him every day, leaving him messages, hoping to get him to the Patriots. Tampa Bay defensive coordinator Jim Bates, who coached Taylor in Miami, was also calling him every day. But Taylor just wanted to go back to the Dolphins. Finally, they signed him, and you'd figure that was the end of it. But then they couldn't get along again after 2009. I don't get it, but what the hell, it's not my problem. I just saw a guy who probably has a couple of good years left in him, who I could use as a super backup. So I pulled out every stop. I did all my homework on everything that had happened, and I was selling Taylor hard. I wanted him to know that I *wanted* him, I *needed* him. And then, well, I'll let Jason tell the rest of the story:

When Rex recruited me, he personally made it a priority to come and get me. That meant a lot. Him knowing the history of the Jets and the Dolphins and him knowing the things I've said. He wanted me despite all that. He said: "I don't care about

all that, I want you on this football team. I need you on this football team." It wasn't like, "Oh, we'll take you, here's the veteran
minimum." I wasn't an acorn that they stumbled upon. He made
me feel special. That meant a lot. I've been an acorn before . . .
I tell you what, if for whatever reason it didn't work out and Rex
went somewhere else, he's one of those guys you follow. If for
whatever reason he wasn't the head coach here next year, there
would be a lot of guys in this locker room who would want to
follow him. He's that kind of guy. He could be a special-teams
coach and you'd want to be there.

Rex is real. He always says it's blunt-force trauma. That's how
he delivers his message, blunt-force trauma. Some people don't
like it. Some people are put off by it. He's boisterous, cocky,
whatever people want to say, but he says it the way it is, he says
what he believes and he believes so much in his players. Even if
the housekeeper says that player is no good, if that guy is on the
football team, Rex is going to believe in him. He's going to make
you feel you're the best player at your position in the league. He
has a very unique personality, a unique way of making people
feel wanted, feel positive. The work environment is very positive.
It's laid back, but when it's time to work, it's time to work. I'm
telling you it comes from the head guy. He treats you like men,
there's no babysitting here. If somebody has something to say,
they can say it. He doesn't tell you how to talk. When you take
guys and let them become professionals, they become professional. When you take guys and you watch over them and treat
them like children, don't be surprised when they don't grow.

There's another very simple, key idea I believe in: In order to
succeed in the NFL, you have to have fun. You have to live by your
love of this game. It's like I tell our players: Remember back to the
first time you put on the equipment, the first time you put on the
uniform. That first time you put pads on, you probably had no idea
how they went on, how you were supposed to wear them. You didn't

know how to put the helmet on, how you pinch the ears out. But you went out and had a blast that first time. You were a kid and you were excited. That's the type of team I want to have. I want to have guys be excited, where they can't wait to come to practice, to get to the building or the stadium and enjoy playing a game. When I played, I couldn't wait to get there. Even though this is a multimillion-dollar business, it should be the same way it was when we were kids. We have such an unbelievable opportunity here, and it's a real blessing to get this chance. I get to be a kid every day. That's what I want them to understand. No matter what the media says, despite all the outside pressures, this is still a game.

It's like my mom told me after I didn't get the head coaching job in Baltimore and I was so disappointed. She looked at me and said, "Are you going to let it bother you or are you going to go out and work as hard as you always have?" She was asking me a question, but she was making a point. This is a job I love—I couldn't let something like that get me down. It's good advice for anyone: Don't let anything take away from what you're doing. These days, everybody talks about how I have to get that next contract or get the next deal. That's not the reason I'm doing this, that's not what motivates me. It's not for the contract, it's because I love doing it. I come to work every day with a smile on my face. If you do what you love, then the money will follow.

It's just like with Steve Bisciotti. That letter may have been a big mistake, but it was saying how much my heart is in what I do and how much joy I got out of it. People tell me that I was Bisciotti's favorite coach on the staff and that's the reason he made sure I stayed even when they hired John Harbaugh. If you look at it that way, maybe that letter helped. I didn't get the exact job I wanted, but the people there respected me and knew what I was about. I can't ask for more than that.

8. Loving Baltimore

The path to becoming a successful NFL football coach is long and arduous. It's a test to see how much you want it. Over the first 12 years of my coaching career, I worked in six different places back and forth across the country. I started in Kentucky, then moved to New Mexico, back to Kentucky, back west to Arizona, then to Cincinnati, followed by a one-year stopover in Oklahoma. The whole thing at Oklahoma was unfortunate. John Blake was the coach there and he recruited some great players, but he didn't have a winning record in three years, so they fired him and the whole staff.

Right after that, I took a job at Kansas State, knowing that I desperately wanted to eventually get into the NFL. Then, out of the blue, I got a call from Baltimore Ravens coach Brian Billick, who I knew a little bit. Billick was calling to interview me for the Baltimore defensive line coach job, and little did I know that I'd already interviewed for it. In Billick's words:

The interview took place in a way he didn't even know he was being interviewed. I had gone up to Montreal to do a coaching clinic when I was still an assistant in Minnesota. I don't know why it was in Montreal. The guy before me was Rex Ryan. I had met Rex before, I had known Buddy, and we had some mutual coaching friends, so I was aware of Rex, but really I hadn't spent much time with him. I get up to this clinic and there is like five guys, nobody there. So I'm sitting in the back of this big, old auditorium and the five guys are up in front. I'm watching Rex Ryan and he is coaching his ass off as if that room was filled with 1,500 high school football coaches. It didn't make any difference to him whether there were five guys or 500 guys. The chalk was flying and he was coaching his butt off. It's then that I said, "You know what, if I ever get to a position as a head coach, I'm going to hire this guy." I was aware of Rex, so I just called Rex and offered him the job. I didn't have to interview him. I didn't even have to talk to him. I knew I wanted him on the staff.

Billick offered me the job, and I was back in the NFL, this time on my own. My wife and my two great boys moved to Baltimore, and life was sweet.

Now, this was in 1999, and when I first arrived in Baltimore there was a lot to work with. I mean, we had some terrific guys on defense, and in my first few years we would get a handful more. I also learned a few things about not only coaching a lot of talent, but about managing a variety of personalities. As our terrific general manager (and Pro Football Hall of Fame tight end) Ozzie Newsome put it: "That defensive line room was a strong room with a lot of strong personalities. It could have gone a lot of different ways. It's a credit to Rex and all of them that it was so successful."

As I recall, by my second year in Baltimore, we had this great nucleus of tough-ass guys in that room and throughout our defense. Ray Lewis had already been in the league for four years, and he was the man. He was already becoming the face of the Ravens. As a coach, you're looking at your typical players and checking if they're dedicated. You want to see if a player can handle the pressure, if he likes the contact, if he's willing to hit and be hit. With Ray Lewis it's totally different, because *he's* looking at *you*—because there's no question about his dedication; he wants to know if you like being a coach, if you're buying into the long hours.

Now, Ray wasn't the only guy like that, he was just the loudest and most obvious. When I got to Baltimore in 1999, that team was loaded with great pros, from Rob Burnett to Tony Siragusa to Michael McCrary. I'm not even talking about offensive guys like Jonathan Ogden and Jamal Lewis. Later, we got Ed Reed, maybe the greatest safety in the history of the game.

But when you coach guys like Ray Lewis, you're not really coaching. With guys like that, it's a partnership; it's a joyful and ridiculously easy process. You show up every day and you can't wait to work with them, because they're going to take your ideas and go further with them than even you could imagine. The only thing you have to do with players like Lewis, Burnett, Siragusa, and McCrary is show them that you know what you're doing and that you're as committed as they are. If you do that, they're with you 100 percent.

Burnett was from Long Island, a smart guy from a really great family who was also wise about people; he had street sense and intelligence. He had been in Cleveland and gone through all the crap when the Browns left there, and had come to Baltimore and become a Raven. He got the whole picture of how the league worked, how the team worked, how the coaches are supposed to handle players and how the players should carry themselves. Plus, he was just a grinder of a player. He didn't do anything flashy as an athlete, which is why he was a fifth-round pick. But he did everything very well. There was no weakness in his game. If you have six or seven guys in your lineup like Burnett, your team is going a long way.

Then we had McCrary, who was one of these former seventh-round picks who came out of nowhere to make it. McCrary was from Virginia, and, like Burnett, he was from a great family, too. In the 1970s, his mother had sued a nearby day-care center that refused to let McCrary attend because he was black. It ended up being a major case about race in the United States, going all the way to the Supreme Court. As a kid and a teen, McCrary was pushed hard by his parents, even to stick with football when he wanted to quit in high school. Eventually, it all came together for him. Think about what a serious kind of kid you're talking about—this is a guy who was taught from an early age that you don't back down from *anything*.

McCrary got there in 1997 and became a Pro Bowler before I'd even met him in 1998, so I didn't change anything when I got there in 1999. I just let him be him, knowing he was going to fly around and make plays. He made the Pro Bowl again, getting 11½ sacks. He was going to hustle no matter what, and never quit. McCrary was important from another perspective, too. He had started his career in Seattle in 1993, when the Seahawks drafted him out of Wake Forest. The next year is when Seattle took Sam Adams with the No. 8 overall pick in the draft. I'll get back to Adams in a minute, but I think having McCrary helped us a lot when Adams was a free agent in 2000. I'm sure Adams thought he was a lot better player than McCrary, but he also saw McCrary come to our place and have a lot of success, and that always makes an impression on a player.

Finally, we had Goose. Tony "Goose" Siragusa was something really special. I still see Goose all the time because he lives in New Jersey, which is where he grew up. He lives right around the corner from our complex. Really, this is a salt-of-the-earth kind of guy—salty, too, no doubt. I think he's one of the few guys who swear more than me, and he ain't much for political correctness, I'll just put it that way. Goose is going to tell you exactly what he thinks. Like Burnett and McCrary, Goose wasn't supposed to do anything in the NFL. He wasn't even drafted coming out of Pittsburgh in 1990. He made it with Indianapolis that year and stuck it out with the Colts for seven years. Goose isn't a guy with a whole lot of moves. In football-speak, he's an all-out bull rusher, one of those guys who just pounds away at his opponent until the opponent quits. There's no finesse to

Goose. In fact, Goose couldn't spell finesse if you spotted him the last six letters.

I mentioned Sam Adams. In 2000, we got Adams as a free agent. Now, Adams is one of the more talented men I've ever had the opportunity to coach. I don't say that lightly. Sam Adams was different. He was just as talented as any of those other guys, if not more so, but Adams was also spoiled and selfish. He was the son of a great player in his own right, former New England guard Sam Adams, Sr. His dad had obviously given his son both the raw physical gifts that come with great DNA, and the knowledge of how to play. Adams was 6-foot-3 and anywhere between 320 and 350 pounds, depending on the season or just the time of year. He had a first step so quick that it was like he was a 260-pound guy playing defensive end. Between his quickness and his strength, he was scary-good.

On the other hand, Adams was also a total pain in the butt to coach, and my job was finding a way to harness his huge potential. Frankly, I can say with confidence I did. Let me jump to Newsome again:

> Rex got more out of Sam Adams than anybody who ever coached him. I think it had to do with Rex's personality and his approach to players. Rex isn't one of those coaches who says, "It has to be this way or else." He can work with someone's personality, finds a way to get the most out of that individual and understand that individual so that he can work within the group.

I've always felt that was a key to coaching in the NFL. You have to understand the guys you're coaching—to be able and willing to work with them in different ways because they're all so different. The most important thing is to earn their trust and get that guy performing at the top of this game. Adams was both physically gifted and smart. In fact, he was probably too smart for his own good, and that's what made him a pain in the ass. He didn't think he knew the game better than you, he *knew* he knew the game better than you. Coaching Adams was a challenge because he didn't believe in coaches. He didn't think you were smart enough to help him.

Well, maybe I didn't teach Adams anything new, but let me put it to you this way: In his two seasons with Baltimore, he was named a Pro Bowl starter twice, which were the only times that ever happened in the 14 years he played. He was a Pro Bowler two other times, but both times as a backup. He was a vital part of one of the greatest defenses in the history of the NFL. He won the only Super Bowl ring of his career.

Now, you don't want to have too many guys like Adams, because if you do, all of a sudden they have a quorum and they start to work together against you. That's an interesting thing about coaching in the NFL. But every team has one or two guys who are so good that you probably have to put up with some crap from them at some point in time. It's just the way it works. If you had nothing but guys like Lewis, it's easy. But I mean, go out and try to find 53 guys who are not only great football players but also choirboys and good students who never miss a day of class. Good luck with that.

As a coach, you have to find a way to motivate that guy who sits in the back of the class, waiting to fire a spit wad at you or somebody else, that guy who's always joking or being a cutup. Hey, that was my brother and me half the time we were in school. So trust me, I know you have to find a way to appeal to their pride to get the most out of them. With guys like that, you have to have the right environment. That's why most of the guys on your team have to be guys who work within the team structure. They can be fun-loving and a little wild out there, but they believe, in their hearts, that football is important and they're going to do whatever it takes to be good.

I like to put it this way: You have roaches and you have ants. With roaches, when you turn on the lights, they all scatter every which way. That's because they're no good and they can't work in a structure. On the other side, you have ants. You can have a bunch of ants in a jar, shake up the jar, and toss them out of the jar onto the ground—and what happens? The ants all get right back in line. In fact, the ants will work so well together that they can carry a roach. Now, they can't carry two roaches, but they can carry one.

That's what we had with Adams, a roach who was carried by a bunch of ants—red, attacking, powerful ants.

Now back to Tony Siragusa. Goose had heart and desire. He set the tone that way. I told Goose my story about roaches and ants and he picked up on it right away. He started saying Adams is "a fuckin' roach, this guy's a roach." After a while, they started calling me Coach Roach. Goose was funny, but he was totally dedicated, all in every time. If I ever needed it, I could just go to Goose and say, "Hey, Goose, let's go, pick it up, get these guys going." He'd jump right in, no matter how sore he was or anything else; he'd get the tempo going for practice, for games, whenever I needed it. He was awesome. I tried to take care of him, but, really, he took care of me.

My first year there, Goose had a great year and decided to hold out the following season. Linebackers coach Jack Del Rio and I joked that we were going to drive to Goose's house and go get him, just to end the holdout ourselves and drag his ass to training camp. See, you have to know the drill. Veteran players know how to get ready, and with vets like that, you're not pushing them in training camp anyway. I remember one year in Philadelphia, my dad had an offensive lineman named Ron Heller, a big tough guy who played right tackle. My dad told Heller not to even show up for the first three weeks of training camp. They kept saying it was a contract thing, but it was just an excuse to give the guy a rest without telling the rest of the team.

So Goose finally showed up late in preseason, and we were already getting set for the opener in Pittsburgh. Remember, this was 2000, our title year—and we knew we had a kick-ass defense. Marvin Lewis was the defensive coordinator; then we had Del Rio, me, and a bunch of other great coaches. We could just feel it was going to be great. As we're getting ready to play the Steelers, I said to Goose, "Look, dude, I need you for like 15 plays. Give me that and we'll be okay." I figured we'd spot him in on first down, stuff the run, get a lead with our offense, and then rest him a lot.

That day in Pittsburgh was brutal. It was the last year they were playing in Three Rivers Stadium, the old multipurpose place where the Pirates also played. The place had Astroturf, or whatever synthetic surface they were using, and it was literally 90-something degrees outside that day—which meant it was even hotter on the field, because the surface retains so much of the heat. You stood there and your feet were physically burning because of the heat.

Anyway, we got to the end of the first quarter and Goose had gotten 15 plays in, so he was on the sidelines. He said to me, "What do you think, Rex? I'm about done, right?"

I shot back, "What the hell are you talking about?"

"Shit, I already got 15 plays—I'm done, right?"

I just went off on him: "That's what I said, about 15 fucking plays a quarter."

"You son of a bitch, you told me 15 plays and that was it."

We were laughing our asses off at this point.

"I said 15 plays a quarter. Now, shut up and get your ass in there." And you know, he was awesome. He played the whole game. He was all over me, too, giving it right back. To this day, he brings it up. We shut Pittsburgh out 16-0 that game. Goose was phenomenal. He's one of the most unselfish guys I've ever met.

He was that way off the field, too. In 1999, we had a defensive end named Fernando Smith. On Christmas Eve, Smith was at his apartment with his family, trying to make a turkey, but it caught on fire because of the grease. Smith and his family got out, but the fire burned up their apartment and a couple of other ones around it. Smith has three kids and all they've got to wear are the house slippers, shorts, and T-shirts they were wearing when the place caught fire. Word got around by the next day, Christmas, when the players had the morning off, and we were supposed to get to the hotel because we had to play Cincinnati the next day.

Goose didn't even like Smith that much, but Goose told me that day, "Rex, I ain't gonna be at bed check tonight."

I said, "I gotcha, no problem." I knew exactly what he was going to do—he was going to get Smith some clothes. Sure enough, he brought Smith $10,000 of unopened Nike stuff for his family. Plus, Goose took presents from underneath his tree that were supposed to be for his own kids and gave them to Smith's kids. That's just the kind of guy he is.

On a football team, you have to have guys like that. Sure, you have to have the premium players, the guys like Lewis and Adams, safety Rod Woodson, the great left tackle Jonathan Ogden, and the great running back Jamal Lewis. We had tight end Shannon Sharpe, who made like every big play we needed in the playoffs. The stars stir the drink. But if you don't have the right ingredients, it doesn't matter how much those guys stir the drink, it's not going to taste good. They're just going to be stirring up crap.

In our defensive line meeting room, it was crucial to have that mix of people. I remember Adams used to come into every meeting and go for the thermostat on the wall—turn the temperature way up, as hot as it could go. He loved it hot, but it was uncomfortable as hell for everyone else. We'd all be miserable, and Adams didn't care. He just didn't give a damn. We started making it a joke. I put a lock on the thermostat one day, but Adams just broke it. Guys would try all sorts of things to get him to stop, but he never did. It became kind of funny and it brought everyone together. Finally, one day Goose went over, turned the temperature down to something comfortable, and just ripped the thermostat off the wall.

That was perfect for me, because I could let the other players police Adams. I didn't have to be the bad guy as much in the relationship, because he wasn't really going to listen to me anyway. With other players, he might not want to listen, but he at least respected who they were because they played. With me, I would be hard on him in practice, but I always did it with a smile on my face, with a lot of enthusiasm. I used every ounce of my energy making sure I kept Adams as pumped up as I could get him.

In the end, what made that Baltimore defense so great was the same thing that separated the 1985 Chicago defense. It was blunt-force trauma, the kind of pain and fear that we could inflict on an opposition. That's where Adams and Goose led the way. The way the NFL works today, defensive tackles aren't the highlight players anymore. It's the pretty-boy defensive ends who can run around and get sacks. The defensive tackles are specialists, playing two downs against the run and then subbing out.

Adams and Goose would come out on passing downs a lot, but not all the time. They weren't out-there-on-every-down guys because of the damage they could do. In 2000, they both had career years. Whatever an opposing team tried to do to us, Adams and Goose just blew it up. They would take out the three offensive linemen in the middle, the two guards and the center, and allow everybody else to run around and do basically whatever they wanted to do. There was Ray Lewis, one of the most physical guys in the history of the NFL, playing his ass off all season because of the whole situation in the aftermath of the murder trial he went through in Atlanta. Lewis had one of the greatest seasons any human being could ever have, and he was able to do that while running around without being blocked. Like I said, I'm not going to say we were better than the '85 Bears, but we were as close as it's ever going to come.

In 2000, we set the NFL record for fewest points allowed in a 16-game season, with only 165. We allowed a record-low 970 yards rushing. Burnett had a career high with 10½ sacks. McAlister and fellow cornerback Duane Starks combined for 10 interceptions. In the playoffs, we were even better. We allowed 23 points combined in four playoff games, including two on the road. In the AFC Championship Game, Siragusa put such a brutal hit on Oakland quarterback Rich Gannon that he knocked him out of the game. It was a free-for-all by the end of the season, like sharks having a feeding frenzy.

And everybody benefited. Like I said, Adams made the Pro Bowl as a starter for the first time. Brian Billick was the AFC Coach of the Year. Marvin Lewis was named Assistant Coach of the Year. Ray Lewis was the Defensive Player of the Year and made the Pro Bowl.

Ogden and Woodson made the Pro Bowl, too. Even kicker Matt Stover won the Golden Toe Award.

For me, it legitimized all the thoughts I had about why I chose this profession. Getting each of these very different guys to play hard told me I could do this job. It made me know that I could be a successful coach, that I could contribute something. All that energy I spent all those years, even when there were maybe only five people listening, meant something.

When I first got to Baltimore, I really thought that would be it. That's really strange to say when you're in this job, but I just had this feeling that my days of bouncing around the country from job to job were over. And really, by the standards of this job, they were. I lasted 10 years in Baltimore, and that's an eternity for an assistant coach. We found our first real home. When we bought it we made sure to be around great schools, because we wanted our kids to grow up there. We celebrated a Super Bowl victory in our second year and that was just an amazing moment. In less than two years, we were entrenched.

Now, that didn't mean I wanted to be a defensive line coach my whole career. No offense to position coaches, specifically defensive line guys. I've been around a lot of great ones. John Teerlinck in Indianapolis wrote his master's thesis on defensive line play. Jim Washburn up in Tennessee is another great one. Clarence Brooks, who worked with me in Baltimore, is awesome. Mike Waufle, who was with the New York Giants in 2007 when they won the title, is one smart guy who knows how to get guys going. Those guys love that job, and they're geniuses with inventing new tactics and new ideas. They love the details. So do I, but I also wanted to be a head coach. I felt like I had a passion for it, and possibly an ability to go the distance with it.

After Marvin Lewis left to spend a year with Washington and then became the head coach in Cincinnati, Mike Nolan got the defensive coordinator job. Like me, Mike is the son of a former coach, the late Dick Nolan. Mike is a good guy, a little uptight but definitely a guy who understood how to run a defense. He's probably a little more conservative than me in calling blitzes, but Mike was really consistent in how he laid out a game plan and explained his thinking to the rest of the coaches. He lasted there until the end of the 2004 season and then got hired as the head coach at San Francisco, which was sort of a homecoming for him, because his dad had been there, just like my dad was an assistant coach with the Jets back in the 1960s and '70s. The most encouraging thing to me was that the Baltimore defensive coordinator job was more and more a good springboard to becoming a head coach.

In 2005, I got the job of defensive coordinator and, man, did I feel ready. For years leading up to that, I had been studying how Billick ran the team, how he addressed the coaches and put in the game plan. Billick is a disciple of Bill Walsh (he even cowrote Walsh's great book *Finding the Winning Edge*), so he had a really specific way of putting in the game plan, of how to run meetings and how to install the things we were working on with the players. Everything was systematic.

There's one problem with all that Walsh stuff—you'd better have a great quarterback, like Joe Montana or Steve Young, to make sure it all works. My first year in Baltimore as defensive coordinator, our quarterback situation . . . well, how should I say it?

Okay, it sucked.

We alternated between Kyle Boller and Anthony Wright. Those guys tried, but we didn't score 20 points in a game for the first 10 weeks of the season. Our 2005 season finished at 6-10, which was sort of a continuation of what we had been doing ever since I got there. We'd be great for a season or two and then we'd really drop off. The reason is pretty simple: We never had that franchise quarterback. We tried. We drafted Boller in the first round and he looked the part pretty well: big guy, strong arm. But he was just too inaccurate. Even in our championship season, we ended up going with Trent Dilfer and then let him go after the season because Dilfer, as tough as he was, just wasn't a franchise guy.

For me, this was another lesson. You know the saying "Defense wins championships"? Well, there's plenty of proof in that. Our title season was a good example. Two years after we won it, Tampa Bay played Oakland in the Super Bowl. It was the No. 1 defense against the No. 1 offense. Tampa Bay killed them.

But here's the other part that even great defensive coaches have to admit: While you can win a title with a great defense and it's more important to have a great defense than a great offense, if you don't have a great quarterback, you're going to be limited to one or two shots.

Just look at the history of the league: There have been 44 Super Bowls; 10 quarterbacks have combined to win 26 of the Super Bowls. What that tells me is that having that one guy, that special quarterback, gives you a chance every year. Look at New England with Tom Brady or Indianapolis with Peyton Manning, even if Manning has won only one title. If you have that quarterback, you have a chance every year if you can just build around him.

In Baltimore, we didn't get a guy who looked like a real franchise guy until my last season there, when we got Joe Flacco. In my four years as defensive coordinator, we finished fifth, first, sixth, and second in overall defense. We were in the top three in run defense three times. But after we went 6-10 in 2005, we went 13-3 in 2006, 5-11 in 2007 (after which Billick got fired), and then 11-5 under John Harbaugh in 2008. We might have been consistently great on defense, but our results were all over the place because we didn't have the quarterback.

That's why I made sure that the first thing I did when I got to New York was to draft Mark Sanchez. Sanchez was a young guy who I felt would be a franchise quarterback for us for a long time, but I'll come back to that in detail later.

The other important lesson I learned during this time is that you have to head off problems right away. You can't be afraid to make tough decisions. In 2006, we made a strong move to go get Steve McNair, a tough, warriorlike quarterback who was let go in Tennessee when they drafted Vince Young. It was kind of sad to see the

Titans do that to such a great leader, but those are the breaks and it helped us. We also already had one of McNair's favorite targets with Derrick Mason, who we signed the year before as a free agent. He was a really good possession receiver with enough ability to hurt you over the top—a complete football player.

We got McNair late in the off-season and he showed up as soon as possible. At the time, Jim Fassel was our offensive coordinator. Fassel, who had been the coach of the New York Giants when we beat them in the Super Bowl, was really good friends with Billick from way back in their West Coast days. Both guys had gone through Stanford and knew a lot of the same people. Fassel had been the head coach of the Giants for seven years and had his ups and downs with players there. Typical stuff. After he got fired in 2003, we hired him in 2004. As I said, our offense wasn't very good in 2004 or 2005, but most of the blame went on the quarterback. There's only so much you can do.

When we got McNair, there was a lot more expectation. Maybe we weren't going to put up 30 a game, but we had a chance to run an offense that could complement our defense, control the ball, change field position, and keep the defense fresh. Well, we got McNair and Fassel was on vacation at the time. He came back for a few days and worked with McNair, then went back to be with his family. All right, I understand that getting time with the family is hard and vacations generally are pretty sacred. But this was a time when you have to look at your family and say, "We don't get quarterbacks like this at this time of the year very often" and they have to understand.

I've never coached a quarterback directly, but everybody was expecting that Fassel would have this guy ready to go. Here you have a chance to work with a really smart veteran who had the potential to take us a long way as a team if he was just decent—and you passed up the chance to grind away with him for a few weeks? As you can imagine, a lot of our offensive position coaches weren't real happy about that. Then we got into the season and the offense was just kind of limping along and not really improving. We opened with two solid games, then went three straight where the offense didn't score more than 16. We held on to win two of those games. We opened the season 4-0, then dropped two straight before heading into the bye week. In the bye week, all of a sudden, Billick fired Fassel. I came to find out that Fassel was spending most of his time on the phone at that point, calling around trying to get a head coaching job. Assistant coaches couldn't get in his office to work with him, so they were getting frustrated. It was ugly all the way around. You just can't have that in the season. Look, I know what it's like to get frustrated when you don't get the job you want, but you don't handle it that way. You've got to keep pounding away, giving your job everything you can. That's how you'll finally get what you really want.

After that, Billick took over the offense and we got rolling. That was a big year for Billick because the owner, Steve Bisciotti, was examining everything we did. We won nine of the next 10, and we scored at least 20 points in all but two games. The whole thing was really coming together. We finished 13-3 and had the No. 2 seed in the AFC playoffs. We had a bye before we played Indianapolis in the playoffs. It was all set up for a big showdown between San Diego and us. Then the setup came apart when we lost to Indianapolis 15-6 and San Diego lost to New England. That's the year Indy ended up winning the title over Chicago, and man, was that frustrating. I truly believe that any of the top four teams in the AFC would have beaten the Bears. I know we would have beaten the Patriots that year in the AFC. We were staring right down the pipe of another title, but we couldn't come up with a score on defense. We had a couple of chances to intercept Peyton Manning, but they slipped through our hands. If we had caught those two passes, we would probably have run them back. They were touchdowns, plays that would have completely changed the game. But I give Manning a lot of credit, because he didn't force a lot in that game. He knew what our defense could do and he played for field goals instead of getting greedy. That's a heck of a quarterback.

Billick got a contract extension after 2006, but things went backward in 2007. McNair got hurt and the offense was inconsistent again.

Our watershed moment that season was probably the Monday-night game against New England in Week 13. The Pats were 12-0, on their way to 16-0 for the regular season before losing in the Super Bowl to the Giants. We were 4-7 at the time, not going anywhere, but our defense still had so much pride on the line. It was just amazing how hard we played that night. Early in the fourth quarter, we got a touchdown to grab a 24-17 lead. We held that great offense to a field goal for the next 12 minutes, and with us leading 24-20 with 1:48 remaining, when they were facing a fourth-and-1 situation. Right as the Pats are about to snap the ball, I called time-out. The ref hears it, but not in time to stop the snap. Tom Brady tried to sneak it, we stopped him, and our guys thought the game was won. But I called time-out. Oh geez. I thought we were in the wrong alignment and we ended up making a great play. I felt like an idiot.

From there, the whole thing really unraveled. Eventually, New England was facing fourth-and-6 and we got called for an illegal-contact penalty. We got them in fourth down again and Brady threw an incomplete, and we got called for another penalty that gave them first-and-goal from the 8. They finally scored on a pass that had to be reviewed. Brutal, just brutal. Our guys just lost it. Bart Scott got called for two unsportsmanlike penalty calls, including one for throwing a penalty flag in the stands. We got called for offsides on the point after. It was all coming apart. Strangely, we almost won the thing on a Hail Mary throw to Mark Clayton at the end, but that loss was just brutal. The Patriots had the greatest offense in the history of the game that year and we stopped them. We should have won.

After the game, everybody was asking Billick about the time-out. They didn't realize right away that I called it. I felt bad for Billick, and he was classy about it with the media. He never said I was the one who called it. He never threw me under the bus. Eventually, they saw on the tape with one of the sideline cameras that it was me calling the time-out. I told our guys it was my fault. What can you do?

The season just petered out from there. We ended up losing nine straight at one point, including an overtime loss at Miami that was the only game the Dolphins won all year. We beat Pittsburgh in the final game, but they were resting most of their guys. The next day, on New Year's Eve, Billick got fired. Really, we all got fired, technically. As a coach, you get conditioned to this happening, but this hurt a lot for me. Billick brought me into the league and he gave me a lot of freedom to do what I thought worked. He didn't interfere and he didn't second-guess. I appreciated that and I was loyal to him, even when some of our players would start complaining.

I ended up interviewing for the head coach job. I also interviewed in Atlanta and with Miami. I had a great interview with Bill Parcells; man, we hit it off. I loved talking to Parcells, but he had his guy with Tony Sparano, the offensive line coach of the Cowboys when Parcells was in Dallas. The Falcons hired Mike Smith from Jacksonville, who did a great job down there and had been with us in Baltimore. Smith and I came to Baltimore the same year, and he stayed for four years before going to Jacksonville with Del Rio. Smith is Billick's brother-in-law. I like Smith—he's a real upbeat, positive guy. I thought I had a better résumé at the time, but then again, you always believe in yourself.

Really, I thought I was the best candidate for the Baltimore job. I thought it was going to be mine. I really did. Again, I thought I'd never leave Baltimore—and maybe that worked against me. Over the next couple of weeks, the Ravens interviewed Jason Garrett and John Harbaugh for the job. They offered it to Garrett, but he turned it down when Dallas gave him a monster contract to stay as the offensive coordinator. Harbaugh was the special-teams coach in Philadelphia, and I had worked with him when I was at Cincinnati. I really like John, great guy, son of a coach, his brother was a terrific quarterback in the NFL for a long time (and recently took over as head coach in San Francisco)—the whole package. John is a really positive, organized, upbeat guy. I can see why anybody would like him. Plus, Bisciotti got a call from Bill Belichick telling him that Harbaugh was great. That's a pretty great recommendation.

Meanwhile, they started talking to me about whether I would

stay as the defensive coordinator if they hired somebody else. I told them Harbaugh was the only guy I would stay for, but I also expected them to help me get a head coach job somewhere else. I wasn't going to be satisfied doing the coordinator job the rest of my career. Our general manager, Ozzie Newsome, was great about that. He said he would help, and he did. I think they announced Harbaugh's hiring about 20 minutes later.

I admit it: I was bummed out by that whole situation. I was probably in dreamland about staying in Baltimore the rest of my career, but I just had a feel for it. I loved that situation and I gave everything to it.

I talked a lot to my family after that, and eventually I got my attitude right again. It's like my mom said: What's the best plan to get what you really want? Are you going to let this get you down or are you going to throw your all at it? To me, that's not even a question. John was great to me after that, too, so it got to be easier. He really sought out my opinion and brought me in on a lot of decisions. He started hiring a lot of guys that I kept saying I would have hired, too, like Cam Cameron to be the offensive coordinator. I really liked what John was putting together, and there wasn't any politics to it. We were really working together as a whole group.

Plus, running our defense in Baltimore was nothing but excitement. When I took over in 2005, three seasons earlier, we had Ray Lewis still at the top of his game, and we had Ed Reed. Again, you're talking about two guys who are maybe the best ever to play their positions and two guys who put football above everything else. You're talking about two players who are willing to put in the time and energy that coaches put in.

Moreover, Ray Lewis is the Baltimore Ravens. He is the face of that team and the heart of that team. I hear some outside people talk about Ray and some of the stuff he went through early in his career, and they have no clue what this guy is about. I'll tell you one other thing: I didn't even dream of taking Ray out of Baltimore when I left to go to the Jets. Yeah, there was a lot of talk about how we were going to make some monster offer to get Ray and Bart Scott. I wasn't going to discourage that because I didn't want to show our hand, but in my heart, I wasn't going to do that.

Ray Lewis can play for only one team. That was my opinion. When it came down to it, I went to Bart Scott's house at midnight of the start of free agency in 2009 and not to Ray's, because that's how I felt. It would have tarnished Ray's image. You're talking about a guy who represents fierce loyalty and passion. He carried that franchise to its championship in 2000. He carried it for all those years. Ray Lewis in the locker room is an amazing thing that people don't see. He runs that locker room and sets a tone for how everybody is supposed to work. Trust me, it was tempting to want to bring a guy like that with me, but I don't think it would have been the same. I think Ray would have been a leader, but it's just not the same thing. It wouldn't have been so natural for him. I think it would have been forced. It was like when I heard that Deion Sanders was telling Dallas owner Jerry Jones to get Lewis in free agency. It made sense, but I just don't think it would have been easy for Ray to feel the same way about the Cowboys as he did about the Ravens.

He's the most intense, passionate guy I have ever seen—just a warrior. If you're storming the beach, he's the first one on the beach and he's going to make sure his guys are with him. It's like the stories they tell about my dad in Korea. Ray motivated me as a coach. That's how good a player he was. That's how intense a competitor he was. He got there before I did, but they told me he took the team over right when he was a rookie. When I got there and then when I took over the defense, all he wanted to know was whether I was genuine and if I could help him. That was it. If you could do those two things, that resonated with him. If you're a phony, Ray Lewis can see right through you in about two seconds. I saw it happen. He'd see coaches or players who weren't with the program and he'd know it right away. When there was something missing with a coach, Ray just wouldn't respond to that guy.

Let me give you a good example of the other side of it. When the Ravens hired John Harbaugh in 2008 and I stayed as the defensive coordinator, our team was looking for a strength and conditioning coach. I was in Hawaii at the Pro Bowl, just there with Ray, Reed, and the other Baltimore defensive guy who made it. When we were there, we met a guy who was working with Green Bay at the time. I knew him a little and figured he'd be a good guy to interview. I don't know anything about strength and conditioning, but Harbaugh wanted me to talk to him, so I interviewed him. I thought he was a hell of a guy. He sounded good to me, but here's what I wanted to do just to be sure: I had Lewis and Reed come for the second interview, because I wanted to see if he could stand up to them, if he could handle them. The guy never flinched. He was great, phenomenal. Now, some of his ideas were a little different because he had more of a baseball background, but you could see he was smart. So when it was all said and done, I asked Lewis and Reed what they thought. Ray told me, "You know some of the things were kind of strange and whatever, but I really like him." I asked Ray why he liked him and he said simply: "He speaks from the heart." Ray knew it right away. In the end, we didn't end up hiring the guy because Harbaugh liked somebody else a little better, but it told me a lot about how Ray picked up on people and what he was looking for.

Of course, the best stories about Ray are from the games or practices, and there are a ton of them. Even after I left, there are stories I love about him. In 2009, there was that play during the end of the game in San Diego, when he shot the gap for a big stop at the end of the game. It was a conservative defensive call, but he saw the play and just blitzed on his own. The football intelligence and the physical ability—it's unbelievable. But even in my first year working with him, I was just wowed every time I saw him in action. The way he hits people is unreal. We were in a "thud drill," where you're just supposed to form-fit the tackle, not go all the way through with the full hit. We had a running back named Eric Rhett, a loudmouth guy out of Florida who played in the league for a while, funny guy. I really liked him, because he kept things loose. Anyway, Rhett was running his mouth through the drill, just running it constantly, and all of a sudden it sounded like a gun went off. *Pow!* I mean, the hit Ray laid on him was unbelievable. Rhett's feet went over his head and he landed literally on the back of his head. I looked over at Billick and said, "How's that for a thud period?" It was unbelievable. To this day it may have been the loudest hit I've ever heard, and Ray would make those hits all the time.

Another time, we were getting beaten by Cleveland. It was a close game and it was still early on. As I said before, I've always believed that one big hit can change the momentum of the game faster than anything—faster than a turnover, faster than anything. Sure enough, Cleveland tight end Kellen Winslow (who's a great receiver) came across the middle and Ray hit him. I mean, he leveled this guy. The ball went flying up and we ended up getting the interception. After that, the tone was set for the rest of the game. The Browns' receivers would come across the middle and they'd be pulling off passes. None of them wanted to take a hit like that so, literally, Ray controlled that whole inside. If you came in there, you knew you were running into Ray's territory and those brakes came on. I've seen more dropped passes inside those hash marks because Ray Lewis is standing there. That's it—he wills himself into making plays.

When you work with people like that, it rubs off on you. If you do your job with joy, you're going to bring joy to the people you work with. Ray was like that for me, and I wanted to be that way for the people I worked with in Baltimore.

Our last season in Baltimore—2008—was a great one. We were No. 2 in overall defense and went 11-5. Watching Flacco develop into a good quarterback as a rookie was really fascinating to me—especially the way Cameron handled him and nurtured him. It gave me confidence going into New York with Sanchez. The only downer to that 2008 season was losing to Pittsburgh in the playoffs. What a game, though—the hitting, the intensity, the big plays.

Honestly, as I've said, I hate to lose. I enjoy winning, but at the end of the day, winning a game in the NFL just means you had a good day at the office. Losing, on the other hand—losing is really painful. But to this day, there are a few losses that I've had in my career that still really haunt me. One that I still haven't gotten over is that last game at Baltimore, losing in the AFC Championship Game to end our 2008 season—and my tenure in Baltimore. As much as I couldn't wait to become a head coach, I would have loved to leave Baltimore on top with a championship. But hey, what you don't get just makes you hungrier.

9. The Perfect Owner

After the disappointing end to 2008 in Baltimore, I had taken a deep breath and was ready to look to the future. And for me, that meant pursuing a head coaching job for 2009. There were some good opportunities around the league, and I had a pretty good feeling that my dream of becoming a head coach in the NFL was about to come true. But once I sat across the table from New York Jets owner Woody Johnson, I knew exactly where I wanted to be.

Let me explain something about Woody Johnson. The man is completely dedicated to making the Jets great, even if that means doing something that seems to run headlong into another idea.

See, here was the idea I brought to the Jets when I interviewed for the job: I suggested we should go away to training camp. I believe it's great for team building, great for the players to really focus on football, get away completely from all the comfort and distractions they have at home and really get to know each other. No problem, right? Well, I was pitching that idea to a man who just spent about $75 million to build the Atlantic Health Jet Training Center in New

Jersey and opened it about five months before I sat down with him to interview. This wasn't like some run-of-the-mill place. Trust me, the Baltimore Ravens have a great training complex in the suburbs of Maryland, but this place dwarfs even that. It's so nice that Atlantic Health signed a 12-year contract just to put their name on the place. Think about that: They sold a sponsorship for the training facility, not just the stadium.

The place is like some gleaming office structure for some high-tech company. Not only is the team there, but so is the entire front office and the business department; everybody who works for the team is in the 130,000-square-foot building. Heck, the weight room alone is around 11,000 square feet. If I ever lose my house, I could probably move my entire family there for a few months and nobody would find us. (Just kidding, honey.) We've got beautiful outdoor fields, a field house for indoor practice, an enormous locker room—every bell and whistle. The other thing is that Mr. Johnson did this after decades of the team training full-time (in-season, off-season, and training camp) up on Long Island, way out in Hempstead on the Hofstra University campus. The Jets were an institution out there. Johnson took a big chance to spend money on the team and break tradition.

So along I come, and the first thing I say to him is, "I want to do something different." That's basically like saying, "Yeah, boss, those company cars you just got for all the execs—they're not quite good enough. We're going to need individual limos." To my credit, I'd never been there to see what it was like. Plus, I really do believe that getting away is important to team building. Still, that was my first idea, and it was going to cost him even more money.

What did Mr. Johnson do? He said okay. He understood what I was trying to do. He listened to my ideas about team building and how important I think it is for a team to get away. That was my first clue that he was a guy who cared about letting people do their jobs as they saw fit, not insisting on having his own way.

Then came the next idea. Fast-forward to training camp, when we were actually up at State University of New York in Cortland. It's way out in the middle of the state, about 35 miles south of Syracuse. Already, everybody was pissed at me for bringing the team there— and I mean everybody: the media, the fans, and even people on the team. Nobody had ever done that in the history of the Jets, so why did I—a first-year head coach—have to, yada, yada, yada. I heard all the complaints, but I had a plan. Of course, the first thing I noticed was something that was going to cost us even more money. We had two practice fields built specifically for our team. Not even the Cort- land team was supposed to use them before we got up there; they had their own practice field. Mr. Johnson spent hundreds of thou- sands of dollars just so those two fields were ready for us, and to most people, they'd be great. But I looked at them and nearly had a heart attack, because the turf was not level. Instead, it was full of little dips and hills. So I said, "We are not putting our team on that field. It's too dangerous. I don't want a player to get hurt. We're all about player safety." I mentioned it to Mr. Johnson and he was pissed that the fields were screwed up. They went in and tore up the whole thing, and we started anew, getting all the sod in. We had helicopters hovering all night trying to dry the field off before we could finally start using it.

While we were dealing with that, it was also our first week of camp and we were getting ready for our green-and-white scrimmage, the first real kind of action that the guys would have. There wasn't quite going to be full hitting, but it would get pretty close. It was a time to let the players show something more, and it was going to be competitive. Just as important, we were going to have a ton of fans coming up for the day to see the scrimmage—which would be held in the stadium at SUNY Cortland. My problem was that the stadium had Astroturf or some other synthetic surface, and I was not going to have our guys practice on it, regardless if we were doing full hitting or not. We were not going to risk the injuries, even if we didn't have a place for the fans to watch. All we had were some little portable bleachers, and the rest of the fans would have to surround the field. I told Mr. Johnson, and he immediately answered, "No problem.

Player safety comes first." I was telling a guy who has just built a new training facility and was in the process of building a $1.6 billion stadium with the New York Giants that I was not going to make the fans comfortable—and he was okay with it. Maybe he wasn't happy, I don't know, but he agreed and he let me do what I thought was most important.

Trust me when I say that coaches in the NFL will tell you that the most important guy on your team is the owner. You can have Tom Brady or Peyton Manning at quarterback. You can have Ray Lewis leading your defense. It doesn't matter one bit if you don't have an owner to make it work. Without that, you're not going anywhere. I'm not going to start naming names, but trust me. You look at teams that consistently win and it starts at the top. Everybody talks about Bill Walsh in San Francisco, but you don't get Bill Walsh unless you have Eddie DeBartolo. You look at all the championships that Pittsburgh has won and you better understand how important the Rooney family is to making that work. Bob Kraft and his family up in New England have made that operation pretty amazing, building that stadium and everything they've done, along with three titles. Heck, look at the New York Yankees, arguably the greatest team in baseball. Do you think they began their climb back to greatness in the mid-1970s without the late George Steinbrenner pushing the buttons?

In this game, there are some owners who care just about the bottom line. I've been lucky. For example, when I first joined the Ravens, they had Art Modell running the show and he was great to my family and me. Modell loved the players and wanted to do anything he could to win. Then Steve Bisciotti came in and he was great to me, too, and to the entire organization. Bisciotti didn't want a whole lot of attention, but he wanted to make sure that everything was done right. In fact, he went to bat for me to get the head coaching job with the Jets. However, as I'll get back to in a minute, Bisciotti could have done a lot to hurt my chances for the Jets job if he had wanted to save some money. Fortunately for me, he didn't.

Now I have Woody Johnson, an owner who wants to do nothing but win. Part of him is still figuring it out, because he didn't buy the team until 2000, from the estate of the late Leon Hess, one of the owners my dad worked for when he was with the Jets. Hess was a good man, kind of a silent owner. Back in 1963, he bought the team with Sonny Werblin and Phil Iselin. Those guys really understood what it took to win. They hired Weeb Ewbank, who eventually hired my dad, and together they brought in Joe Namath. They understood how to get a great coach and a great quarterback, two guys who were very different but who could handle the whole New York atmosphere. Weeb was the grinder and Namath was the good-looking, talented face of the team. Namath was "Broadway Joe" with the mink coat, and had all the personality and flash. Meanwhile, Weeb was getting the team ready to play. It was a perfect marriage, and that's how they took the league by storm so fast; it's just too bad Namath's knees didn't last. The key in all of that, though, was a group of owners who understood what it took. They had a plan and they carried it out.

Hess bought out Werblin and Iselin in the 1970s and ran the team from afar after that. Bless his heart, he'd put some guy from his company in charge of looking over the team, but he just wasn't involved in the daily business. That's kind of a problem, when you really think about it. You can't have some middleman in charge, because he's always going to think he has to prove himself to the owner. Either he has some impact on winning or losing, or he's keeping the costs under control, or he's making sure that the players and coaches don't do something stupid in public. Whatever it is, that middleman is always thinking he has to justify his job, and most of the time, he really doesn't know that much about football. That's starting to change around our league. You see Bill Parcells and Mike Holmgren getting these "advisor" jobs. Those are football guys, former coaches who are hired by owners to oversee the operation. Those guys are really part of the program. In Miami, Parcells had a big say over who the players were going to be. In Cleveland, Holmgren has a big influence over how the future of that team is going to be set up. So even in those situations, you have football guys who are involved with the team and with the coach. They have to prove that they're worth something to the owner. It's just human nature. If you hire me and pay me a lot of money, I have to do something, right? Heck, I remember when the Dolphins hired Dan Marino to be a kind of football advisor back in 2004. He started showing up at the Senior Bowl and doing a number of other appearances, but he lasted only about three weeks. I think he realized very quickly just how much work it was going to be to do that job for real. It probably takes 80 to 100 hours a week. No joke.

That's why I think it's so important for the owner to have direct contact with the people who are making decisions. An owner can be out in front or behind the scenes, but he has to be there. That's how Woody Johnson is. He's there. Look, he could spend his time doing a lot of other things, making a lot more money than he makes day-to-day with the football team, but he wants to be there with us. He wants to help in whatever way he can, just like when he went down with me to Fort Lauderdale before the 2010 season to talk to our gifted cornerback Darrelle Revis. When Mr. Johnson went down there, he didn't talk to Revis about unemotional details like money or the contract. He was talking about the big picture, about being one of the greatest Jets of all time, about being a Hall of Famer. That was huge, because I think it made Revis understand that this wasn't only a business deal about a certain number of dollars on a page. Mr. Johnson was looking at Revis and saying: "I want you to be great. I want you to be a Jet for life." That's a whole different level of commitment.

When Mr. Johnson took over the team in 2000, he had that kind of structure in place with Parcells. Parcells had just retired as the head coach but was going to stay on as the general manager, the guy in charge but not talking. That's when they had the whole weird thing with Bill Belichick, who was supposed to be the next head coach but who abruptly resigned with some strange handwritten statement. Whatever it was he wrote, it didn't go over so hot. Then they got Al Groh to take the job, and he did okay, going 9-7 in 2000, but his heart just wasn't in it. He wanted to coach at the college level and ended up eventually taking off for Virginia. After that, Parcells quit as the GM, which they knew was going to happen. Still, in the space of less than a year after Mr. Johnson bought the team, Parcells retired as coach, Belichick left, Groh left, and then Parcells left as the GM. Okay, I've never run a real day-to-day business like Johnson & Johnson or even a coffee shop, but I don't think it's easy to have your top managers leave every other day.

The Jets hired Herm Edwards after that, and Herm did a good job. Again, some people would say, "What are you talking about? He had a losing record in five years." True, Edwards was 39-41 in five years. That's a winning percentage of .488, which most people would say is kind of lousy. Hey, if I did that, I'd probably be disappointed in myself. You have to put it in perspective, though. In the history of the Jets before I got here, there had been 16 head coaches. Edwards has the fourth-best record of all of them. Seriously. He went to the playoffs three times. That's more than any coach in the history of the team, Parcells and Ewbank included. I kid you not. What that says is that winning with the Jets has been tough.

As things were winding down with Herm, Johnson was trying to figure the whole thing out and he did exactly what so many of us do: He hired somebody from a team that was doing good. He hired Eric Mangini away from New England. Now, trust me, Eric is a good coach. My brother worked for him in Cleveland before going to Dallas, and he also worked with him in New England under Belichick. Mangini is smart as a whip and really knows how to teach, particularly defensive backs. I have nothing bad to say about Mangini. He just does his deal differently, and I'll explain that a little later in the book. And I totally understand why he got hired. You weren't going to find anybody more successful than the Patriots. Everybody wanted a piece of that team, which is why guys like Romeo Crennel, Charlie Weis, and Josh McDaniels also got head coaching jobs coming out of there. Mangini also had a really great first year, going 10-6 and making the playoffs. The second year was down, and then they were having a great third season in 2008 until it came apart. They were 8-3, the best record in the league at that point; Brett Favre was playing great (give Mr. Johnson a lot of credit for going out and getting that trade done)—and then they lost four of their last five games and missed the playoffs. The bad part of all of that was that they kept swinging from one extreme to the next. That's hard for the fans to deal with. You get way up there and then you fall. It's rough.

An unforgiving spotlight can shine on an NFL coach. We all get that. Trust me. This job is not built for people who can't ride the wave. You might wonder if I feel bad about taking the job from a guy I know pretty well and who's a friend of my brother. Not really. I wasn't cheering against Mangini. I didn't want to see anybody fail, especially someone who is close to my family like Mangini is with Rob. We all know how it works, though. It's not personal at that point; it's just how this business operates.

That's where I also have to give Mr. Johnson credit. He made his decision to change direction, and this time I think he really looked deep into the overall picture. Look, there's no manual for being an NFL owner. There's no manual for how to be a coach, either. There are certain things you learn along the way. From what I can see, when the Jets searched for a new coach and hired me, it was deeply researched. They wanted to find out everything they could about everybody they interviewed. One of the ideas they had for doing that came from Bruce Speight, our senior director of media relations. Speight has been around the NFL for a long time. He was with Carolina before he joined the Jets, and he really understands how the whole league works. From what I'm told, the Jets were talking about how to really find out about the candidates; Speight suggested that everybody on the team who ran a department should call their counterparts from the teams that the candidates work for. This way, they could find out what their peers thought about the guy, and whether the candidate knew what was going on with the different departments on his own team.

From there, the Jets compiled all the information and analyzed it. Trust me, this was tough, because they also had three great candidates from inside their own building: special-teams coach Mike Westhoff, offensive line coach Bill Callahan, and offensive coordinator Brian Schottenheimer. Those are sharp guys, all of them. There's a reason I kept them on staff when a lot of new coaches might have gotten rid of a guy who was trying to get the job. I'll talk about that some more later, but you have to understand how thorough the Jets were in really looking at all the information and not just letting one interview or some appearance lead them to making a decision.

While we're talking about appearance, let me address that head-on: I know I'm overweight. I'm not living in denial. I've tried all these crazy diets over the years, losing a bunch of weight, then just putting it right back on and then some. This is who I am. It's my problem. That's why I finally had the lap-band surgery, because I knew I couldn't do it the way everybody else did. It just wasn't going to work. Still, here I am, all 300-something pounds of me, or whatever I am, and I can see how people react to me. I can see it in their eyes, and I know what people say about fat guys. If you're fat, you're lazy. Look around the NFL at the head coaches. You don't see a lot of heavyset guys, do you? Andy Reid in Philadelphia is one. Mike Holmgren—you could see he battled it, and he wasn't even that big. There simply are not many guys like that. I remember when Charlie Weis was up in New England and talked about how hard it was for him to get a head coaching job and he thought it had a lot to do with being overweight.

Let me tell you something: Just because I'm a fat guy doesn't mean you're going to outwork me. That crap about being lazy? I'll take on anyone. Don't worry, I'll be there to put you to bed every night when you need to get tucked in. Back in 2008, I can't help but think that was the reason I didn't get a job. I interviewed with Parcells down in Miami, but that wasn't going to work because he already had his guy with Tony Sparano. I also interviewed with Atlanta, and that one really frustrated me because that was a job where I really felt like I fit. That made a lot of sense to me, and I think I would have been great there. They hired Mike Smith, who, as I said, I think is a good guy. But in the back of my mind I was thinking that maybe it was my appearance, that maybe I wasn't exactly what they were looking for from the outside, and that was really tough to take.

Finally, I interviewed with Baltimore after they cleared out the staff, but it just wasn't going to work. As much as I wanted to be the head coach of the Ravens, I could feel that the interview wasn't going my way. You see, I knew I had to be honest with Bisciotti about what had gone wrong. By that time, Brian Billick had lost the team. I knew it. It had been 10 years. It wasn't necessarily Billick's fault. Heck, even he had said in the past that a great coach has a shelf life of about 10 years. Unless you are clever, after that long you've given every speech you can give. You've tweaked every ego in every way you can. Heck, that's why it's so hard to last even three years in this business. When you're on a roller coaster the way we were those last couple of years, it's hard. You go from the AFC Championship Game to 5-11, back into the playoffs, then down again. It's just like with fans, where you build up expectation and then it comes crashing down really fast. You run the risk that when people get down from that big adrenaline rush, you can lose them. It's hard to keep them on board that way, and Billick did it for a long time. It's like the old saying from some coaches about how some owners and some coaches don't mind going somewhere between 7-9 and 10-6 every year in the NFL. You're just good enough to keep selling the fans and the players on hope, but you're really not making any big strides. To me, you're not doing anything; you're just playing around.

Anyway, as I was sitting there with Bisciotti, he asked me point-blank what had gone wrong and I had to give an answer. Well, when I told him what I thought the reason was, I felt like I was basically saying I was part of the problem because I was telling him something was wrong with the guy I was working for. I'm a team guy. I was part of that. As soon as I said it, I knew I had killed my own chances to get the job. I could feel it; it just wasn't comfortable at all, because I had to be honest about what I thought. Sitting there, I felt like crying about the situation. It just went very wrong, so I knew I wasn't getting the job. I also felt, at that point, that Bisciotti didn't know the true me. I mean, I know he liked me and I always heard I was one of his favorite guys, but it wasn't the same thing as truly having his respect. I think I earned it after that year, when I worked so hard to make sure that we could be as successful as we could after they hired John Harbaugh. I think Bisciotti really understood how dedicated I was and how honest I was about making it work for the team.

That's why I think Bisciotti stood up for me the next year when I interviewed for the Jets job. Billick was trying to get the Jets job at the time and, trust me, Bisciotti had a good reason to hope Billick got the job. After Billick was let go, he still had three years and about $10 or $12 million left on his contract. If the Jets had hired him, Bisciotti wouldn't have had to pay off that money—the Jets would have, or at least most of it. Yet there was Mr. Johnson calling Bisciotti to get the word on who he should hire, and Bisciotti said me. I can't tell you how grateful I was to him for saying that.

When it came down to it, though, the final touch was Mr. Johnson. Again, he could have taken one look at me with my big belly, my kind of scruffy look, and not-so-classy way of speaking, and said, "What the heck? We're going to hire *this* guy?" Instead, he listened. He listened to me. He listened to all the people who gave him information about me. I heard there wasn't one person in the entire Baltimore organization who had a bad word to say about me. That was pretty amazing to find out. You're in a place for 10 years and you don't royally piss somebody off somewhere along the line? I was proud of that.

When I was sitting in that interview with Mr. Johnson, I realized something that was so uplifting: He was comfortable with my being who I am. I was open about everything, my weight, the dyslexia, everything I could think of. He was fine with it all. Here was a man who hangs out with the top people in New York society, the upper crust of the upper crust, and he told me, "Don't sweat it. Be yourself."

Do you realize how important that is for a guy like me, a guy who has been dreaming of getting here but struggling with some of the politics that comes with it? It's an incredible burden getting completely lifted from my shoulders. I can't tell you just how much that means. During the interview (and I did only one interview, which really surprised me. A lot of the time, they make you come back a second time), I explained to him my whole plan for team building. The thing he says to this day is that they had always talked about team building, how important it is and how much they wanted to do it. Yet I was the first guy who really came in with a plan about how to do it—what gets guys to fight for each other, what gets guys to understand and accept each other. It's just like what I said at the start: I had my idea for doing it and Mr. Johnson understood how important it was to the team. He realized it was more important than trying to save some dollars, even when he had already spent a ton. That's the kind of owner a football coach would want to be around. I heard some stuff before the 2010 season about how we didn't want to sign Revis because Mr. Johnson didn't want to spend the money. That's crazy. He'll spend it on whatever he thinks we need to spend it on, and he wants to hear from Mike Tannenbaum and me about what's important.

Just like every other part of his life, Mr. Johnson is devoted. He helps run several charities and gets me involved with them, too. One time, my wife and I were at a charity event with Sting, Uma Thurman, Catherine Zeta-Jones, Michael Douglas, and some other big stars. I looked at my wife and said, "Who are the two people who don't belong here?" We pointed to ourselves and started laughing. It was crazy. As the dinner went on, I was supposed to be the fundraising leader of our section. Really? Me? I was supposed to be leading Sting and a group of industry titans? Mr. Johnson would encourage me to be myself with all these people, have fun, laugh a lot, have a

great time, and do something good. Mr. Johnson is devoted to terrific causes, like the Juvenile Diabetes Foundation and others. But
he's not just donating, he's hosting events at his place in New York.
He's active; he's being a part of it.

He does the same things with us and the football team. You can
feel that vibe every day, and it radiates through the whole organization.

10. Changing the Culture of the Jets

There's a tendency for guys who become head coaches to say, "Okay, I'm going to run this my way. I'm in charge now." There's no question you need some of that. It helps to establish that you're the leader, that the buck stops with you and that you make the final decisions. That's the whole point to being put in charge. If you're afraid of that, you shouldn't have applied.

At the same time, the show is not all about just you. As the head coach, your job is to bring everybody together and make them understand that you're there to help the team work as one unit. I know I'm a pretty good coach, but I can't do everything myself. I'm not smart enough to do it all alone, so I need everybody pulling with me, working together to get it done—which is why after I got to the Jets, I changed some things right away.

The first thing was my office. When Eric Mangini was coach of the Jets, he wanted some distance between himself and his players. The head coach's office in the Atlantic Health Jets Training Center has this floor-to-ceiling window that looks out over the rest of the offices and cubicles. But when I arrived, the windows were all painted over. I believe that people working there, the assistant coaches, the players, everybody should be able to look in and see the head coach; but for whatever reason, Mangini had them covered. I don't know exactly why because I never asked him. I want my players and coaches to know they are welcome to come up to me anytime. I want them to see me and feel comfortable. Not only is the door open, the windows are open. I'm an open book for those guys.

I want my players to know who I am, just like I want to know who they are. I want there to be that connection as people. That's valuable when it comes to figuring out how to motivate somebody. It's valuable because I want that guy to fight for me, just like I want to fight for him. Again, I'm all in, everything is on the table. I want those guys to know about my family, that I've been married for nearly 25 years and that I have two sons. I want them to get to know my family. Now, I know there has to be a line somewhere, which is why I don't go out with players. I don't go drinking with them. I don't go out to dinner. Sure, we have some big meetings and stuff, but that's not what I'm saying. You can't have it where some players get to be the coach's favorite in the eyes of the other guys. That divides your locker room. It puts guys against each other, and that's not constructive. I'm human—some guys I'm going to like better than others. That's just life. But I don't want to make it obvious to the point that it makes other guys uncomfortable.

I also don't want it to cloud my judgment. This job isn't easy from that perspective. You have to make decisions about guys all the time. Who's going to be on the team? Who's going to be cut? That's the business side, and you can't get around that. If all of a sudden I'm keeping a guy around because I like hanging out with him and not because he's the best guy for the team, then I've screwed up. Staying within that, you want to bring guys in to really understand who you are as a coach. If they know what I'm really like, then it's no problem for me to make stupid jokes like how Beyoncé wants me.

I'll say to the guys, "Yeah, tell her to quit calling me." I'm just talking some trash to get those guys to crack up and relax a little. Hey, what does Jay-Z have on me?

Don't answer that.

Anyway, the first thing I did was get that window taken care of. The next thing we changed was the media policy. With Mangini, the policy was basically that he talked and maybe Brett Favre, the quarterback at the time, talked. Other than that, everybody was supposed to stay shut. The orders seemed to be, simply: Don't say anything. When Woody Johnson and Mike Tannenbaum were interviewing me, they asked, "What's the policy going to be with the media?"

I thought, "What do you mean, 'what is the policy?' There is no policy." Everybody can talk, the players, the coaches, everybody. I don't want people to be scared to say something.

I just have one rule: When guys talk, it's their job to mention at least two teammates and one coach every time they answer questions. The first time I did that was when I was back at the University of Cincinnati and I was the defensive coordinator, and I've kept it up ever since. It gets to be kind of a game with the players after a while. They'll start talking about teammates and then we'll say, "Okay, now you have to name three players, then four, then five." Next, maybe we'll say you have to throw in somebody who's not a coach or a player. They'll start by talking about the owner or the general manager, but then they get talking about a cook or a janitor. It gets to be fun, and they're learning about everybody who works in the building. During the season, if we pick up a new guy, you'll hear somebody say, "Okay, I got the new guy from Dallas." It gets to be funny, something the guys laugh about. In its own way, it's team building.

Now, when I first told the players about it, they looked at me like I was crazy, but then they went out and did it. As a result, they start reading quotes from teammates and they start thinking about what other people are saying about them. It also gets guys out of the "I and me" routine. It's not about them anymore; it gets guys thinking outside of themselves and only what's going on with them. They have to think about what other guys are doing and what's going on around them. It helps them get a better picture of how they make a play, and they're able to see that they have to depend on somebody else to do his job in order for them to do their job. Maybe Shaun Ellis will get two sacks one week and he'll talk about how Robert Turner, who's a backup offensive lineman, did a great job of getting him ready in practice.

The other thing it does is it keeps the tone positive. If you're thinking about somebody other than yourself, then you're not being negative and worried all about yourself. That's something I can't stand—negative thinking, selfish, greedy thoughts. But I'll get back to that later, because it is very important to me. Say our quarterback, Mark Sanchez, has a bad day. He throws a couple of interceptions or misses some big throws. Heck, he had a game last year when he threw five interceptions but we still almost won the game. Hey, young guys are going to struggle, but having to talk about his teammates got him away from feeling sorry for himself. I'm not saying he would get stuck in that kind of negative thinking, but our interview rules are a tool to change a player's way of thinking. If the reporters ask him what happened, he can say, "That's unfortunate. I tell you, our defense is phenomenal. I felt like I really let our guys down. Braylon Edwards was open a couple of times, I just overthrew him. And then there was Thomas Jones, who rushed for 320 yards. There were just so many positive things." That's all you have to do. You've taken something completely negative and done nothing but make it a positive thing by talking about your teammates. It's such a simple thing, and it really builds up everybody else.

I even had the assistant coaches do the same thing. Our defensive coordinator, Mike Pettine, talks about Dennis Thurman, who talks about Jeff Weeks, who talks about Bob Sutton. Trust me—when somebody says something nice about you, it changes your whole viewpoint. On those tough days when you're having a hard time, instead of saying, "Man, why am I going to work?" and feeling down, think to yourself, "I can't wait to get there." If somebody consistently says something good about you, you want to give that to somebody else. That's how it spreads. It's unbelievable.

I've never told the media about this and I don't know if they've noticed. I'm sure some of them have, but it's not like I'm trying to trick those guys. Again, the media has a job to do. In New York, everybody believes that the media is trying to trick you or trap you. Maybe that's true for some of them, but it doesn't really matter. What I do know is that all of those reporters are looking for quotes and they just want some cooperation. You give them some courtesy and that goes a long way. If you tell them they can talk to anyone they want to, what are they going to complain about? You're making their job easier, and it's not such a hard thing to do. In the meantime, you can do some team building.

The other thing you need to understand about letting people talk is that it's part of letting them become professionals. Are guys going to say the wrong thing from time to time? Sure, that's how you learn. I want our guys to be more than just people who mimic what I'm saying or just say whatever I tell them to say. I want them to think. I want them to have ideas. I want to bring that guy out so he's part of what we're doing. The only way to do that is to let guys actually talk. They develop. Look, my owner tells me to be myself. He wants me to say what I feel. Should I tell the players something different? This is what the owner signed up for, although he probably wishes he didn't sometimes.

The other thing I changed were the ongoing, absurdly late nights. I heard stories about how they used to call for meetings at 4 A.M., and it wasn't a rare thing. I wasn't there, so I don't know why they did or didn't do that, but it was made quite clear by Woody Johnson that he didn't want that anymore. He didn't feel it was productive. I'll let him tell it in his own words:

Eric Mangini is different. He is kind of the mad scientist, as well. I guess it was something that we didn't really know each other as well as we thought when we hired him. That's one of the reasons we went through the kind of search process we did when we hired Rex. It was so elaborate so that we really understood what we were getting into with every candidate. One of the things I was very sensitive about was making sure we didn't keep our coaches in the office unnecessarily. There was so much time spent there that they wouldn't be spending time sleeping or doing something other than football, like spending time with their families or whatever it may be.

Rex assured me and we saw that in Rex—he was going to do his job and go. He's not going to have four-in-the-morning meetings with his staff and make his coordinator wait for him. No, thank you. His management style is more akin to my own, which is "do the job and let's go."

When I was the defensive coordinator with Baltimore, I used to notice something. All the assistants would stay until I was done, even though I knew they were finished with their work. Like in most work environments, nobody wanted to leave before the boss. Well, after a while, I'd start leaving the facility, then just head to the mall down the street from our place. I'd go for a snack, or just kill an hour and then I'd come back. All of my assistants would be gone. I could get back to finishing whatever I had to do, and they'd get some rest.

—————

Now, I could go on and on with all the little things we changed with the Jets, but that's not really the answer. Again, it's not always about what you change. It's about having the guts and the knowledge to leave certain things the same—to keep people who can help you—even if those people wanted your job.

As I said, when the Jets interviewed me, they also interviewed three guys from the staff: offensive coordinator Brian Schottenheimer; offensive line and assistant head coach Bill Callahan; and special-teams coach Mike Westhoff. You could have made a really good argument for any one of those three guys if the Jets had wanted to hire them. Schottenheimer is going to be a head coach in this league one day very soon, and I'm pushing for him. He's a great offensive mind and his demeanor is great. You can see how much he soaked up from his dad, Marty Schottenheimer. Schottie doesn't ever overreact when things are going extremely well or extremely bad. He completely keeps his composure.

Callahan was the head coach in Oakland the year they went to the Super Bowl against Tampa Bay. Before that, he had been the offensive coordinator for the Raiders under Jon Gruden, running Gruden's version of the West Coast Offense. He made it to the title game in his first season. The next year, things fell apart, but that's because that team was so old and all the leaders got hurt, guys like Rich Gannon, Bill Romanowski, Jerry Rice, and Tim Brown. Look, my brother was out there for five years as the defensive coordinator. I watched that team closely and I wanted them to be good—not better than our team in Baltimore, but I wanted them to be good. That team just fell apart in a hurry, and they had some really negative guys on the roster. That's the big reason why the Raiders struggled for years. Callahan was the first guy to take the blame for that, but after you go through coaches like him, Norv Turner, and Art Shell, you start to realize it's not just the coach. Again, that's part of the deal in coaching. It's not like they're actually ever going to fire the players. You hear owners and GMs talk about dumping the players all the time, and maybe they get rid of one or two guys, but that's only after the coach goes first. Trust me, we all get it.

The point is that I have a chance to have a guy like Callahan on my staff and I'm going to keep him. He's been involved with offensive football for close to 30 years. He was doing a great job running the show in Nebraska after he left the Raiders. If they had just been a little more patient in Nebraska, it would have been amazing. He came to the Jets in 2008 and started working with our young guys, like Nick Mangold and D'Brickashaw Ferguson. That's why we have one of the best lines in the league. I'm not messing that up. That's the culture of the team you want to keep intact.

Finally, there's Westhoff and he's a beauty. Everybody should get a chance to know a coach like Westhoff. The man is hilarious— really sarcastic, has great one-liners in practice and, really, all the time. He'll come up to a guy who is screwing up and say something like, "My man, a doctor told me how to cure your problem. Walk up a flight of steps, jump down, and land hard on both feet. Your head will fall right out of your ass."

More important, Westhoff is all in. You talk to Westhoff and you know that football is his life's work. For him, it isn't just about money, or winning, or glory. It's about ideas; it's about finding different ways to do things. It's about teaching guys how to think, not just how to run plays. It's all that higher-level stuff that you can do in the NFL because everybody can be so focused on just doing football.

It's also the reason we get results. Since Westhoff came to the Jets in 2001, through my first year as coach in 2009, we had 13 kickoff or punt returns for touchdowns. That's the most in the league. Our coverage units always have ranked right at the top of the league. In today's NFL, where everything is so tight and one or two plays can make your season, special-teams play is critical.

Westhoff has been coaching in pro football since 1982, with all but one year in the NFL (he went to the USFL for a year back in the 1980s). He spent 15 years in Miami, working for three different coaches (Don Shula, Jimmy Johnson, and Dave Wannstedt). Now, it should tell you a lot when an assistant coach spends 15 years in one place. I thought I was doing pretty good at 10 years in Baltimore.

See, we're just scratching the surface with Westhoff. In 1988, he was diagnosed with cancer in the femur of his left leg, the section that runs from your hip to your knee. The first time he had surgery he almost died because the doctor thought it was a back problem. Not only was it misdiagnosed, the doctor accidentally cut through one of Westhoff's arteries. After they finally found out what was wrong, Westhoff had 10 surgeries on the leg, removing cancer, removing bone, replacing it with pins and screws, grafts, and more hardware than you find at Home Depot or Lowe's. It's crazy when he starts to tell you this stuff.

The best part is, he never quit. Westhoff used to hobble around on a cane or drive around practice in a golf cart. He said one time that he looked like a pretzel after a while because of all the surgeries. Along the way, this one doctor told him that he was going to end up in a wheelchair one day. Still, he never flinches and never quits. Think about all the chances this guy had to feel sorry for himself, to say enough is enough with all the pain and just take the benefits and go. But he never did it. Finally, a great orthopedic surgeon, Dr. John Healey of the Sloan-Kettering Cancer Center in New York, suggested a procedure for Westhoff. Healey specially designed a titanium rod to go in the leg and replace the femur. That was in the winter of 2008, and Westhoff had to go through some serious rehab. That was the one time he really had to quit working with the team, right after the 2007 season ended. He wasn't going to be able to do anything for months.

This wasn't just some three-hour routine surgery—it was 12 hours. It was so long that they had to have two different X-ray technicians. First, Healey had to take out all the screws and previous stuff. At one point, Westhoff said that the only thing keeping his leg attached to his body was the soft tissue. Brutal. Then Healey put in the rod, which Westhoff said looks like something you would jack your car up with. (On a side note, you should know that Healey has done this surgery only once before, because this is a totally unique case. You don't get this kind of cancer situation very often.) So everything finished and Westhoff did the rehab he needed to do. Slowly, he started getting stronger and stronger so that by training camp of 2008, before I took over, he was in good enough shape to be walking and the Jets realized that they had some problems on special teams. They begged him to come back, but he still had so much healing to do so he said no. They waited awhile and asked again, and because he's just that kind of an intense guy, he came back.

Now you watch him and, aside from a little limp, you'd never know he's been through anything. You don't see the scar that runs from his ribs to his left knee. The guy is amazing, and the bottom line is that I want guys like that on my side. You don't hear him complaining about his life, and that's an inspiration to all of us.

Here's another interesting story about Westhoff that applies to this situation with me coming in after he didn't get the job: He went through exactly this same kind of situation earlier in his career. Back in 2000, right after the Dolphins lost a horrible playoff game to Jacksonville 62-7 and Jimmy Johnson quit, the team hired Dave Wannstedt. Most everybody knew that the job was going to Wannstedt, because Jimmy Johnson brought him in that year after the Bears fired Wannstedt. Wannstedt and Jimmy went way back to the start of their coaching careers, basically as best friends. Wannstedt was the first defensive coordinator of those great Dallas teams that won three titles in the 1990s before the Bears hired him away. Wannstedt did a great job running Jimmy's defense.

After Jimmy officially quit, Westhoff asked to interview for the head coach job the same way he did with the Jets. He sat down with then–Dolphins owner Wayne Huizenga, but the team ended up hiring Wannstedt. Okay, that happens. Westhoff came back with the staff and Wannstedt started to believe that Westhoff was bad-mouthing him and fired him. Now, I wasn't there, so I don't know, but it doesn't sound like the Westhoff I know to talk negative about anybody.

To me, Westhoff is the kind of guy you really want to keep around. Not only that, you give him all the responsibility he can handle. Guys like Westhoff love it. The more you give them, the more they want. Before I ever got here, Westhoff would do our scouting report on officials before every game. I wanted him to keep doing that. He would bring in officials each week and tell them how to call certain stuff to give us a better look for Sunday. I wanted him to keep doing that, too. This is on top of having a great special-teams unit. Oh yeah—did he mind if I kept him doing that?

You know what happened with Westhoff? It didn't take long before we were completely on the same page. He told a reporter one time—before we had ever played a game in 2009: "I like Rex, I really do. And you know me, I don't like anybody."

Like I said, he's a funny man.

Guys like that, like Westhoff, Callahan, and Schottenheimer, you want them around. You can't be afraid of guys who might want your job. If you are, then you're going to end up hiring bad people who are not motivated to do more, who aren't going to work as hard as you need them to work, and who aren't going to challenge you with new ideas. How are you going to get better if you don't have good people around? The thing you do with good people is you help them out. You don't stifle them and you don't control them. You make sure that they know you're doing everything you can to help them, because then they'll fight for you. Someday, I would love to have five or six guys from this staff become head coaches in the league. It would be awesome to sit back and say, "Wow, these are guys that worked with me, and look at them now!" That would be great. I'll find some other great coaches and we'll be okay; but if you had that kind of success, the guys you hired after them would do anything for you because they'd know how much it helped those other guys. You want that type of culture.

It's funny. After our first year, when we made the AFC Championship Game, Schottenheimer was invited to interview for the Buffalo job. He declined the interview. Really, that was surprising. Again, there's only 32 of these jobs and you don't always get a chance, but if that's what he wanted to do, I'm happy. I want that guy on my sideline for as long as he wants to be there.

The funny part is that Woody Johnson ran into Schottenheimer down at the Super Bowl in Miami after all that. He said to Schottie, "Those jobs don't come around often—what made you decide to stay?" Schottenheimer told Johnson: "To be honest about it, I've been in this business for a long time and this is the first time I've ever had any fun. My wife is having fun and I'm having fun. I just don't want it to end. It's not worth leaving."

That makes me proud—that I'm creating an environment where people want to work, where they want to stay. That's important. At the same time, it takes work and it takes tough decisions sometimes. It's not like we're just sitting around eating Oreos all day and telling jokes. For me, I faced a tough call to fire one of the guys I brought in during my first year. It just wasn't working and I had to fix it. The one thing you can't do in this job is sit around denying that you made a mistake. You have to take care of things.

I had to do that halfway through my first year. I had hired Kerry Locklin, a guy I knew from my college days, to be our defensive line coach. The problem was that the guy was a negative thinker, and when our situation started to go south for a stretch, it just got worse and worse. Eventually, it got to the point that I couldn't take it anymore. I never want to see negative things associated with us, talking negatively about a teammate or any of that junk. The day I got to the Jets' HQ, I talked with our general manager, Mike Tannenbaum, and he gave me the pulse of the type of people we had. Anybody who was considered a negative guy—players, coaches, anybody—I said we were going to get rid of. I didn't care whether they could help us or not—they were not going to be leading my team. No way in hell. I don't want anybody negative around me. I can't stand negative people, and that includes coaches.

So that meant that Locklin had to go. We were in the middle of a bad run, having just lost five of six after opening the season 3-0. We were 4-5 at the time and I made the move. The media thought I did it to get the blame off me, but that wasn't it at all. I took the blame. I hired the guy, after all. I had known Locklin for almost 20 years and this was his first season in the NFL. Unfortunately, his mind-set didn't fit with us. He never respected his players. That pissed me off, and I kept telling him, "You have a job here; they're putting food on your table." Yet he didn't have the time for them and wouldn't respect them. He wouldn't listen to them; he'd talk down to them and take a negative tone. So I said, "Fine, you're gone." That was it. I'm not going to have that on my coaching staff. I'm not going to have it in the locker room. We may not win every game, but I know one thing: I'm not having any form of disrespect. I want to surround myself with positive people and guys who think the glass is half full.

Players feed off the energy of the coaches. That's just how it is. You would think that players are motivated by themselves to be great, and a lot of them are. There are plenty of guys out there who you don't have to say two words to and they'll get going. It's like going to church. At church, you have all of sorts of people who want to be inspired. If the preacher gets up there and has no energy or no strength, you see people fidgeting, dozing off, and not paying attention. Coaches are the same way. They get the mood going. They turn on the engine for those players.

It's like how I've been dealing with Vernon Gholston, a guy the Jets drafted No. 6 overall in the 2008 draft. That was before I got here and people were thinking it would be easy for me to just get rid of him. Truth be told, I didn't like the kid coming out of college. He's a good athlete and a smart guy, but I thought he was a phony. We had him come to Baltimore, and I just didn't believe in him. I even told Mangini not to draft him. Well, suddenly he was on my team and I was going to have to work with him. I was not just going to give up on him—that's too easy. I thought, "He's one of my guys now, and I'll be damned if he's going to feel like that. He's going to know that I'm in his corner and I'm trying like hell to get him to play better." I want him to see everything I'm about, so all those pictures I painted of him back in 2008—you know what I'm going to do?

The same thing I did with the paint over the window in my office. I'm taking it down.

11. Mark Sanchez

Coming into my first year as head coach with the Jets, we knew there was a pretty good chance that Brett Favre was planning to leave. If we were going to be successful, the most important person that we had to draft was someone who could lead. It had to be someone who could take control of this franchise. For a quarterback, we set our sights on Mark Sanchez.

For the record, let me clarify that previous statement. Mike Tannenbaum and I set our sights on Mark Sanchez. Mike and I were determined to draft Sanchez. Of course, now that he's become the first quarterback in NFL history to win four playoff games in his first two seasons, everyone in our organization says they wanted Mark!

Who wouldn't want to be responsible for making Mark a Jet? There isn't a single person in this franchise who doesn't respect him as a person and as a player. Honestly, the kid is unbelievable. He's not just a guy with GQ good looks and a good arm. He's the real deal. He has all the intangibles: talent, charisma, intellect, and leadership abilities. I believe Mark's going to be extraordinary in the

NFL. I have believed that since I first met him. I refer to him as "my baby." I know that may not be the most masculine way to put it, but it's the truth, he is absolutely my baby. He wasn't just my first draft pick as an NFL head coach; he was the first of many important decisions I was going to make for this franchise. He's my guy, and I'm damn proud of it! I still have his draft card at home, tucked away in a drawer. I plan to get it framed one day.

Statistics say that if you are a rookie head coach and you use a first-round draft pick on a quarterback, you will not make it more than four years in that head coaching job. Those are the numbers. Frankly, I think that's BS. You have to have a franchise quarterback. Look around—you can't win in this league without one. So when the time came, the last thing I was going to do was let a few facts and figures keep me from going after Mark.

I'll tell you this, though: We weren't the only ones who were after Sanchez. Other teams liked him, too, and we sat relatively low—too low to draft Sanchez—with the 17th pick in the 2009 NFL Draft. Needless to say, finding a way to make that pick happen wasn't easy. Mark's coach at USC, Pete Carroll, wasn't used to his quarterbacks leaving school early. Heisman Trophy winners Carson Palmer and Matt Leinart and John David Booty stayed for their senior seasons at USC. Carroll made it clear he thought Sanchez should do the same.

A fourth-year junior, Mark waited until the last day that players could announce their intention to enter the NFL Draft early to make his plans known. At the press conference called for him to make his announcement Sanchez and Carroll sat together at a table, and Carroll looked as if that was the last place he wanted to be. Carroll knew Sanchez intended to leave, and he wasn't happy with the decision. He believed that Mark, who had only started 16 games at USC, could benefit by another year in college. Carroll actually left the news conference before Sanchez could take questions. It appeared awkward, but both downplayed Carroll's exit, and I know for a fact that the two are still good friends.

While NFL personnel may have been concerned by Sanchez's lack of experience, Sanchez believed all four years of his time at USC—not just the 16 games he started—actually helped his preparation. He cited the team's talent—many of his teammates had gone on to the NFL—and the opportunity to play in the Trojans' pro-style offense.

When Sanchez declared for the draft, he was considered a first-round prospect, but his stock climbed during the months leading up to the draft to the point that no one would have been surprised if he was picked in the top five. Sanchez was described as a player who could be groomed to become a leading man in the NFL. He was exactly what we needed in this franchise.

I was part of a group of Jets officials that included Woody Johnson, Mike Tannenbaum, Brian Schottenheimer, and Matt Cavanaugh that met with Sanchez in March 2009. We sneaked him through a back door at the California hotel where the NFL meetings were being held. We gave him an X's and O's quiz that he aced, no problem. All of us were so impressed by him.

The next day we watched him throw in a private workout at his alma mater, Mission Viejo High School. I couldn't believe it. Schottenheimer put Mark through every workout known to man and he passed every one of them with flying colors. We knew, I think right then, that this was the guy we really wanted. Still, it wasn't just because of his arm that I wanted Mark. It went deeper.

We had gone to Kansas State earlier to meet and watch Josh Freeman. He was a great quarterback prospect, big, strong, and talented. You want to like Freeman the best, and, of course, he's now a starter in the NFL with the Tampa Bay Buccaneers. Yet just two receivers showed for Freeman's workout when we visited. Two. We worked out Sanchez and the guy had 24 receivers there. Twenty-four! That's more than enough players to field two football teams. They had come as volunteers because they wanted to help Mark as he was auditioning for us. I have to tell you, in all my years, I've never seen 24 guys show up to another guy's workout.

That's not all. When we arrived at Sanchez's high school, a field hockey game was scheduled for the field. The two teams, with no questions asked or complaints, delayed the game so Mark could get his private workout in for us. The teams had absolutely no problem with it whatsoever. Why? Because they LOVE Mark Sanchez and both teams and their coaches respected him that much. The kids sat and watched Mark's entire workout. The coaches actually asked Mark if he needed more time. Everyone pulled for this kid. To me, that spoke volumes about Mark Sanchez. My mind was made up; he had to be a Jet.

This is also a young man who lived an hour away from Southern Cal; yet he'd bring his receivers to his home in the off-season for workouts. They'd eat, train, go to a local theme park—and Mark still found the time to wash and fold everyone's laundry. I don't know what it is, but it is amazing, that charisma. I can't think of anybody who doesn't like Mark Sanchez. Anybody.

Naturally, the NFL scouts liked Sanchez, too. He made all the throws—in the pocket and on the run. He was a leader. He was confident and poised. Sanchez handled the pressure of playing for a national championship contender at USC and of playing in a large news media market like Los Angeles. I knew he could handle New York. I didn't believe Mark was afraid of the big stage at all.

The trouble was, other teams such as Seattle (No. 4 pick), Cleveland (No. 5), and Washington (No. 13) expressed serious interest in Sanchez as the draft drew closer. At No. 17, we were sure there was no way Sanchez would be available when it was our turn to select.

Quarterbacks, of course, are the face of a franchise. They usually make the most money and are placed under the most scrutiny. In the 10 years from 1998 to 2008, a quarterback was chosen first overall eight times in the NFL Draft. That equaled the number of times a quarterback was picked No. 1 in the previous 30 years combined.

Honestly, quarterbacks weren't in high demand in 2009. Stafford, Sanchez, and Freeman were considered first-round selections, but

NFL staffs had to dig a lot deeper to find other early-round quarter-back gems.

That's why the pressure was on Tannenbaum. We wanted Sanchez, and Mike needed to make a deal that would give us the top-five pick required to draft Sanchez. Tannenbaum worked his magic and turned to an unlikely source—Eric Mangini, the coach he fired after the 2008 season—to make the blockbuster trade that allowed us to draft Sanchez.

Tannenbaum and Mangini remained on good terms and their professionalism allowed both to do what they felt was best for their teams. This was business. On the day the draft started, Tannenbaum pulled off a five-for-one deal with the Browns to give us the fifth overall pick. Many in the media called us the splash team of the draft, and that was our intention.

To acquire Sanchez, we traded our first- and second-round choices (No. 17 and No. 52), plus three players—defensive end Kenyon Coleman, quarterback Brett Ratliff, and safety Abram Elam.

Only Coleman was projected as a starter for us. We liked Ratliff, too, and he had the potential to be our quarterback of the future. But I believed in Sanchez and was prepared to make him the Jets' highest-drafted quarterback since Joe Namath was selected first in the 1965 AFL Draft.

The NFL Draft took place at Radio City Music Hall in New York City and consisted of seven rounds. It's always a big event that attracts the die-hard fans. It's a party. The 2009 draft was televised by both the NFL Network and ESPN and was the first to have cheer-leaders. The Detroit Lions, who became the first team in NFL his-tory to finish a season at 0-16, used the first pick in the draft to select Stafford, as expected.

The next three picks—Baylor offensive tackle Jason Smith to the Rams, LSU defensive end Tyson Jackson to the Chiefs, and line-backer Aaron Curry to the Seahawks—were announced, though it seemed to take an eternity for each team to hand in their cards. Thankfully, it was finally our turn, and Sanchez was our man.

The media called it an aggressive move; I called it a smart one. Mark was at his agent's offices in Irvine, California, at the time and was watching the draft on television. He busted into a wide smile, pumped his fist, and pulled on a Jets cap. I don't know who had the bigger grin—Mark or me.

I also knew there were teams that were bluffing during our negotiations to trade up for Sanchez, asking way too much in return. We were on the telephone with St. Louis Rams general manager Billy Devaney. I've known Billy for years, and he tried to hire me once. Billy suggested they may have an interest in Mark and asked me, "Rex, if that happens, what are you going to do?" I told him I was scheduled to take the next flight out, heading to Hattiesburg, Mississippi, and I was determined to talk Brett Favre into coming back to play for the Jets.

If we hadn't traded up, our plan was to select Florida receiver Percy Harvin. And then I was going to head straight to Mississippi to get Favre to come back to New York. Instead, I have the quarterback who will be here with me for the next 10 years, count on it.

———

Honestly, Mark and I are a lot alike. He feels a constant need to prove his doubters wrong, all those people who believe he needed to remain in college for his senior season. I am the same way.

When I kept getting passed over for head jobs and finally was hired by the Jets, I told the team, "You know what? I am going to take it out on the NFL." Sure, I held a grudge. I told anyone who would listen, "My guys are going to be better than they have ever been, and that's a fact. We're in a preseason game against Atlanta and don't think for a second that I had forgotten what I had promised. Get frickin' ready, because I am going to show you." That's just who I am. Mark Sanchez is the exact same way.

I told Mark when we drafted him, "Hey, buddy, get ready. We'll be together for 10 years." And the funny thing is that 10 years would nearly be a record with the Jets for a head coach. I am the Jets' 14th head coach since Coach Weeb Ewbank lasted 10 years (1963 to 1973) as the top man for the Jets. In fact, only Walt Michaels (1977–82) and Joe Walton (1983–89) coached longer than five consecutive years.

The pressure in New York City is different. The New York media will kill you if you're not successful. If I wanted security, I could have gone to St. Louis or somewhere else more forgiving and out of the glare of the major media outlets. But, no, I came to New York City because I am competitive, and that's what I told Mark. We are going to do it; we are going to make this work.

Among the things I love most about Mark is that he's focused, he's funny, and he keeps it light.

One night after Mark, Mr. Johnson, and I ate at a Mexican restaurant—my assistants call it "Rexican" since it's my favorite food—we headed out the door. There was a gorgeous, high-end motorcycle parked out front. What did Mark do? He straddled the thing like he was going to crank it and ride it home. I was thinking, "Oh, shit, we can't have this." But Mark was just having fun. He climbed off and admired it, making sure he left no smudges on the machine. That's him. He has a quick wit and doesn't take himself too seriously, yet he's competitive as hell. He's one of those "I will show you" kind of guys.

The guy always thinks of others, too.

I weighed 310 pounds at the start of the 2009 season and have actually gained 30 pounds since the Jets hired me. I have tried every diet known to man over the years, including a liquid diet during the 2009 training camp. I dropped 20 pounds but quickly gained it right back. I knew I was too fat, so I decided to have a lap-band procedure. It's not an invasive procedure, but it can be dicey. A plastic band is inserted and encircles a patient's stomach, effectively shrinking it and curbing the appetite. After I had lap-band surgery at NYU Medical Center in March 2010, Mark was the only player who telephoned and stopped by the house to see how I was feeling. I wasn't the only member of the Ryan family that Mark cared about. He never missed one of my son Seth's high school freshman football games. He came to every single one, sitting in the bleachers like any other fan.

Of course, the Jets also made sure Mark could buy a ticket to Seth's games! In June 2009, Mark became the highest-paid player in Jets history. He signed a five-year contract that included a team-record $28 million in guarantees.

It was a credit to Tannenbaum and Mark's representatives—David Dunn and Mark's brother, Nick Sanchez—to get the deal done so quickly. Sanchez also handled the announcement of his contract with his usual grace and style. He said his contract was accompanied by a lot of responsibility, just like being the quarterback for the New York Jets. The bottom line was that Mark wanted to make sure he could be in training camp on time and compete for the starter's role with Kellen Clemens. He was just the second of 32 first-round picks to sign, which is rare for a quarterback picked that high.

It should come as no surprise that Sanchez's family helped prepare him to be a success on and off the field. Mark's father, Nick Sr., a fireman and former army sergeant and junior college quarterback, taught his three sons the importance of leadership and put them through a rigorous workout routine to prepare them for sports. Mark's mother, Olga, focused on teaching them the importance of manners and generosity. As an infant, Mark attended the football games of his oldest brother, Nick, in a stroller. He was the water boy when his brother Brandon played. Mark's parents made it a point to make sure their sons could be best friends for life.

Sanchez is what our quarterbacks coach Matt Cavanaugh calls a "people pleaser"—an engaging, but maybe sometimes naïve, person who wants to help everyone and make everyone happy. In an interview, Cavanaugh once very correctly told Greg Bishop of the *New York Times*: "Quite honestly, I tell him sometimes you better learn how to say no. Sometimes, he gets distracted, and we've got to pull the reins in. You're known and admired because of the game you play. You don't want to forget that."

Mark also has openly embraced being a role model for children, especially those who share his Mexican-American heritage. At USC, he had a rabid following, with fans often wearing Mexican *luchador* wrestling masks and sombreros, and chanting "Viva Sanchez." As Ohm Youngmisuk of the *New York Daily News* wrote, "Sanchez represents so much more than the latest Hollywood quarterback from Southern Cal who likes to surf, play the guitar and sing James Taylor songs to his mother."

Other quarterbacks of Mexican descent have played in the NFL, including Tony Romo, Jeff Garcia, J. P. Losman, Joe Kapp, and Jim Plunkett. Yet Sanchez is the only person of Mexican-American heritage who has started at quarterback in the history of the NFL.

It's still about winning, though.

Look what he did for us during his first two years. Twice he helped lead us to one win away from the Super Bowl. He has shown the competitive fire, the pocket presence, and the awareness that, in my opinion, make quarterbacks special. Yes, he has occasionally been mistake prone, but I could see steady progress in his ability to read defenses, to put himself in the right positions to make plays, and to trust his receivers. Mark is mature enough to take the praise with the criticism.

Mark is also a well-rounded guy. He has lots of interests outside of football, including theater. He loves attending Broadway plays — he was even a presenter at the 2010 Tony Awards.

And I'm here to tell you his character is top-notch. I've never seen a young man who always puts his teammates and team personnel first. He took D'Brickashaw Ferguson to the White House and equipment manager Vito Contento to watch the Mets. Sanchez bought shoes for each player he tossed a touchdown to during his rookie season.

During the off-season in July 2010, Sanchez took the initiative to work with his offense in a setting away from the team's practice facilities in Florham Park, New Jersey. The workouts were called "Jets Camp West" and were held in Mission Viejo, California, at Sanchez's high school. A number of players, including receivers Santonio Holmes, Jerricho Cotchery, Larry Taylor, and David Clowney, tight end Dustin Keller, and quarterback Kevin O'Connell, participated.

Sanchez used the video cutups of each receiver from the 2009 season, and they'd meet for an hour or so to discuss how they could all improve. Mark also ordered all the equipment for the players, from their shoes to their pants to their specially designed jerseys that said "Jets West." It looked like a crayon drawing of an airplane. Mark arranged for the players to stay at this phenomenal place.

I took my son Seth out to California to visit Mark during that time. He ran routes and even won a quarterback challenge over Sanchez in one of the little contests Mark had set up for the guys to work on to sharpen their skills. They'd throw up Gatorade bottles and had to hit them with the ball on the way down. It takes a perfect throw. They also had to hit the goalpost crossbar. Seth hit it two times in a row to win it. It was just hilarious to watch.

Mark made sure all the players also enjoyed some good leisure time together, playing golf and attending Major League Baseball's All-Star festivities in nearby Anaheim and the Espy Awards. You name it and Sanchez did it. He had everything arranged to help HIS team grow together.

That's Mark—he's all about doing the little things. And Mark knows that little things add up to big things. He's a winner.

12. Filling Out the Roster

You have to do two things after you take over an organization. First, get rid of the guys who don't fit your system, be it mentally or physically. Second, bring in guys who do fit your system. Two guys I dumped in a hurry were tight end Chris Baker and linebacker Eric Barton. Take Barton, for example: His idea of trying to motivate Vernon Gholston was to rip the guy, yelling at him all the time about how he wasn't giving enough effort, that he wasn't playing hard, that he wasn't measuring up. That's not showing respect. Those guys never respected the guys they played with. They were negative guys, and I'm not going to have negative guys on my team. That was the message I got from the people I talked to in our organization.

When I arrived in New York I used a different tactic to learn about our players. I talked to lots of people, like our equipment guy. You'd be surprised at how much the equipment guys on a team know about the locker room and what the players are really like—and no one ever asks their opinions. It was the same concept that the Jets used when they were looking at the head coach candidates. I talked to the people who were around the players the most. I wanted to see how the players treated other people on staff, the people who have to help them every day—whether it's getting a pair of socks for practice or getting a DVD of some plays they want to study when they go home. If you just talk to the players you only get one view, and players have a hard time being really straight about the guys they play with—and that's understandable. In fact, it's kind of important for those guys to really stick together, because they're the ones who fight together. They have to deal with the little things they don't like about each other and still be able to work as a unit, to trust each other. That's why I had to ask around to get the whole picture. It was hard, because when I was about to make some of the moves I knew were necessary, some guys came up to me and said, "Rex, you'll love that guy. He's a great player." No, I knew what kind of leaders they were by that point and I didn't want them on my team. Our first year, we got rid of about nine players on the defense, including three or four starters.

Clearly, those decisions didn't hurt us, because we ended up No. 1 in the league in defense. After the 2009 season, I traded Kerry Rhodes, another guy who didn't fit. He was a selfish-ass guy. He wouldn't work, and he was a Hollywood type, flashy and needing attention. I don't mind flashy, but your work ethic had better back it up. He was a talented SOB, that's for sure, but he wasn't one of us. So we traded him. For most of those guys I let go, I didn't even wait to see if I could trade them; I just got rid of them. What you have to understand is that we're not running a day-care center here with the Jets. I'm not trying to have a group of guys who sit around the campfire singing songs. Heck, if you saw *Hard Knocks*, then you know there probably aren't too many day-care centers that would allow me in the front door these days. I can see it now: preschool teachers cringing as they imagine my pep talk: "Hey, kid, that's a great f—ing finger painting." I will say this about any preschool I might go to—I know we'd have a great time. Hit the playground and wrap things up on a positive note . . . "Let's go snack!" I'd be a hero.

Anyway, my point is this: There are times you have to correct people by getting on them, really laying into them; however, you had better have a strong foundation of positive thought so they'll be able to deal with it when you give them an earful. If you're always telling a guy, "You suck," how long do you think it's going to be before he tunes you out? Really, that kind of ripping approach just doesn't cut it unless a guy trusts you and believes you're trying to help him.

The toughest decision I had to make coming to the Jets in 2009 was about Brett Favre. After I got the Jets job in January, I had a conversation with Favre and told him I'd be happy to have him come back. Part of me really wanted to coach Favre and I think we would have been great with him, even for the $15 million he was supposed to cost us if we kept him; but he said he was retiring, and I could just feel that he didn't want to play here again. It was obvious he wanted to play for Minnesota so that he could try to get his revenge on Green Bay. It's funny—when I got the job, Adalius Thomas, who played for me in Baltimore and then went up to New England as a free agent, and knows Favre really well, was telling Favre, "You're crazy, you should want to play for Rex with the Jets." But Favre wanted to stick it to Green Bay. I get it. He told us "No" in February and announced on February 11 that he was retiring. (Not that anybody in the media believed it.) In fact, I remember Woody Johnson joking that Favre was like that Sears commercial where he wants to buy a TV but can't make a decision.

Anyway, we had come to the conclusion that we were going to go get a young quarterback in the draft. As long as we could do that, we'd let Favre go after the draft, and that's what we did. Now, if we hadn't drafted Mark Sanchez, I would have flown down to Mississippi just like Brad Childress did, and I would have brought Favre back to New York no matter what it took . . . but that wasn't really our first choice.

We didn't want to wait for Favre and have our whole team held hostage by his off-season routine. We needed leaders in the locker room right away, not in a few months. I understand that Favre sits around in the off-season and doesn't know what he wants to do about the upcoming season. Heck, I know plenty of veteran players who don't want to be around for the off-season. Really, how much more is a guy like Ray Lewis or some other 10-year vet going to get out of the entire off-season program? But you see, the off-season is about everybody being there and working together. You develop many of the relationships between guys by having them work together. Football is a game about collective suffering. It's about guys putting the pressure on each other to fight through the pain so they can make sure they're ready in games. For a quarterback, there's even more of that. You have to be in synch with your receivers and understand where they want the ball. The other thing is (and you hear this especially from the offensive coaches), the quarterback has to be your hardest worker. He has to be the guy who is first in and last out—especially a guy like Favre, who is the face of the team. If he doesn't think he has to put in the time, what are the rest of the guys going to think?

I give Favre a lot of credit for what he ended up doing in 2009 with the Vikings, coming in a few weeks before the season and putting up a career year. Trust me, there were times I looked at that and wished we had an experienced guy like that. I love Sanchez and at the time I knew he was going to be great, but there are always going to be growing pains as a young player develops into a seasoned veteran. I mean, in 2009 Favre threw seven interceptions the entire regular season. Sanchez threw five in one game. That's the way it is in this league for a rookie. Favre has seen everything in this league. Sanchez was four years old when Favre was first drafted. Sanchez is now well on his way with two terrific seasons under his belt, and I'll say this: If he plays long enough and well enough that he feels like he should miss an off-season, well, then we picked a good player. I won't agree with him and I'll tell him to get his butt in here, but you could have worse problems with the quarterback.

Getting back to 2009, after we made the decision about Favre, I had to work on getting some leaders in here. Enter Bart Scott, Jim

Hey, anybody got a snack? That's me reaching for one.

Double trouble . . . I'm on the left, and Rob is on the right.

I was feeling pretty dapper here.

Here I am in my goalie gear for our all-star hockey team . . . what a long-haired trend-setter I was.

Just before we graduated college (I'm on the left), Dad spent two days teaching us the 46 defense. It only took me one day . . . took Rob two.

*My father being carried from the field after the Chicago Bears
won the Super Bowl by beating New England in 1986.
What a great day in the Ryan household!*

*Three Ryans on the same sideline! My father hired both Rob (right) and me (left)
to coach with him in Arizona; here we are in 1994.*

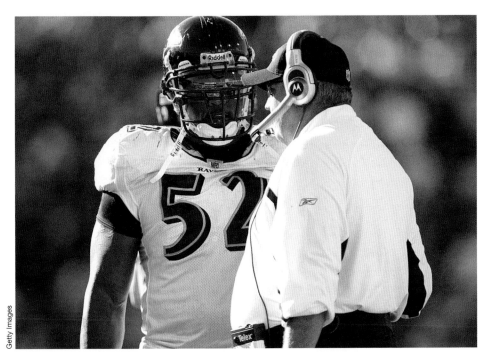

As defensive coordinator in Baltimore, I had the chance to coach some of the greatest defenders of all time, including linebacker Ray Lewis.

A picture of my beautiful wife, Michelle, and me at the Kerry Rhodes Foundation dinner in 2009. With her, I definitely outkicked my coverage!

Mark Sanchez was my first draft pick as a head coach, and I believe he will be the face of the Jets for many years. That started here, in his first-ever preseason game in 2009.

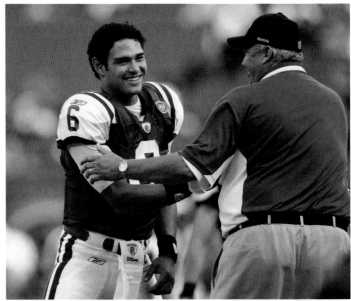

Getty Images

It's no secret I love defense, so I wanted the perfect defensive coordinator for my aggressive style. Mike Pettine is that guy.

Al Pereira

Look at that form . . . and you'll know why I never played quarterback!

Al Pereira

Al Pereira

Al Pereira

Top: Two of my favorite USC guys—Dennis Thurman and Mark Sanchez. Dennis and I have been together for 10 years, and the three of us plan on making it another 10.

Left: After a huge fourth-and-1 conversion to beat the Chargers in the 2009 playoffs, Brian Schottenheimer, our offensive coordinator, knew he could count on me for a big hug.

*One of the best parts of winning is celebrating a plan well-executed.
Here Jim Leonhard helps me hit the showers after beating Tampa Bay in 2009.*

*After losing the AFC Championship Game to Peyton Manning and
the Colts in January 2010, I wished him luck . . . but, oh, that was hard.
It gets old getting beat by him in the playoffs.*

Bringing the heat!
June 2010 at Citi Field.

It was an honor to drop the first
puck of the year at the Islanders'
season opener in October 2010.

*This job is so much easier with an owner like Woody Johnson
and a GM like Mike Tannenbaum on my side!*

*Many people questioned our signing of Braylon Edwards, but I have to tell you,
I love what he has brought to our team.*

Before our game against Cleveland, where my brother Rob was defensive coordinator in 2010, I decided to have a little fun with the fact that he still sports long hair and a bigger stomach than me.

Rob and I talking before the game. We always dreamed of coaching in the NFL . . . and here we are.

Three studs . . . my father, Rob and me on the sideline before our game at Cleveland in 2010. A proud day for all of us!

Post-game celebration after beating the Chargers in January 2010. I told our guys, "Three home teams and the f—ing Jets!" Nobody but us thought we'd get that far.

In the locker room after our big game at Pittsburgh in December 2010, Darrelle Revis and Santonio Holmes made sure the rest of their team knew how huge the win was.

*I love breaking it down
in practice.*

*Santonio Holmes wanted to see my "ups" after
a score against Philadelphia in the preseason
of 2010. Clearly I was on the way down!*

*Darrelle Revis, the best defensive player in the NFL,
shows the Steelers why I say that about him.*

Calm before the storm . . . Revis heads to warm up before facing
· Peyton and the Colts in the 2010–11 Wildcard game.

The big ending to our big playoff win against Indy was sparked by Antonio
Cromartie's clutch kickoff return with less than two minutes to go.

Braylon Edwards and Mark Sanchez told me this play would work . . . and they were right. We drove the field against Indianapolis in the 2010–11 postseason, and set up Nick Folk's chip shot field goal to win the game and send us to New England.

Much as I love the way Peyton Manning plays, I enjoyed seeing him grimace as he walked off the field. It was about time!

"The Madbacker," Bart Scott, who is an integral part of our success.

We brought in Santonio Holmes to make big catches . . . and he delivered. The bigger the stakes, the better he performs—he's a prime-time player.

Two of the main reasons why we beat New England in January 2011— Sanchez and Tomlinson.

These guys definitely know how to fly like Jets. Cotchery, Edwards, and Holmes enjoyed letting New England fans see their wings.

We weren't going to bury this game ball . . . and Sanchez clearly wasn't letting go of it after beating Tom Brady and the Patriots.

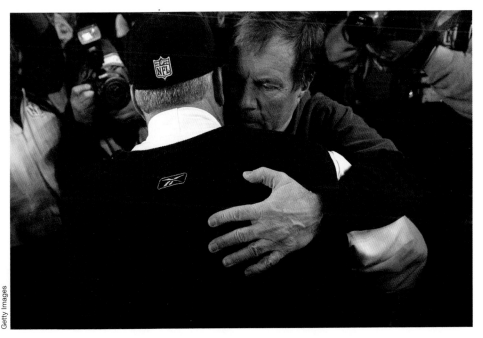

I have enormous respect for Bill Belichick. His kind words after our win against the Patriots will be something I remember for a long time.

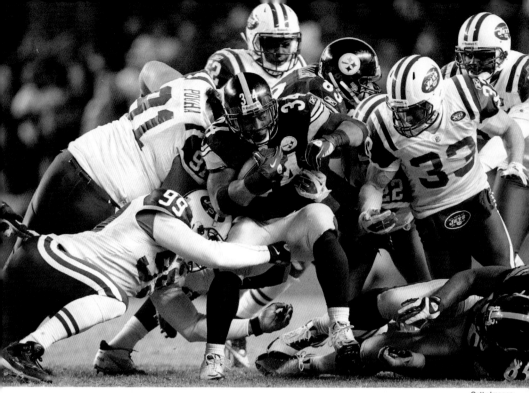

*The Steelers made sure to pound the football at us in the
AFC Championship Game, playing the game just as we like to play it.
On that day, they played it a little bit better.*

*Shonn Greene busted through the Steelers' line late in the game.
Our inspiring comeback fell just short . . . but we'll be back!*

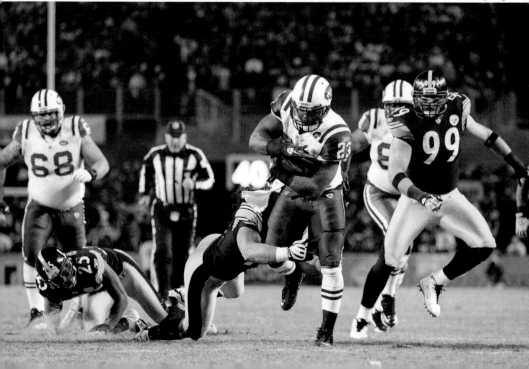

Leonhard, Marques Douglas, and Howard Green. These were the guys from Baltimore who I brought to the Jets during my first year here. The next year, I got Trevor Pryce, a great veteran player who was with me in Baltimore and was a first-round pick in 1997 by Denver. Those first four guys, though, were especially important as I took over the team—and not because they were all great players. Douglas and Green were cut the second year, in fact. It was because they all have a certain toughness about them. They have the right mentality. It's a lunch-pail mentality, like those guys who work manual labor their entire lives. They show up for work no matter how bad things are. They might not be feeling good, they might have had a big argument with the wife that morning—whatever it is, they will show up ready to work. They were a lot like Siragusa, Burnett, and McCrary in Baltimore. You have to have that work ethic on a football team. As we say around here all the time, "Your talent sets the floor, but your character sets the ceiling."

Every team relies on its most seriously talented players. You have to have those game changers, those five or six guys on your team who can make a play. It's hard to have a team that's just about the stars, though; you have to have guys who are going to go to work and set that tone. It's great if those guys are also your stars, but that doesn't happen all the time. That's why you have to have guys like Scott, Leonhard, Douglas, and Green. Obviously, Scott was the most important guy to bring aboard the Jets, because he's both a star player and a grinder—which is why we spent $48 million on a six-year contract to get him and why I was at his house at midnight the second free agency started. Scott is a kind of kindred spirit for me. He's the reflection of everything I believe a player should be and how one should act. I like to tell him he's my brother-from-another-mother. He's a guy who is all in every day and doesn't hold back on anything he has to say. At one point, he said I am the Charles Barkley of the NFL. You can't help but love someone who sees you that way!

In fact, in an interview Scott once said, "You ask us a question, be prepared for the answer. We ain't going to bullshit nobody. I don't have time to live that lie or live that story by trying to be somebody who don't want to beat the hell out of somebody, that don't want to knock a quarterback out of the game. Why lie? That's why I play, because it's fun." Man, is that ever music to my ears! My other favorite comment from him ever was during the off-season after he signed in 2009, when he told the New York media we were "swaggerlicious." If you look it up online, you'll find the term in the "Urban Dictionary" and Scott gets credit for it. I think *Webster's* is putting that one in the next edition of their dictionary; if not, they should. What a great word.

But the thing I really appreciated is what he said when he signed with us, explaining why he wanted to come to this team rather than go back to Baltimore, even though the money was pretty much the same:

> Anybody, I don't care who it is (you can get the last guy who may not make the team) and Rex is talking to him. He'll hit them with one of those "What's up, mother lovers." Just crack you up, but he's getting him comfortable, on his side. The reason I came here and left my comfort zone in Baltimore was not for the money, because the Ravens weren't too far off on the money. It's because I wanted my success—I took for granted I was going to have success—to be linked to Rex. Whatever success I have would be beneficial to him. I wanted my legacy, or whatever that is, to be linked with his. I wanted to come and play well so that he could be successful, because I think he deserves it. I think he goes about football in a nontraditional way.

That's powerful for me to hear. It means that my message is getting through and that's exactly the kind of enthusiasm for the team that I'm trying to create. I want people like that to be around the program I'm building, because they know I'm going to do everything I can to help them and I'm going to pull in other people—assistant coaches, trainers, and so on—to do the same. This is a total team approach. I'm not just about making sure we take care of the stars or the headline-grabbers.

Now, some people might think that some of Scott's statements are negative, but they don't get it. First of all, the positive stuff always outweighs anything else; he's such a joyful guy at every moment. Second, the stuff he's saying stops short of being really personal. What he's doing is testing a guy, but he's not going to humiliate a guy. It's just competitive stuff.

During the entire off-season and into training camp in 2009, Scott was on Mark Sanchez's case, our rookie quarterback, every day—just pushing the kid's buttons to see how competitive Sanchez would be. Again, it wasn't ever personal or mean. He would just say stuff to challenge Sanchez like: "Rookie, what you got? You gonna make a play or you gonna fold?" And what happened? One day in practice, Sanchez looked across the line, told Scott to shut the hell up, and hit a big pass in a situational drill. Everybody was laughing; it was great! That was when we all knew that Sanchez wasn't going to get scared. He might struggle a bit as he learned the ropes, but he wasn't going to fold just because some veteran was talking trash to him. I talked to Scott about that one after the practice and he was grinning as he told me how much he loved it. That's what he was trying to get out of Sanchez, and it worked. Nobody will fight for a teammate more than Bart Scott. That's why I wanted him so badly. Our team needed that more than they needed Ray Lewis's intensity. Trust me, Ray Lewis is great, but like I said, he represents the Ravens. He doesn't represent the Jets. We needed guys who would represent us—who would bring out the best not just in themselves but in the other guys in the locker room.

The other thing you'll notice about the guys we brought in early—Scott, Leonhard, Douglas, and Green—is that they're all guys who were either undrafted or were late-round picks who bounced around. Green was a sixth-round pick in 2002 who didn't make it as a rookie and didn't play for anybody in 2006. Scott, Leonhard, and Douglas were never drafted. They all had some big defect in the view of scouts, but the bottom line was that they could all play football. When I brought them in, I wasn't thinking about our similarities, but when somebody pointed out our parallels, I sat back and really thought about it: Maybe I was drawn to them as players because I'm a guy like that, a guy who has been passed over a bunch of times and then finally got a chance to prove himself.

Those guys made it the hard way into this league. Scott's story is a great one — you may have heard it. During his junior year at Southern Illinois, he got into this argument with the defensive coordinator, a guy named Mike Vite. Vite got on Scott for eating an apple during a meeting. It might have even been during a game. That's a new one on me. In fact, during games, you want your players to have a piece of fruit so they don't get dehydrated. Whatever the case, Vite went nuts over it and suspended Scott for the final six games of the season. Seriously. After that season, the whole staff was fired and the school brought in Jerry Kill, who ignored all those stupid warnings about Scott, instead calling him a leader and a great player. Kill really promoted the heck out of the kid, Scott made all-conference, and we eventually signed him in Baltimore as an undrafted guy. It was a sweet move for us, and (just so you know what Scott is like) every game day he puts an apple in his locker to remind him of that whole incident from his college days. This is another thing you should know about Scott: After he got to the NFL and was in the league for three years, he went back to Southern Illinois and ended up getting his degree in economics. And that was from a kid who didn't even qualify academically coming out of high school in Detroit. Now, that's determination.

In fact, with each of those early guys I sought out for the roster, nobody gave them much of a chance coming out of college and they made it because of their own grit. Nothing was handed to them. They had an intangible hunger that never let them give up. That's what I'm looking for. When you get to this level, you have to have ability, but you can't make it on ability alone. You have to really love the game. Well, I take that back. Some guys have so much ability that they can get by without really buying in. Sam Adams, who I talked about before, he didn't have those intangibles to get everything out of himself. You had to really work him. But trust me when I say that guys like that are the exception. At any time in the league, you might have 10 guys who are so incredibly gifted that they can get by without loving the game. But that's it. It's just too hard to get through all the pain and hard work without having passion for it.

That's where you get to a guy like Leonhard, who has more passion and pride than most locker rooms full of players. Here is a guy who is all of 5-foot-8, maybe 190 pounds on a good day, but he won't back down from anything. When we signed him in Baltimore in 2005, we already had Ed Reed, maybe the greatest free safety in the history of the game. We were pretty set at the other spot, too. We were in talks with Leonhard, and he wasn't sure about signing with us because he didn't know how he was going to get a job on a team with such great safeties already. I told him, "You're going to make it, because we *keep* good football players." That was all he needed to hear. Sure enough, one of our safeties got hurt, and Leonhard came in and played great for us, just pouring his heart into his game.

Now, with the Jets, Leonhard is a guy that the rest of the defensive backs really look up to. You see him with Darrelle Revis and Antonio Cromartie, and they're always asking him all sorts of questions. The same goes with Brodney Pool, a free-agent safety we brought over from Cleveland. Those guys just know that Leonhard—even though he's a little guy who doesn't look like much—is a player who can help them. They're loyal to him, because they know he's going to be loyal to them and help however he can. That filters down to everything we do and everybody we hire. We have guys who want to get into coaching, like former defensive lineman Larry Webster. Webster is a great guy. He was part of the rotation of our championship team in Baltimore. He had his problems with substance-abuse issues, but he battled them. That can be a daily issue for some guys. Still, I'm going to be loyal to a guy like Larry, because he's one of my guys and he has been loyal to me. I've brought him in for an internship three times. I'm going to keep working with guys like that, developing their pride in themselves and in our program.

The most amazing part of this game is really all the different types of people you run into. There was a kid who we brought in one time, he had just a horrible personal life. The dad was never in his life; his grandmother went to jail for close to 40 years for selling drugs; then his mother went to jail for 20 years for selling drugs. He went to live with his aunt, but she ended up marrying a guy who the kid just hated and couldn't stand to be around. Then he went to live with some other family that took him in, but there are drugs there, too, and he didn't want to be around that. He ended up living with his uncle, who is a pastor, and he finally had a chance at something like a normal life. And then the kid ended up in college and being a first-round draft pick. I look at young men like that and just shake my head in amazement. He had an opportunity to quit or go so many different directions, but he was strong enough mentally to stay with it. Guys like that are an inspiration to me.

At the same time, you run into some very tough situations when you go through cuts, because there are guys who have fought through terrible backgrounds but who just aren't good enough to keep on the team. That is pretty emotional. As much as you try not to get emotional about it, sometimes you can't help but worry about what's going to happen. Some of these guys have nothing else. I don't just mean no team to go to; I mean they have no real prospects if they can't play football. These are guys who have put everything they have into it, but once they're cut they will have nothing to show for it in the long term. They've dropped out of school early; they're not on track to get a degree; they have a terrible home life they were hoping to escape—all those types of things. That's rough, because you just know the kid is going to struggle once he leaves the team. Those are the toughest cuts. Some of those guys will call you back later, and I try to talk with them whenever I can. They know I was fair with them. They might not agree with me initially, but they all know I did what I had to do for the team, and eventually they understand that the choices I made were right.

We had one young man in training camp in 2010, Kevin Basped—a big, strong kid with a great-looking upper body. He was 6-foot-4 and 254 pounds, just an ideal project as an outside line-backer in our system. And he could play. We talked about him a lot in *Hard Knocks*, because he was such an interesting player. But beyond that, he has an amazing story. When he was 14, his older brother (who was basically standing in for his dad) was shot in the face and died. When he was 19, his sister died of diabetes. He grew up in this terrible neighborhood in Sacramento, with every bad story you can imagine. When he was being recruited by Arizona State, the coaches were visiting his home and had to duck and hide inside because gangs started shooting outside. When you think about all the odds he beat, it just tugs at your heart. The problem was that he probably had more fluid drained from his knees than a ship taking on water. It was clear to all of us that his body was not going to make it on the field. As it was, he went undrafted because his knees were bad. Then he got here and everything that the doctors said could be the worst-case scenario happened. In a case like that, you're not just telling a guy he's not good enough—which is not exactly the case with him, since he had some ability—you're really having to tell him that it's over. His dreams are shot—he can't play in the league. We let him go, as much as we hated to do it, and he ended up playing for a team in the United Football League. He loves it, but part of me wants to say, "Son, what are you doing? You're going to need a knee replacement at 30!" And now he's playing for a league where he's not going to get that kind of stuff covered by insurance.

You get guys like that and they keep coming back, thinking they're going to make it, that they're going to be the one who finally breaks in. And every once in a while, you get one who does make it, like Pittsburgh outside linebacker James Harrison. From 2002 to 2004, he got cut four times—three times by Pittsburgh, then once by us in Baltimore after we brought him in late in the season and then sent him to play in the World League for Germany. After we let him go, the Steelers signed him again. He makes their team, finally, and helps them win two Super Bowls, wins the Defensive Player of the Year in 2008, and returns an interception 100 yards for a touchdown in the Super Bowl that season. And, of course, he was a formidable piece of the Steelers defense we just played in the 2010 AFC Championship Game. You want to know the reason we cut him in Baltimore? Our special-teams coach never liked him. The guy never made it into one of our defensive meetings. That will make you shake your head and ask "What if?"

That's part of the nightmare of building the roster.

13. The Perfect Formula

Once we filled out our 2009 roster, I knew our defense was going to be great. Now we had to figure out offensively how we were going to play the game. How were we going to play to win? Even though I brought in Brian Schottenheimer (who's known for wanting to throw the ball) as my offensive coordinator, I wanted to create an all-weather offense.

It's funny, because I think most people look at me as anti-offense, that I make fun of the offensive guys for being too soft; but you have to understand that as a defensive coordinator that was my job. I was going to crush you. That's what I was paid to do. I was going to build a unit with a goal of being so dominant and believing in each other so much that they were going to go out and pummel an opponent's offense.

Now that I'm a head coach, I get to build a whole team around that philosophy—offense, defense, and special teams. That's the beauty of it. It's not about me. Yet I know that this is what we're building and I know we have the players and the coaches who are going to give us the opportunity to build this team, to build this model. My coaches, my players, the entire organization—they all know that I believe it so much and they know what my heart says. It might not be 100 percent accurate, but they're going to know that it's from my heart. Maybe that's why I get the respect that I get in the locker rooms. It's because they know that I'm telling it the way it is. Believe it or not, I don't ignore our offense. I like those guys. I actually talk to them and I'm as nice as I can be, too, regardless of what you might hear. I installed our defense during my first year in 2009, so I was involved with that unit from the beginning. Once we got to training camp, I turned the defense over to Mike Pettine so I could sit in on the offensive meetings. One day I just said to Brian Schottenheimer and the offensive staff, "Okay, I'm going to let you know what I think and just go from the heart about what wins in the NFL. This is how we're going to build our team." I told them point-blank, "We are going to run the football. We will have a ground-and-pound philosophy and we're going to lead the league in rushing. I want to lead the league in rushing attempts and pass completions."

We accomplished two of those goals in 2009. We led the league in rushing offense with an average of 172.3 yards per game. That was 10.3 yards more than second-place Tennessee. Our NFL-high 607 rushing attempts was also well above the league average of 440.3. In 16 regular-season games, we had 2,756 rushing yards with 21 touchdowns—one less than Tennessee and Miami—and averaged 4.5 yards per attempt.

Our tailback, Thomas Jones, had 1,402 rushing yards to finish third in the NFL behind Tennessee's Chris Johnson (2,006) and St. Louis's Steven Jackson (1,416). Fifteen runners had 1,000-plus yards. Jones also averaged 20.7 carries per game to rank fourth. He was complemented in our backfield by Shonn Greene (540 yards) and Leon Washington (330 yards). Our ground-and-pound philosophy worked, and it was the same approach I carried into the 2010 season behind veteran LaDainian Tomlinson and Greene. Our passing game, however, wasn't as efficient in 2009. We ranked 31 out of 32 NFL teams in passing offense, throwing for 2,380 yards — 304 yards more than last-place Cleveland and 2,274 less than first-place Houston. In fairness, winging it down the field every play wasn't our approach. We attempted 393 passes — six less than Houston completed! Okay, we didn't accomplish my goals to lead the league in rushing attempts and completions in 2009, but when you combine the two, it does work. Is it the only way to win in the NFL? No, but it's the best formula to win. I am not the smartest guy in the NFL, but I am smart enough to at least look at the history of this league. It made sense. If you run the ball more, you're generally ahead. I am just telling you mathematically that when you look at the factors involved in wins and losses, running the football wins games. When you study it and start formulating it, you think, "Holy shit!" It's right there in front of you, in black and white. You try like crazy to build your team that way, and that's what I did. I think it's important because of the wind in New York and the bad weather, plus we've got a young quarterback in Sanchez and you can't just let it fly every time. I also believed we'd be more balanced in 2010, but I planned to rely on that running game, no question.

I realize that a lot of people thought we ran the football as often as we did during my first season because we had a rookie quarterback in Sanchez. Honestly, I would have had the same approach if Brett Favre was still our quarterback. When I talked to our offense, I just told them passionately what I expected from them and they knew where I was coming from. I told them I wasn't going to call plays, but I wanted to make sure they knew they were going to play with my mentality. My mentality is always that we are going to get after our opponent's ass. That's how we are going to play the game in every phase — offense, defense, and special teams.

Of course, there are so many variables in winning, too. Everybody also knows turnovers play a huge role in games. In the snap of a finger, turnovers can do so much to change the complexion of a game. It's the old plus-minus game. If you look at rushing attempts plus completions, if you are ahead in that category, then you win about 80 percent of your games. It's a proven fact. Then tie in protecting the football and getting turnovers on defense with rushing attempts and completions, and presto, that's all you've got to do. The facts back me up. For example, in our 19 games in 2009, we had a plus-turnover margin in 10 of them. We won all 10 games. It sounds easy, right? According to Randy Lange, who works for the Jets on our website NewYorkJets.com, if you count all games (playoffs and regular season) since 2003, NFL teams that get at least one more turnover than their opponent win nearly 80 percent of the time. Generally, if you go plus-one with turnovers, you win 70 percent of the time. If you go plus-two, it jumps to 80 percent, plus-three is 90 percent, and plus-four is almost 100 percent.

During the 2010 season I was asked by the media why the Baltimore Ravens were so tough to beat. I thought it was simple to explain: Their front seven is as good as any team in football in stopping the run and getting after the quarterback. Plus, they almost always win the turnover battle, having done so some ridiculous number, like 45 out of 47 times, since 2003. My point was that Baltimore protects the football, and when it does, it usually wins.

Actually, I wasn't too far off with my math. Since 2003 and over a span of 51 games, Baltimore had won 48 of them (.941 winning percentage) in which it had at least a plus-one turnover differential. Incredible! That's how close that mark is to being perfect over the past five years. My way is not the only way to win in this league, but I do think it's the most effective. Still, 99.9 percent of coaches in the NFL will say you need to play good defense, stop the run, and be able to run the ball, and I think they'll still probably tell you that. But I also know the game has changed. They will say you better have an explosive offense, because the game has gotten so physical, so multiple, and so complex that you need to have the ability to gain yardage in large chunks. If you are going to be good, if you are going to be a champion, you better be explosive. Naturally, the biggest chunks of yardage come in the passing game.

People will counter, "No, you have to look at the numbers and you have to look at what really does win championships." There are other head coaches, however, who believe that you can't use any form of criteria that encompasses the last 10 to 15 years, because of the way the rules have changed and the quality of quarterbacks we have now. Protecting quarterbacks had a huge impact on the success of the league. Taking away hits to the head and shots to the knees allowed more quarterbacks to play with comfort, and the stats were telling. There were 10 quarterbacks who threw for at least 4,000 yards and 12 had at least 25 touchdown passes. Think about it: Five years ago, there were two quarterbacks who threw for over 4,000 yards; in 2009, there were 10—Matt Schaub (4,770), Peyton Manning (4,500), and Tony Romo (4,483) were the top three. With quarterbacks passing for so many yards, it can change your approach.

Hey, I am a guy who helped win a Super Bowl with the Ravens in 2000 because of a great defense. A great defense is easier to build financially because it takes less money. If you want to be great offensively, you have to have the marquee quarterback, and that gets expensive. Defensively, you have to have that shut-down corner and you have to have the rush end, but financially it is easier and less expensive to build a topflight defense than it is put the resources into a topflight offense.

Take Indianapolis, for example. It's an organization that says, "Hey, we're going to put our assets on offense, and defense, well, you've got to hang on because we are going to wrap ourselves around our unique, talented quarterback Peyton Manning." Manning had the highest salary-cap figure ($21,205,718) for the 2009 season, but he ranked sixth among all quarterbacks with a $14 million average.

Indianapolis owner Jim Irsay said before the Super Bowl that Manning would become the highest-paid player in the NFL. Manning's contract expired after the 2010 season and he was named a "franchise player" by the Colts so that they could keep him from becoming a free agent. On top of that, Manning's brother Eli, Philip Rivers, and Jay Cutler have raised the ante on what it costs for quarterbacks. Of the top 10 highest-paid players in the NFL, according to the *Sports Illustrated* "Fortunate 50" list, the top four were quarterbacks and just three defensive players—linebacker Terrell Suggs of the Ravens, defensive lineman Albert Haynesworth of the Redskins, and defensive end Julius Peppers of the Bears—made the cut.

Honestly, football is like any business. Aside from salaries, all businesses are made up of the same three things: structure, personnel, and chemistry. Offense and big plays are the same thing. It takes a certain level of talent obviously, the ability to physically do the things that it takes to be explosive, whether it's speed, leaping ability, accuracy, or throw power, whatever it may be. It does take a structure. Shoot, even fast-break basketball has a structure. Particularly in the game of football there has to be an integration of all 11 guys on the field for these things to happen—that's your personnel. As far as the chemistry part of it, there has to be the proverbial 10,000 hours. You have to have repetition; there has to be a "you wink, I nod" sixth sense that we have about one another to make these things happen. Occasionally, you just have a phenomenal freak at a position, a player who just does something ungodly during the game. Yet for the most part, to consistently do it and win takes those three things: structure, personnel, and chemistry.

As a head coach, you also have to learn how to give up control of your team and delegate power and responsibility to your assistant coaches. It can be difficult, but it's something you have to do. When I was with the Ravens, Brian Billick used an analogy that I always thought was interesting. He said, "Coaching is like observing a work of art. The assistant coach is so close, just like the person who stands right up against the masterpiece that you can see the brushstrokes, the texture; you can smell the canvas almost. You lose a little bit of the bigger picture, but you're right there in it." That's what an assistant coach is. He's right there in it with his players.

When you step back as a coordinator, you now have a little bit of a bigger picture—not the total picture, but a bigger picture. You have stepped away from the canvas a little bit. You lose just a little bit of that interpersonal connection, but you still have it to some degree. When you become a head coach, now you've got the big picture. You see the total scope, but it's hard to maintain that up-close-and-personal relationship, that standing close to the canvas, so to speak.

It's hard, because it's no different from the principal who longs to be back in the classroom at times, or the detective or desk sergeant who misses the beat. The thing that drew you into the profession is what you miss, but it's offset by the fact that you're moving up the chain of command and there are rewards there as well. I remember Brian Billick telling the story of how Denny Green had a big team meeting and Billick got up and did his thing as a coordinator for a little bit. He must have gone a half hour or so, and then he turned it over to the assistant coaches because they need individual time. After Billick walked out of the room and passed by Denny's room, Denny said, "Now I know you are going to be a good coordinator."

Billick asked, "What do you mean by that?"

Green answered, "Because you are finally getting the idea that less is better and that the more you can turn them over to your assistants, the better off you are going to be." I always remembered that.

While the entire team is my responsibility as head coach, there are times I have to hold back and let my assistant coaches coach. Even so, I've always pushed my coaches toward the teaching process. That's where I felt like I had the biggest impact. Hey, we are all good coaches and they know what they're doing, but the one thing I did want to control was the way we taught. I want it to be specific. I want it to be energetic. I wanted the players to get exactly what they need instead of the mind-numbing dump of "You know what? I'm going to throw so much shit at the players that even if it doesn't go right I can rest well at night at least to say I covered it, so it's not my fault." That's not teaching. If you emphasize everything, you've emphasized nothing. So the teaching progression has always been the most important thing to me, and that's where I felt I could impact the coaches the most. For example, when I was at Baltimore, I would teach my guys to watch the quarterback's hand under the center. When his hand twitched and flashed open, that gave us a little bit of a jump, because the ball was about to be snapped. It was a simple lesson, but it was specific.

My brother Rob and I both like to study the opponent and understand what they do; and when we do pressure, we make sure it's something that will hit the quarterback. We always read protection and usually try to set up blitzes that will hit their quarterback with a wide-open blitzer. That's when you are a good pressure team. It's an art; it's how to study it, however much time you put in. You get to those last situations, and the NFL is great. In college football, very few games are decided by a touchdown or less. In pro football, hell, they all are. So the last seconds of any game are absolutely critical.

You know the old saying that the NFL is an easy game complicated by coaches? That's the truth. My dad told me that, and it is as true now as it was then. Football is an easy game made complicated by coaches. I try to carry that over with our guys. Some people have that KISS philosophy—Keep It Simple, Stupid. We have the KILL philosophy—Keep It Likable, Learnable.

We have a great scheme, a great system. It's proven. You look at our defense and it's proven, year in and year out. Our blitzing, gambling defense embarrassed a lot of players and teams in 2009. We had the best defense in the NFL; even so, you can always be better. Mike Tannenbaum and I agreed that the Colts exposed us after we led Indy by 10 at halftime of the AFC title game and lost. Mike told the story that part of the moves we made in the off-season go back to when he hired me and had called Ozzie Newsome in Baltimore to ask about me. Ozzie made the joke that I'm the sort of guy who's always standing out on I-95 with a sign around his neck that says, I NEED CORNERBACKS. He wasn't far off.

Well, guess what? We always talked about this. It's not the position of the player, it's his disposition, and we do have that kind of mentality. Cornerback Darrelle Revis has that kind of mentality. Linebacker Bart Scott has that kind of mentality. Mark Sanchez has that kind of mentality. I understand the philosophy of players. I know when to give guys time off. I don't want our assistant coaches meeting all day with players. I want to keep our guys fresh—not only their bodies, but their minds, too. I want it to be a stress-free environment.

There's already enough pressure. Players all understand that they have a job to perform, and if they don't perform they are not going to play for the New York Jets or me. I am not going to be uptight and be an asshole about it, but I'm still going to get my message across. Coaches and players are linked together. I might cut a player today, I might fire a coach tomorrow, but eventually it's going to come to the head coach. I understand that the better players perform, the better the team performs and the longer I will be the head coach. When everyone has respect for the guy above and below them, and you have a respect for his place in an organization's success—and you communicate it that way—that makes everyone want to elevate their game to protect each other, and that's why it goes back to disposition.

Let's go. Let's get it done. This back is going to block you. What are you going to do? I am going to run his ass over. I am going to kick his ass. That's right. If he beats you, okay. I am going to beat his ass on the next play. I am telling you, making mistakes on the field is part of the game. It's the part where we will come back and create something. That old saying "Momentum is heading our way" is the way we approach it. Even if we are down—if we go into halftime and we're down 7-0—we say we have them right where we want them.

Think about it. First of all, the skill of some of these players is amazing. The competitive balance of the league is always in play, so your team might go from last to first in one year. You all have the same money. It's fair. The system is fair and the system works. I think that's the beauty of it all. That's the reason the games are so competitive. How many games get down to the last minute with the game in jeopardy? The teams are so well balanced, and I think that's a great feature of the NFL. They are trying to protect players, which I think is terrific. They are protecting the quarterbacks, protecting the guys who don't see it coming. Even the defenders now, they are trying to do right by the players, trying to protect them. You don't want your players crippled. You don't want that to happen, but there are always going to be injuries. When you play New England, you want to see Tom Brady at quarterback. The only thing that got me riled up until 2009 was hitting a defenseless defensive player. You couldn't hit a defenseless receiver, yet you could hit a defenseless defensive player, so I am glad they cleaned that up.

Obviously, you have to build for the season, too, from start to finish. The NFL wants to extend the regular season to 18 games. In fact, they're probably negotiating as I write this, so who knows how it will turn out? They are proposing to cut two preseason games and, in place, start the season two weeks earlier and make each team play a total of 18 games. That is, each and every member of the starting lineup must be healthy and playing for at least 18 games. Me? I like it the way it is with four preseason games. The way you adjust it, you play a quarter, then a half. You basically get five quarters in and you are ready to go by then. You go into the regular season and you are ready. You're also given an opportunity for some of your younger players to step up and make the team. It gives you the opportunity to see what you have. If they extend the season, it will be hard sometimes to get healthy players to the game.

I hope it doesn't change. I hope they keep it the way it is, but I doubt it. I can see them going to 18 games and two preseason games. I understand what they are saying from a fan's perspective, that you would rather pay to see a regular-season game than a preseason game, but I'm afraid the product would suffer. At the end of the day, you want what's best for the league. It's a pretty good thing right now as it is. Fans complain a little bit about the preseason games, but in a way they still enjoy it because they get to watch the young guys battle. I don't want to lose that.

All I know is I am not going to change the way I coach, the way we prepare, or how I build my team. I know we are going to be great on defense. And I want us to be great on offense, too. That's a proven formula. I know we are a pain in the ass to play against, really a pain in the ass. Yet it's also simple. It's an easy philosophy to teach. Once you learn the concepts, it's easy to play our system. It allows you to be really creative as a coach. Let's do this. We may blitz all corners. We may blitz whomever. We may run the ball behind the center.

If my plan works—and I honestly believe it will—I'll join Bill Parcells as the only first-time NFL coaches in New York to rely on a kick-ass defense and a ground-and-pound running game to win a Super Bowl. And here's the thing about Parcells: He really had to struggle to get there in 1986. That was his fourth year in the league and he almost got fired when he went 3-12-1 in 1983.

You always have that one goal, but it's so hard to win that Super Bowl. Like they say, it doesn't take just one or two great players. You have to have 11 good players on defense or you are not going to win. If you only have 10 good ones, they are going to exploit the other guy. So you better have 11 good ones on defense and you better be ready to chase the quarterback in the fourth quarter. On offense, you don't have to have 11 great ones, but you have to have enough that you can put the ball where you want to and you have to be able to run it and control the line of scrimmage.

In 2009, I decided to take a more active role in the offense. Sanchez was struggling and I was being criticized for not coaching the entire team. It's no secret that I believe in defense first, last, and always. Our entire team is built on that brashness and aggressiveness. I guess I am considered a throwback with my offensive philosophy. I've been called conservative. I've been criticized. I can handle it.

And I won't abandon my formula. It works.

14. Taking Risks on Players (and Making My Own Mistakes)

I know what a lot of people are going to say after reading my chapter on getting guys like Bart Scott, Jim Leonhard, Marques Douglas, and all those other lunch-pail attitude guys: "Sure, Rex, all that stuff about building your team is great, but what about the risks you took on other guys? How about Santonio Holmes, Antonio Cromartie, and Braylon Edwards? They were all troublemakers on their previous teams, but you couldn't say no to their talent. What about LaDainian Tomlinson and Jason Taylor? They both looked like they were done, but you rolled the dice that they had something left."

No question, we brought in some interesting guys, players that other people didn't feel like they wanted anymore. Hey, it's just like in Baltimore when we brought in defensive tackle Sam Adams, or tight end Shannon Sharpe, who was 32 when the Ravens got him from Denver. Sharpe ended up being our biggest weapon in the passing game in the playoffs. Both Adams and Sharpe were crucial for the Ravens.

The key is, they weren't the first guys in the door. When you're building your team, you had better have your foundation right. It's just like building a house. You screw up the foundation, that house is not going to stand. Well, we had foundation guys. We had Scott, Leonhard, and Douglas to be the grinders that I need, the guys who set the tone. We had some great veterans, too, like Shaun Ellis and Brandon Moore. We had some young, up-and-coming stars like Darrelle Revis, Dustin Keller, Nick Mangold, David Harris, and D'Brickashaw Ferguson—guys who were there before me. All of those guys, every one of them, is a good character guy, the kind of guy who is going to do all the work, every last thing you need. You're going to win a lot of games. Then we added our quarterback with Mark Sanchez, so we had a guy who was young but was going to put in the work.

Now, you can take some chances. You can get some guys who have had some issues here and there because you have a foundation of players in your locker room who are going to do a couple of things for you. First, they're setting the tone more than those new guys. The new guys have to fit in, because everybody else has already established how the team is going to be run. Second, those guys who have already set the tone for your team, they police it for you. If somebody gets out of line, they take care of it or they let the coach know what's going on. Even then, what chances are you really taking on some of those guys? Yeah, Tomlinson and Taylor are getting up there in age, but you can't buy that kind of character, that work ethic, and (most important) that little extra desire both those guys have. But I'll get back to that in a minute.

With guys like Holmes, Cromartie, and Edwards, I still don't see it as taking a chance. If you look at all of them, they have all been great players. They've done it on the field and they've done it pretty consistently. Maybe not as consistently as they wanted to, but still pretty consistently. You're talking about a Super Bowl hero and two Pro Bowlers. These aren't lazy guys just out of college, who have all the ability but aren't willing to work now that they think they've "made it." These guys have all put in time. All I have to do is channel their ability and make them want to play for me.

When it comes to getting guys interested in coming to the Jets, right now, I think I'm on a roll! If you don't believe me, check out what the players say. *Sports Illustrated* did a big poll of players this past season. They had 279 players respond this year, and yours truly came out No. 1 among coaches when players were asked, "For which other coach would you like to play?" I got 21 percent of the vote. Mike Tomlin of Pittsburgh was second at 12 percent.

I think the reason is that I focus on how to deal with guys individually. I'm going to find some way to connect with them, make them know that I'm on their side and to get them on my side.

Let's take Santonio Holmes, for example. The first thing I did with Holmes, right after we traded for him, is I called NFL Commissioner Roger Goodell; I'm lucky, because he's right up the road in New York. I called him and said, "Roger, I need your help. Can you come down and spend an afternoon here?" He asked what I needed, so I told him that once we got Holmes I wanted Goodell to come down and talk with Santonio after one of our minicamps. Then I said, "I'd like for you to try to bring him closer to me." Goodell said okay, but he wanted to know what I had in mind. I said, "When the three of us sit down, I want you to take the first 10 minutes of our conversation to rip my ass in front of Santonio — about what I've done off the field, how I've embarrassed the league." That's all true about me. This is a couple of months after the Super Bowl, when I got fined $50,000 by the team for flipping off that fan in Miami.

But for this visit on this day, I asked the commissioner to rip me good right there in front of Santonio. Then I asked if he would turn and give both barrels to Holmes. I wanted the commissioner to let Santonio know that he hadn't done what he should either in being a good employee in the NFL.

My goal was that at the end of that conversation, Goodell would leave . . . and Santonio and I would be left in the same boat. I wanted him to know that we needed to be better, not just for the league, but for each other.

Anyway, Goodell made that trip to my office and he chewed us out, and I think it actually brought Holmes and me closer. There he was, not just out there alone feeling like he did something wrong, which had led Pittsburgh to trade him for an embarrassingly low fifth-round pick, but instead he's hearing about how I've done something stupid, too, and how the league doesn't like it. All of a sudden, I have a bond going with Holmes. Maybe I played it up a little, but it was all true. I've made mistakes in my life. I don't want these guys thinking that I'm some saint. I want them to know I'm human just like they are. I wanted Holmes to understand I'm going to be in there fighting for him and I need him fighting for me. You should see it now; we're as close as I've ever been with a guy after this much. He'll come over during practice and we'll put an arm around each other. It worked.

The other thing I did with Holmes is I went out to California at one point to see him. At the time, he wasn't doing everything perfectly, like calling his counselor exactly when he was supposed to, so I wanted to check on him. Now, one thing you have to realize about this guy is that he's as stubborn as a mule. If you try to force him to do something, he'll go kicking and screaming. As I've said many times, until they know how much you care, they don't care how much you know. I'm serious about that.

Some coaches think they can come out and bark orders and expect that players will just jump. Some will, but you're not really forming a bond. If you really want somebody to do something, to really put their whole heart into it, you have to show you care about them, that you trust them. So I started thinking about how I could show that kid that I trusted him. Well, what's the number-one thing that I have in my life, the thing most important to me? It's my family, of course. So I brought my younger son Seth, who is a receiver on his football team, with me to see Holmes in California, and the favor I asked of Holmes was "Can you teach Seth about getting off press coverage?" Then I just walked away. I left the two of them to just be together on that practice field. For an hour and a half, I left them together and Holmes was working and working. I mean, he was really into it. I don't think he was just trying to please me; you don't do something that long just to please the coach. I think he really felt good that I would leave my son with him, that I trusted him to take care of my kid. They just worked and worked and worked. And after that, I couldn't get Seth away from Holmes if I tried. Holmes was phenomenal with Seth.

As a football player, Holmes is one talented guy. My last year in Baltimore, Holmes was playing for Pittsburgh and was a complete nightmare for me to deal with. The Steelers, who had won the Super Bowl the year before, had drafted this kid with the No. 25 overall pick in the 2006 draft. In fact, they traded up to get him. They had the last pick in the first round, the No. 32 pick, and moved all the way up to get him at No. 25. You have to know this—Pittsburgh isn't very big on making moves in the draft, so you know they had to be convinced about this guy, even if he had a rough background.

Holmes grew up in Belle Glade, Florida, which is right next to this other town called Pahokee. That part of Florida is where they grow half the sugarcane in the country and a ton of citrus fruit.

And a ton of football players.

Joel Segal, an agent who has represented a great number of guys in this league over the years, represents Holmes. Segal also represents Michael Vick, Reggie Bush, and Randy Moss. We're talking about some serious players and guys who came from really rough backgrounds. But Segal said that in all the years he has been representing guys, Holmes came from probably the toughest background he had ever seen—all kinds of brutal stuff.

That's part of the deal with Holmes; he doesn't have many people around him he trusts. He has a huge heart and he's a good kid and a charismatic guy. Really, you talk to him and he's a sweetheart of a guy, but he doesn't trust people and that makes it hard. At the same time, it's part of what makes guys great football players. If you want to get out of the environment where you grew up, you have to throw yourself into the game with nothing to lose, and that's part of the reason you see so many great players with backgrounds somewhat similar to Santonio's.

Holmes will tell you stories about chasing rabbits for dinner. You want to become quick, that's a way to do it. Before the Super Bowl in the 2008 season, Holmes admitted that he sold drugs when he was a teenager growing up there, but he quit when his mom told him he had a future to worry about.

Holmes had his problems right off the bat—he was involved in an incident even before he got to the Steelers that started his challenges there—but on the football field, you could tell right away that he was special. He's a skinny, little dude at 5-foot-11, 192 pounds. You'd think you could break his skinny ass in half, but to do that, you have to catch him first . . . and that's the problem.

In this kid's career, he has averaged 5.8 yards after the catch. In football lingo, we call that YAC. You always hear quarterbacks telling their receivers, "Get me some YAC." Oh, those greedy quarterbacks, they love those five-yard throws that turn into 25 yards when the receiver breaks a tackle. For those quarterbacks, Holmes is the guy. Most people will think, "What's the big deal about 5.8 yards after the catch?" Put it this way: That's better than the career numbers for Chad Ochocinco (3.3), Larry Fitzgerald (3.4), Randy Moss (3.9), Wes Welker (4.6), Andre Johnson (4.9), and Terrell Owens (5.3). Now, I'm not a huge stat guy because a lot of stats in football don't mean much, but if you're taking a stat and comparing it to some great players, that is when the stat means something. If Holmes keeps himself straight, he's on the way to being a truly great player.

Trust me, I saw it coming firsthand. As I was saying, in 2008, this kid started dominating. You didn't see it right away in the stats, because the Steelers aren't this big passing team. They throw it pretty well with Ben Roethlisberger, but that's not their bread and butter. They play hard, brutal defense and they want to run it. In the AFC North, you have to play what we call December football—ground-

and-pound style, as I call it here. When the weather gets cold and you're playing outdoors like they do in Pittsburgh, New York, and Baltimore, throwing a bunch of deep passes gets harder and harder. Yeah, New England still does it, but they do it because they have Tom Brady. When you have one of the greatest of all time, you can do stuff like that.

So when Holmes was in Pittsburgh, he wasn't getting eight or 10 throws a game going his way on a regular basis. He had to make do sometimes with four or five opportunities per game. He was also splitting the chances with guys like Hines Ward and tight end Heath Miller. In Baltimore, we played them three times that year, and in those three games he caught a total of eight passes for 152 yards. Nothing out of control, right? Wrong. That kid killed us. He scored one touchdown in every game against us and they beat us by three points the first time, four the second game, and nine in the play-offs. The worst part is that in the 2008 AFC Championship Game between Pittsburgh and Baltimore, he turned a broken play into a 65-yard touchdown—ran right through our defense at the beginning of the second quarter to give the Steelers a 13-0 lead. The thing about Holmes is that he never stops running and he understands how to play the game when things break down. He knows how to hustle to come back to the quarterback. He knows how to find open areas when the quarterback scrambles, which was big with Roethlisberger, who loves to get out of the pocket and extend the play.

So after Holmes got done beating us—that game is going to bug me for the rest of my life—he went to the Super Bowl and dominated. You've probably seen his game-winning catch . . . every Sunday for the past two years, six or seven times a day. It's only maybe the greatest catch in Super Bowl history. He was MVP of Pittsburgh's win over Arizona, catching nine passes for 131 yards. Most importantly, he was amazing on the final drive.

The next year he was even more dominant, catching 79 passes for 1,248 yards, living up to everything people thought he could be. All the crap from earlier in his career seemed to be fading.

Then, as everybody knows, Roethlisberger got in trouble down in Georgia in the 2010 off-season. On the heels of that, Holmes was in the news twice. First, he was accused by a woman in Orlando of throwing a glass at her. Then Holmes was suspended for the first four games of the season for violating the NFL's substance-abuse policy. You put that all together and the Steelers felt like they had to do something. Hey, the quarterback isn't going anywhere. I know there was some talk about them getting rid of Roethlisberger, but are you kidding me? Do you know how hard it is to find quarterbacks in this league? So the Steelers decided, at least in my opinion, to send a message by dumping Santonio. I think they wanted everyone, including Big Ben, to know that they had limits.

Just before we made the deal, I was checking around about Holmes. Mike Tomlin, the Steelers' coach, was done with Holmes by then, tired of dealing with everything. He told other coaches around the league that Holmes would never play another down of football. The whole league believed him, which is part of the way we worked out the deal. Nobody was offering anything for the guy. Look, we were definitely in the market for a receiver. We wanted to put more guys around Sanchez to make the job easier for him. At the time, we were talking about getting Brandon Marshall, who Denver eventually traded to Miami for two second-round picks. The Dolphins also gave Marshall a new contract: five years at $47.5 million.

We could do that or get Holmes for a fifth-round pick. Are you kidding me? We kept our second-round pick and sent that to San Diego for Cromartie. Some people in New York were saying it was a bad deal, but I don't know what they were thinking. We gave up a fifth-round pick for Holmes. On good teams, you're lucky if your fifth-round pick makes the roster half the time in the first year. I'm just talking about making the squad. I'm not even talking about whether the guy contributes. This was a no-brainer.

Could it have blown up on us? Sure. I've been around long enough to know that some guys have a hard time with staying straight. With all the temptations that come your way in the NFL, it doesn't matter what kind of background you come from, it's not easy; but you do your best as a coach to get that guy to buy into the program, to be loyal to you, because that way he has something else and somebody else he's responsible for.

Santonio bought in. Thanks to a little help from Commissioner Goodell!

With the other guys, like Cromartie and Edwards, the problems were different. Cromartie has a pretty complicated life. He has a lot of kids with a bunch of women. I'm not casting any stones. Like I said, I have my issues and I've made plenty of mistakes of my own. Among the most publicized after my first year with the Jets was the previously mentioned "moment" in Miami. It was bad, but it actually could have been a whole lot worse. I went down there to a Mixed Martial Arts event to see some of the guys who are trainers and to see Jay Glazer, the NFL reporter for Fox who also does MMA training. I had heard that several NFL players were developing themselves by getting into MMA training, and I wanted to see what all this was about for myself.

Well, I was at the event and there were a bunch of fans screaming at me, but this one guy kept getting into it with me. At one point, he spit at me and I really almost went after him. Look, I'm a man, you're not going to do that to me; but I thought better of it and just let it go. Then, of course, the people running the event introduced me and gave me the microphone. I was in Miami—what do you think I was going to say? "Next year, we're coming to beat you twice."

Oh, that went over big. I had to stop them from throwing flowers. The love was just too much for me to handle. Once that was over and I was done meeting with the MMA trainers, Glazer and I were on the way out and who did I run into again but this same guy. Only this time he had a bunch of his buddies, and they were cussing at me and giving me the finger. I'd had enough at this point and flipped him the bird. The next day, there was a picture of me in the New York *Daily News* and I was thinking, "Oh, crap, what am I going to do now?"

I'd been there before, in even worse situations, which probably hurt my chances of getting a head coaching job in the past. In other words, I know how much a mistake can hurt your career. It can take away your chance to chase your dreams. I know what players who make mistakes go through, and I think I know how they feel. I'm not afraid to share my past with my players because, frankly, it lets them know that I know how they feel and, for some, it gives them a connection to me.

I think Cromartie feels that, because he seemed so comfortable coming to play for us right away. He really settled in here with the Jets; he just needed a change of scenery. From what I hear, he got to the point that he was butting heads with a lot of people in San Diego. The front office (they seem to butt heads with a lot of guys), the coaches, teammates—it just got real sour. Again, that stuff happens. They said he was a bad teammate, but I know otherwise.

Just like Holmes, players like Cromartie don't come around very often. I remember working him out when he was coming out of Florida State. Now, remember this: He missed the whole season before he was drafted with a knee injury and this guy was so talented, he was still a first-round pick. That's how great of an athlete we're talking about. When I saw him way back then, it was the most freakish workout I have ever seen. Ever. He has long arms, long legs; he's 6-foot-2 and has amazing acceleration. He is one of those guys who can throttle his speed up or down and you don't even notice it. He just glides. Oh yeah, and his hands are amazing. First, they're huge. Second, he can catch absolutely anything: tipped balls, leaping one-handed grabs, everything. He had three interceptions in one game against Peyton Manning, including a one-handed grab along the sideline. Then there was that 109-yard return of a missed field goal he once had. Go find that on YouTube someday. He leaps up to grab the ball with one hand, manages to land inbounds, and then returns the thing. I mean, like I said, he is freakishly good.

Cromartie was just the guy we needed to play the defense we really wanted to play. Yeah, he's not a great tackler, but he's fearless when he's covering a wide receiver. Early in the 2010 season, we put him up against Randy Moss twice, the first time when Moss was with New England after Revis got hurt and then again after Moss was traded to Minnesota. Moss had one big catch against Cromartie for a touchdown, but otherwise Cro was all over Moss—shut him down completely. We needed him badly, because with the way we play defense, we have to have man-coverage guys. I need a guy who can play cover one, which is where you have only one safety behind you. Sometimes you have to play cover zero, where we're not giving you any help over the top, no safety at all. He matched up on Randy Moss like it was nothing. He just went out there and said, "Okay, I've got to cover Randy Moss man coverage. No problem." Where most guys wouldn't sleep all week, Cromartie was ready to go.

So we made the deal to get Cromartie. Again, he had one year left on his contract. I knew his agent, Gary Wichard, really well and that helped make Cromartie happy. Now, obviously, he has made some mistakes and made his life difficult with all the kids all over the country, but he's not hiding from it. He's not running away from trying to be a good dad. He talks to his kids all the time, either by phone or by computer, doing the video chat. I think he honestly wants to be a good father, but that's hard in this situation. That has to be pressure on a guy. On top of that, you're dealing with a lot of women in your life. That's not easy. You have lawyers and money to pay. Hey, it's hard to be a good dad even when you remain married to the child's mother!

The first guy we picked up who people really wondered about was Braylon Edwards, who we traded for in the 2009 season when the Browns wanted to dump him. I heard all the bad stuff about Edwards from the Cleveland coaches, but let me tell you the one person I talked to who really mattered: my brother Rob, who had been there for about nine months when we made the deal. My brother told me, "Don't worry about it, Rex, you'll love this guy." Rob saw through all the negativity and the anger from the team and from the kid. That was a bad situation with the team trying to retool. That happens. At the time, Cleveland was going through a big rebuilding phase. They got rid of tight end Kellen Winslow before the season, then cleared some other guys out, too. I think Edwards was getting fed up with it and didn't like the town anymore. At least, that's what he said. I heard all kinds of stuff about how he dropped balls and didn't block.

Well, Edwards gets here, and let me tell you, we couldn't have made the playoffs that first year without him and all the plays he made, especially all the great blocking down the field. Did he drop some balls? Yeah, but all receivers drop some balls, and we continue to work on that with him. We're going to do whatever we can to help him. In the meantime, he's doing whatever he can to help us win, sacrificing himself and his stats, and throwing his body around. I'm serious when I say that he is a huge part of our running game. When he lined up for us, he was so dominant that he was getting double-teamed, which was opening up the running game. Then he was blocking, which helped us get some big runs.

He may have looked like a risk to some, but I'll take a risk on a guy like this every day of the week.

Finally, we went and got Tomlinson and Taylor last year. Again, in my mind, this is not a risk. Yeah, they have some mileage, but this is football. It's not like I'm re-creating the Over the Hill Gang. You pick and choose a couple of spots. With L.T., we had a tough choice to make on whether we were going to keep Thomas Jones or not, and he ended up at a place where he was earning more money than we thought we could pay. I love Thomas Jones, he's my kind of guy. He's going to get you that tough yard, just like he did on that big fourth down we had in the 2009 playoff game at San Diego. We also had Shonn Greene at the time. As much as I love Greene, I wanted Jones in there for that play and he got it.

Unfortunately, when you have money decisions to make, it's tough. Jones was going to make something like $5.8 million with us in 2010, and it was more than we could afford with all the other moves we had to make, like re-signing Revis, Mangold, and Ferguson. We took a gamble by letting him go and going after L.T., especially when L.T. went up to Minnesota and they offered more than we did. This is where I went on a serious sales job. I called everybody L.T. knows. I even called his wife, LaTorsha, and told her how much L.T. meant to us, and how we needed him so badly. I did the same thing with Taylor. I called and called and called. I knew Taylor wanted to go back to Miami, but Bill Parcells wasn't going to do it. I respect Parcells a lot, but if he's going to turn down a guy like Taylor, I'll gladly take him.

With L.T., it was a little different. Things just weren't working out in San Diego. Part of it was just bad luck. He had been hurt his last couple of years in San Diego. During the playoffs in 2007, the Chargers made it to the AFC Championship Game, but he carried only two times and they lost at New England. The guy had a bad groin injury; what can you do? The next year, he opened the season and got a toe injury but gutted it through every game, but then it was the same thing in the playoffs. He could only carry it five times in the first playoff game, and then he couldn't play after that. That was frustrating for everybody.

In the end, it seemed to me like L.T. didn't feel appreciated there anymore. You don't let that happen with great players. Trust me, if you treat guys like that, what does that say to the rest of the locker room? It's like broadcasting the message "We don't care how hard you work, we're going to treat you like a piece of meat in the end." Look, players get it. They know if they're not good enough, the team isn't keeping them, especially when salaries mean so much. Regardless, there's still a way you treat people. You don't make a guy who works that hard twist in the wind. The Chargers did that during the 2009 off-season. They busted his chops over money, and they made it public and it set the whole tone for the 2009 season. Tomlinson had another down year, gaining only 730 yards. They were not playing him on third downs, and against us in the playoffs, he got only 12 carries and we held him to 24 yards.

Despite all that, I could see he was just a little off in his game. Plus, the Chargers were having offensive line problems all year, so the timing on that team was never right. On top of everything, they had Philip Rivers, who was becoming one hell of a quarterback. I don't think people realize just how great that guy is. You're talking about this era's version of Dan Marino, the way he gets rid of the ball so quickly and accurately. He may not have a cannon arm, but he's one of the best deep throwers in the game. What I was seeing out of L.T. as I was watching him that season was a guy who just needed to heal his body a little and get with a solid offensive line. You could see by the way he was running that he still loved the game. He was just frustrated. The kid is a warrior, a guy with a lot of pride. By that time, everybody in the NFL knew the Chargers were letting him go, so when we had to make our decision on Thomas Jones, it was time to go get L.T.

It's funny—I had my lap-band surgery at the same time that L.T. was making his final decision on whether he was playing for us or for the Vikings. When I woke up from surgery, the very first thing I asked was "Did we sign L.T.?" I just knew that if we did, we were getting one really motivated guy. He was going to prove people wrong, and he certainly showed that all training camp and all season.

With Taylor, I had the same idea. You're talking about one of the best all-around athletes the league has ever had. He's a great edge pass rusher, terrific in coverage, great motor, everything you want with a guy who plays that position. Most important, he has amazing pride and is very driven. You just see it in how the guy walks around. Clearly, he's a good-looking guy, one of those guys who could be on the cover of GQ or *People* magazine every week. I know he has big plans to get into the movie business, too. That's great for J.T. You can just tell how serious he is about being good at everything.

So again, the only risk we were taking is that both L.T. and Jason didn't get hurt. Neither one ended up playing full-time in 2010, but they both ended up being terrific for the Jets this postseason. L.T. started a lot of games, and we mixed it up and had Greene carry the ball a lot. He's a beast. With Taylor, he was in there mostly on passing downs, and both guys were really effective. If we manage the situation right, which is what they pay me to do as coach, the truth is that you can't look at either of these as real risks.

So that's how you build a team. You look for opportunities—moments some call risks—and you figure out how to manage those moments to create BIG moments. The five guys showed that, in fact, this can be done and done well!

15. Sharing the Big Apple

One of the biggest challenges, and one of the reasons I think I am the perfect fit for the Jets, is that they are the ultimate underdog team. When people ask me what it's like to share New York with the Giants, my response is always I am not sharing it with them—they are sharing it with me.

Some people like to say the Giants are the big brother team and the Jets are the little brother team. I know it's going to piss off every Giants fan to hear this, but here you go: I really don't care. We came to New York City to be the best team in the NFL, not just the best team in New York City. And I have news for you: We are the better team. We're the big brother. People might say they are the big, bad Giants, but we are not the same old Jets. That was the big thing in 2009, my first year. We were the same old Jets? Oh, you mean the same old Jets who led the league in defense? The same old Jets who led the league in rushing? The same old Jets who have been to back-to-back AFC Championship Games and are considered serious Super Bowl contenders going forward?

I know the Giants were in New York first and are considered part of the old guard. They had a lot of success when Bill Parcells was the coach and they recently won a Super Bowl (2007), so in a way they have had a much richer tradition than the Jets. They are based in East Rutherford, New Jersey, and the Jets were Long Island's team, so lines had been drawn in the sand long ago.

I am going to be honest, though. To me, it seems clear that right now we are the better team and we are going to remain the better team for the next 10 years. Whether you like it or not, those are the facts, and that's what is going to happen. I know it's going to happen because our style of football is different. We are going to take over the town whether the Giants like it or not, so those fans on the fence that like both teams are going to be Jets fans in the end. The truth is, if I am going to watch one game, I am going to see the Jets, without a doubt. We are better.

I love the fact that people tell me that no head coach has coached past six years with the Jets since 1990. Bruce Coslet (1990-93), Pete Carroll (1994), Herman Edwards (2001-05), and all of these guys— none of them made it six years. Even an agent for one of my own players told me, "Quite honestly, Rex, we have got to do what's best. You are not going to be here."

That definitely got a response from me: "Number one, you are dead-ass wrong. I'm going to be here as long as I want to be here. It's going to be hard to fire ol' Rex with the success we are getting ready to have."

I am a coach who's big enough for this city, and I don't mean that because of my waistline. This city is filled with heroes from all walks of life, and they want us to go for it all. They expect us to go for it all. I'm not a coach who is going to sit quietly by, be a bump on a log, and not stand up for our team, their team. I'm not that kind of coach. I never have been and I never will be

I have promised from day one what the New York Jets would be. I promised we were going to be the most physical football team in the NFL. We were—check. I promised we would have the most dominant defense in the NFL. Check. I promised we would have an all-weather offense that would run the ball when we needed to. Check. We have one major thing left—we have to win a Super Bowl. That's it. We've come pretty darn close in my first two years and we're well on our way. That's the last thing on our original list of things to check off.

I told our team when I arrived that I wanted to be the team in the NFL that nobody wanted to play. By the end of both the 2009 and 2010 seasons, I could promise that nobody wanted to play us. We established that in my first season and we built on it in my second. In one year we were able to capture that identity, and that's what bodes so well for us moving forward. We're going to tell you what we're going to do—and then we're going to go out and kick your ass. That was the bravado I wanted to have with our team. We are not a fly-under-the-radar team. How can you be that kind of team in New York, the most populous city in the United States? New York exerts a powerful influence over life, from finance to athletics to entertainment to the news media. It's my kind of city, and the Jets are my kind of team. I know we have a lot of bull's-eyes on our back, but you know what? That's okay, because we are going to plant a bull's-eye on your chest, and that's the difference. That's our mentality. That's my mentality. We don't have to sneak up on you; we are coming right at you.

Our opponents know that they have to play their asses off to beat us. I know there are teams and players out there who say, "I can't wait to beat that loudmouth. I can't wait to kick the shit out of the Jets." Well, when that ball is kicked off, you will get the chance to prove it and kick our ass. We'll see if you can do it. I think that's part of the chip on our shoulder, being the younger brother in town to the older brother Giants. (Notice, though—I didn't say we are the little brother.) That's the mentality that we embrace in New York. People say I need to be careful what I say because of the media in New York City. Why? Who gives a shit? All we have to do is go out and win. If we don't win, they are going to laugh at us anyway.

I love New York City, the Big Apple. Come on, it's a sports town. The New York City metropolitan area has nine teams in the four major North American professional sports leagues, each of which also has its headquarters in the city. The state is actually represented in the NFL by three teams—the Jets, Giants, and Buffalo Bills. Yes, the Bills, the only NFL team that actually plays in the state of New York. The Jets and the Giants play in the New Meadowlands Stadium in nearby East Rutherford, New Jersey. Like I mentioned earlier, the Giants have always been considered by many people to be the more popular team because they have been around the longest. The Giants, who have the third most titles in NFL history with seven, joined the league in 1925. To tell you what kind of infant state the NFL was in back then, there were five teams that joined the league that year. The Giants are the only one still around. The Jets, who were originally called the New York Titans, were founded in 1960 as a charter member of the American Football League. They changed their name to the Jets in 1963 and joined the NFL as part of the AFL/NFL merger in 1970 (45 years after the Giants).

I loved the Jets as a kid. They were my team. As I said earlier, my dad was the Jets' linebackers coach from 1968 to 1975 and helped the team win Super Bowl III in 1969 against the Baltimore Colts. That game is regarded as one of the greatest upsets in sports history and was the first game officially known as the "Super Bowl." The Jets and "Broadway" Joe Namath beat the Colts 16-7, giving the AFL its first Super Bowl victory. Namath guaranteed a victory in that game, and his bravado brought much-needed interest to the game since the Colts were nearly a 20-point favorite. Many people regarded Namath as an arrogant loudmouth—now, who does that sound like?—and that gave them more reason than ever to root against him, but Joe had his supporters and they happily applauded his bravado. I know the entire history of the Jets. Everybody just kind of looked down on them while I celebrated their history. If I had been offered the job of head coach by the Giants at the same time as the Jets, it still would have been an easy choice. I'd pick the Jets, because that's who I am.

Let me tell you something I love about the New York media: it enables me to talk to the fans every day. Who I am as a person, and as a coach, was made clear in my first news conference when I said we are not the "same old Jets" and I expected us to win a Super Bowl. That caught everyone's attention, both in the sports world and the non–sports world. But I honestly believe that and I know we're going to deliver.

I love the mentality of New York City and the mentality of the New York Jets fans. It's like the perfect marriage. I am not the only one with a chip on my shoulder. Our fans have one also. All you have to do is stand on the sidelines of our amazing new stadium on game day. The roar you hear from our fans—the energy and dedication—it's just something to behold. We're going to win a Super Bowl, and I know our fans feel it, too. Are we setting ourselves up for disappointment? I don't think so. We are going for it.

I talk about it all the time, but a big part of what makes the situation so special is being surrounded by people like Woody, people from the top of our organization all the way down. I have a great coaching staff. The entire organization, we are a team. I have always said this: "I am set up to succeed. I am going to have a tough time failing." I truly believe that. It's really because of the ability of all the people in this organization.

Why does everyone say there's extra pressure in New York? It is probably in large part because of this town's incredible sports history. The Knicks represent the city in the NBA; the Rangers in the NHL. Queens is host of the U.S. Tennis Open, one of the four Grand Slam tournaments. The New York City Marathon is the world's largest. And don't forget the Boys of Summer. Baseball is hugely popular, and you are not going to find a bigger baseball fan than me. I had the opportunity to meet Yankees third baseman Alex Rodriguez, and he was great to my guys and me. I was shocked. I don't know what I was expecting, but it wasn't that. He was phenomenal. The Yankees are phenomenal. There have been 14 World Series championship series between New York City teams, in matchups called the

Subway Series. New York is one of only three cities (Chicago and Los Angeles being the others) to have two baseball teams—the Yankees and the New York Mets.

I know some people liken us to the Mets—they are considered by many the "second" team in New York behind the Yankees and we play second fiddle to the Giants. Sorry, that's not the way I see it—not as long as I have anything to do with it. The Yankees have won more championships than any other team in baseball. They've won 27 World Series championships and 40 American League pennants. Those numbers make them the greatest championship franchise in all of North American professional sports, exceeding the 24 Stanley Cups won by the Montreal Canadiens. And their list of all-stars is staggering—from Babe Ruth to Lou Gehrig to Mickey Mantle to Reggie Jackson to Derek Jeter to Alex Rodriguez. I could go on and on. They have 46 players in the Baseball Hall of Fame. The Yankees talk about winning the World Series every year. They expect to win it every year. That's the kind of culture I want to create with the Jets.

I was told Yankees fans tend to root for the New York Giants (who once played in Yankee Stadium) and the New York Rangers, while Mets fans tend to root for the New York Jets (who once played in Shea Stadium) and the New York Islanders. Trust me when I say that is not entirely true. There are Mets fans who also root for some or all of the teams Yankee fans root for, and vice versa. New York fans are not going to let anyone tell them where their loyalties should lie. I love the fans in New York. I absolutely love the city's atmosphere. It's exciting. It's a sports town, and everyone wants a winner. That's why I talk about winning every chance I get.

People think that's pressure. For me it's an opportunity to talk about my team. If you believe in yourself and you believe in the people around you, what's the big deal? Sure, if you don't win every game you are going to get ripped by the media and fans whether you're in New York, San Francisco, Tampa, or Dallas. You know what? If you don't win or play well, you should get ripped. It's the media's job to talk about what went wrong. I respect the people who have the pen, because they are writing for a living. It's my job to find a way to be successful, and then maybe the media will change what they are writing about us. The media has a job to do; I respect it and I make myself available. I don't go into our news conferences with the New York media just trying to get through it. I go in there, be myself, and enjoy the process. I try to be true to myself from start to finish—win, lose, or draw. I am going to be the same guy.

Hey, losing stinks and I have a difficult time with it. It hurts. But the next week I am ready to go, because, by God, I know we are going to win and that's the way I approach it. My work has just started in New York. I can't wait to win, to be the first coach in New York Jets history to win two Super Bowls. I can't wait to have the most wins in the history of this team as a coach. I want to be here forever. Remember I said someone told me nobody coaches more than six years with the Jets? Well, I'm going to coach 16 years with the Jets. That's my mentality, that's what I'm going to do. I think our fans embrace that approach, too.

Let me say a few words about our new stadium and our hometown rivalry with the Giants. It was tough to play our home games in Giants Stadium in 2009. We were the visitors for our home games, for crying out loud. We were considered the stepchild to the Giants in the Meadowlands. We just had to look at the name on the building as we drove in—Giants Stadium—to feel that way. The Giants-Jets rivalry is all about proximity, not any real impact on the league from a games standpoint because (unlike the Jets-Patriots rivalry) the teams don't play each other that often.

We play each other in the preseason every year and occasionally meet in the regular season—11 times overall, and the last time in 2007. Still, when we played the Giants in our preseason opener in August 2010 at the new $1.6 billion venue at the Meadowlands in East Rutherford, New Jersey, it had a playoff atmosphere. It was actually the first time since the 1983 season that we had met for our opening preseason game. The exterior of the 82,500-seat stadium was lit in green instead of Giants blue, since the Jets were the designated home team. It was an incredible sight, and I'm sure it irritated a lot of Giants fans.

The teams have identical-size locker rooms and the advertising for each team can get changed electronically. While we shared old Giants Stadium for 26 years, this is the first time one stadium had been built with the idea of sharing it between two teams.

There's not a bad seat in the house, and it feels like the fans are right on top of you. I mean, some of the seats are 46 feet from the sidelines! The stadium is equipped with four massive, high-definition video display scoreboards and more than 2,200 high-definition video displays that are located throughout the facility. Earlier in 2009, NFL owners voted to put the 48th Super Bowl in the new stadium. Until this point, the league had never gone to a cold-weather city that didn't have a domed stadium for the Super Bowl. The league made an exception for the New York area—and New York only. According to the league, the 2014 Super Bowl will be played on February 2, 9, or 16, depending on the format of the season and schedule. While there had been other events held in the stadium, from college lacrosse tournaments and soccer exhibitions to concerts, our preseason opener against the Giants was the first NFL game.

And it was a doozy.

New York *Daily News* columnist Gary Myers cited the game's intensity and said in his story that it was time to move our preseason meeting to the regular season. Myers reminded everyone that the Jets and Giants practiced against each other in training camp for one day in 2005—and they needed a boxing referee, not a football referee. We have not practiced against each other again in the last five years. Myers said, "There is a natural rivalry between the Jets and Giants. I don't think the Giants hate the Jets as much as they hate the Eagles, Redskins and Cowboys and the Jets certainly hate the Patriots and Dolphins more than they hate the Giants, but they are still battling for attention in the same market, which has always made their annual summer get-together more meaningful than any other preseason game. This year it was taken to a new level."

Eli Manning suffered a bloody, three-inch cut to his forehead. He had to leave the game, which the Giants won 31-16, to get a dozen stitches because there was blood all over his face after his helmet got knocked off. Fortunately, he didn't suffer a concussion and got sent home. That's what fans probably remember most from that game. I tipped my hat to the Giants. They put a clinic on us, and it showed that we had a lot of work to do, specifically with our reserves.

Over the years, the results of our games against the Giants rarely have had a lasting impact. I know the Jets beat the Giants in 1988 in the last game of the regular season to keep the Giants from the playoffs, but since then there probably hasn't been a matchup with as much weight. The Jets-Giants rivalry isn't about beating the other team for strategic reasons, simply because we don't play each other enough. With the Jets and Giants, it's more about ruling the roost. Each of us has a large and devoted fan base, and each of our home games is usually sold out.

Even so, we could not have exited old Meadowlands Stadium as the "home team" in any better fashion than we did when we beat the Cincinnati Bengals 37-0 on January 3, 2010, in our regular-season finale. We clinched a playoff spot with the victory. Between our offensive line pounding away and our defense being so dominant, we didn't let Cincy get a first down until seven minutes were left in the third quarter. With a first-year head coach and a rookie quarterback, not many envisioned a playoff run at the beginning of the season — except for those of us in that locker room who stuck together all year.

It was very nice that our organization also paid tribute to the 26 years the team played in Meadowlands Stadium, from 1984 to 2009. Each season was represented by at least one Jets player from that year's team at halftime. A video of highlights took fans and players alike back through the history of Jets football at the Meadowlands. Players who made it back included Bobby Jackson (1984), Wesley Walker (1986), Marty Lyons (1988), Wayne Chrebet (1995), Vinny Testaverde (1998), and many others. It was just a great, memorable way to close out Meadowlands Stadium.

———

Jets right guard Brandon Moore called the night "an electric feeling from pregame warm-ups on." He told the *New York Post*, "We wanted to do it for the fans and do away with that least favorite phrase of mine, 'same old Jets.' "

I keep telling you we are not the same old Jets.

Just ask the Giants.

16. 2009 Season

S o let's look at a few highlights from our 2009 season. With all the pieces in place, we went into 2009 thinking that we really had the opportunity to do something special. And we did, reaching the AFC Championship Game and finishing one game shy of our ultimate goal—to win the Super Bowl.

As I said in the opening lines of this book, Peyton Manning, who won his fourth MVP that season and who has been a pain in my backside, brought the Colts back in that championship game. We were up 11 points and he threw three touchdowns to beat us 30-17 in the AFC title game on January 24, 2010. It was our first road loss in six games, a brutal way to close that great season. And what made it even more brutal for me was that was two years in a row I had helped coach a team that was beaten in the AFC Championship Game. I was defensive coordinator with the Baltimore Ravens in 2008, when we lost to the Pittsburgh Steelers 23-14. You get so close and yet you don't find a way to get it done. It definitely hurts. But, then again, I was so proud of our team.

When you're 4-6 at one point in the regular season, or you lose two of your best players (Pro Bowl players such as nose tackle Kris Jenkins and tailback Leon Washington) to injuries, a lot of teams would burn out. But not the 2009 Jets; our team found a way to get it done. We fought. We believed in each other. We believed in our system and in our way of doing things, and that's great.

But we didn't deserve to beat the Colts.

Even after I looked at that film — maybe especially after I looked at the film — I realized we deserved to lose. The Colts won the game. No question about it. It was a nightmare watching Peyton Manning do that again to us. There are some very positive things that happened in the game, though. We had that lead, we felt great about it, but we never felt comfortable about it. They scored a touchdown right before the half and I felt in my gut that the momentum was shifting. It really didn't matter where they got the ball in the second half. We struggled to stop them. That was the main issue.

I knew we were done at halftime. That might come as a shock, but I knew we were in serious trouble. When cornerback Donald Strickland was injured, I was like, "Oh boy." I told the coaches, "Guys, we are in fucking trouble." We all knew it, because there was no magical "We can do this" halftime speech. We knew that Manning knew it. We were in trouble.

What made it nearly impossible was that we allowed that touchdown right before halftime. We were on top, but Manning responded. He marched the Colts 80 yards in four plays. We blew a pair of defensive coverages and Manning hooked up three straight times with rookie receiver Austin Collie, including the 16-yard touchdown pass that made it 17-13 with 1:13 to go in the half. We honestly believe that we would have been okay had we not given up that touchdown. I told everyone before the playoffs that we were the Super Bowl favorites. I believed it — right until halftime.

Going into the 2009 season, I told our players that I wanted to be the team that nobody wanted to play. We played a physical brand of football, and I don't think a lot of teams were looking forward to facing us. From the emails and calls that I received from opposing coaches and guys who I really respect in this game, I think we accomplished that mission. I was a rookie head coach, but I think our guys believed that I was going to tell them the truth and talk straight with them. The way our guys accepted the coaching, accepted our standard, and built our standard will help us going forward. When we bring in players, they have to perform to our standard. If they don't hit the practice field with a mission to get better, they are gone. Not caring is not the way we do things. We wanted to establish that in 2009, and I think we did.

Overall, the season was like a yo-yo. We started great and then we just about hit rock bottom; but we fought back and came right back up again . . . and then, unfortunately, we hit rock bottom again against the Colts. That may sound a little dramatic, but that's the way it felt to me, because there was no tomorrow. At least not in the 2009 season. But the great thing was that our players and coaches had a vision and believed it.

When you consider that we finished ahead of 28 teams in this league with a brand-new defense and a rookie quarterback in a brand-new system, that's really a good thing. I told our players to wear their Jets stuff and be proud of it. There's no reason each one of us shouldn't be proud to be a New York Jet.

We actually defied the odds over the regular season's final months. Even though I declared us mathematically eliminated from the post-season race after we lost to the Atlanta Falcons 10-7 in Week 15, we won our final two games, against Indianapolis—we ended the Colts' perfect-season run and their 23-game regular-season winning streak—and Cincinnati and entered the playoffs as the AFC's fifth seed. On the road through the playoffs, we upset a pair of division champs in Cincinnati and San Diego. We were the only team in NFL history to make the playoffs with a pair of three-game losing streaks during the regular season. And, best yet, rookie quarterback Mark Sanchez grew up before our eyes over the final five weeks.

I believed we saw our future in Mark over that last month or so. I really did. I named Mark our starting quarterback a few days before our third preseason game—that's how much faith I had in him. His teammates believed in him, too. They talked about how relaxed he was in the huddle and that nothing seemed to rattle him. I was encouraged by how he handled everything and, best yet, how he led his team to the playoffs. That's where and how quarterbacks are judged, and I think he handled it all with his usual class.

I knew our fans wanted me to be diverse on offense, instead of just the run first–, run second–, run third–type mentality. I still think we need to run the ball, but I think we can do other things. As comfortable as Mark got in our system and in Schottenheimer's system, you just saw him growing by leaps and bounds. Our team was able to really enjoy seeing him develop as a professional; we knew he was great to begin with, but it was simple reality that he needed more experience. After his leadership the last two seasons, no one has any question that Mark knows how you win games and also how you lose games—and that's how a top-shelf quarterback should be.

———

We all saw the 2009 season as it unfolded, but I want to share a few of its highlights from my perspective. I will always be able to say for the rest of my life that I opened my career as an NFL head coach with a win. And you should have heard how we prepared for that first game against the Houston Texans. Man, I was throwing everything at my team. I was telling our players that we outworked every team in the NFL, particularly the Texans, and it was going to pay off in the season opener. During our team meeting the night before the game, I reminded the guys about how many weights we lifted in the off-season and how hard and long we ran in the awful New Jersey March weather—and how the Texans had probably not done it the same way. I said the Texans were as soft as Charmin tissue and we were going to blow their doors off because our weakest guy is stronger than their strongest guy.

I wanted my guys to go to bed that night thinking they were King Kong and there was no way we could lose to Houston. I really did believe we were the better team, plain and simple. I was jacked up, too. After the meeting ended, Mike Tannenbaum, our general manager, asked me if I wanted to go watch some videotape of Houston. "Tape?" I said. "No way." I went out and ate Mexican food; I was hungry and I wanted to snack. I mean, at that point, there was nothing else I could do to be more prepared, and nothing else I could do to get my team thinking any tougher.

And it worked. We beat Houston 24-7 in what should have been a shutout, since Houston scored in the fourth quarter on a fumble return for a touchdown. Sanchez threw his first career TD pass, a 30-yard strike to wide receiver Chansi Stuckey. Thomas Jones added a pair of touchdown runs. I knew we would win. I set the Texans up. Everything I ran in the preseason on defense I changed. I never ran one thing in the preseason that would get them ready to play us. I couldn't give two shits about the preseason. I will set up an opponent in a New York minute. Because it works. They had no idea how to read us or prepare for anything we brought.

I was so proud of my guys. As I told the media after the game, "Not bad for two rookies." Sanchez became the first Jets rookie quarterback since Richard Todd in 1976 to win his opener.

I presented Jets chairman and CEO Woody Johnson with one of the game balls. Mr. Johnson was the one who made the decision to select me as the Jets' new head coach, and I will always be grateful. I was emotional, too. I cried in the locker room after the game, but I wasn't embarrassed in the least. My players had my back and I had theirs. I predicted we would have a great defense. That unit didn't allow any points and held the Texans to 183 yards. Our ground-and-pound offense rushed for 190 yards. I received the ceremonial

Gatorade dunk and bath in the game's waning moments. What made it even more special was that I had won my first NFL game as a head coach in the city where my father, Buddy, was defensive coordinator for the Oilers in 1993.

I told our team, the media, and the fans that it was just the beginning. We were 1-0 and that's what we expected to be. It was a tough game against a good football team, but our guys were up to the task.

We beat New England and quarterback Tom Brady 16-9 the following week in our home opener. We didn't sack Brady, but we blitzed the hell out of him.

A week after holding Andre Johnson to four catches and 35 yards, our cornerback Darrelle Revis limited Randy Moss to four catches for 24 yards. I also became the first Jets rookie head coach since Al Groh in 2000 to win his first two games.

We followed that win with another, a 24-17 victory at home over the Tennessee Titans. Sanchez became the first rookie quarterback since the AFL-NFL merger of 1970 to win his first three games. Also, it marked the first time since 2004 that the Jets began a season at 3-0. It was the greatest start to a season I could have hoped for. The entire team—coaches, players, and assistants—everyone was phenomenal and did their jobs perfectly.

But even good times have to end. We suffered our first defeat the following week at New Orleans. My guys were devastated in the locker room, but I wanted to make sure that they had a little perspective. I looked at them and said, "Guys, we lost the game. Did you fucking really think we'd go undefeated?"

All the guys answered, "Yeah."

I smiled and said, "Yep, you are dumb as me. I thought so, too." That's the truth, because that was our mentality. We believed we would win every game.

Of course, that didn't happen. And rarely does. But I didn't see what was waiting around the turn. We dropped five of our next six games to fall to 4-6. I was miserable. We all were miserable. One of those defeats was a 24-22 home setback against Jacksonville on November 15. Really, what it came down to was that the Jaguars wanted it more than us. They went 80 yards for the winning touchdown after we had taken a 22-21 lead on Jones's 1-yard touchdown run with 5:04 remaining. They drove it down our throats with simple plays that we had prepared for all week. I told the media that if we kept playing like this, we were going to get embarrassed.

I also caught some grief from the media because I cried at a team meeting the following Monday. But this was different. I told my players how much I believed in them, that I still thought we were the best team in the league. I was criticized by the media for losing control of my emotions; they believed that once that happened, I would lose the team. That was bullshit. My players know that I am emotional. They know I care about them. They see a personal side to me every day. I don't lie. These guys know I care about them, and no way did I think crying in front of them in a team meeting was a negative. We just needed to stop thinking that wins would automatically happen. We had to go out and earn each game on the field.

After word got out about the crying incident, I decided to have a little fun with it. In my next press conference, I started off by slapping a big box of tissues right on the podium. Was I looking for a new sponsor? No. I just wanted to take a potential negative and turn it into a positive. Hey, I can take it.

I was as surprised as anyone that we were losing, but the great thing was, we still believed in one another. There wasn't any question about that. I knew we would still get it done. I know fans had to be tired of hearing me say we had a good football team even though we were losing—but I knew at the end of the day somebody was going to have egg on their face and I was pretty sure it wasn't going to be me.

Even Mark Sanchez made an opening statement to the media following the Jacksonville game. He said he wanted to send a message that it was up to everyone in our locker room. It was up or down, win or lose, or whatever anyone wanted to call it. But the point was simple: Our season wasn't over. We just needed to win some games and we needed to win a lot in a row.

After we lost to New England the following week, that's exactly what we did. We won five of our last six games to qualify for the playoffs. We pulled back to .500 at 6-6 with a 19-13 victory over the Buffalo Bills. We went to 7-6 with a 26-3 victory over the Tampa Bay Bucs. We lost to Atlanta to fall back to 7-7, but we won our last two games—against Indianapolis and Cincinnati—to finish 9-7 and advance into the playoffs.

Of course, the 29-15 win at Indianapolis in Week 15 wasn't without controversy. The Colts were leading by five when coach Jim Caldwell decided to pull Peyton Manning and other starters in the third quarter. They had already qualified for the playoffs, and Caldwell wanted to rest some of his players and give some others who were injured extra time to heal. It didn't matter that the Colts were undefeated. Caldwell wanted his team rested and prepared for the playoffs. As I said after that game, Indianapolis had earned the right to make the best decision for its football team and for its organization. That's a heck of a football team. They didn't have to apologize to anybody about anything, and neither did we. We won the game. We ended up doing what we had to do, no matter who was on the field for the Colts. Unfortunately, Caldwell's decision meant that not enough credit was given to our football team after that win, and that was unfortunate. Our guys made the plays that won that game. We won by 14 points. I believed it was a big win for our franchise, because it set up the opportunity to advance into the playoffs if we won our regular-season finale against Cincinnati. I knew our team was excited.

And we couldn't have kicked in the New Year, 2010, any better. We shut out the Bengals 37-0 in front of our home fans in our final game at the Meadowlands. The Bengals had 72 total yards of offense (all rushing), while we finished with 320. Our players took a victory lap (at my suggestion) around the stadium in a snowfall of confetti to thank the fans for their support. It marked the Jets' second postseason berth in four years, our fifth of the decade, and the 13th in franchise history. We entered the playoffs as the AFC's fifth seed.

Not only did we set the franchise record with 2,756 yards rushing, we also finished with the league's No. 1 rushing attack for only the second time since 1970. Jones also set a career high with 1,402 yards rushing and set a Jets record with 14 rushing touchdowns.

It was encore time in the opening round of the playoffs. We traveled to Cincinnati to face the Bengals in a Wild Card Game just one week after having beaten them at home. The result was just as good. No, make that better. We won 24-17 to extend Cincy's playoff drought. Sanchez was incredibly efficient over the last three wins, leading 14 scoring drives (eight touchdowns and six field goals) while not turning the ball over even once.

It was also our first postseason victory since we beat the San Diego Chargers on the road in the 2004 AFC Wild Card Game. It was an emotional win, too. We dedicated the victory and gave the game ball to owner Woody Johnson, who had experienced the passing of his daughter during the week. We felt like we had really put our hearts into that game for his family. People can say we backed into the playoffs, but I didn't care. To borrow a baseball axiom, I knew we would be a tough out.

We headed to San Diego the following week. Bringing his A-game once again, Shonn Greene rushed 23 times and chalked up a total of 128 yards, including a 53-yard touchdown. That score was the Jets' longest postseason run ever, and it put us ahead 17-7 with less than seven and a half minutes left on the clock. We thought it was over at 4:38, when San Diego missed a 40-yard field goal, but then they managed to get one into the end zone for a touchdown with just over two minutes left and the suspense started to build again. The onside kick went our way, though, and when the clock finally hit zero we had broken San Diego's winning streak by handing them their first defeat in 12 games.

It felt great. We were on our way to the Jets' first AFC Championship Game since 1998, and Mark Sanchez became only the second rookie (besides Joe Flacco) in the league's history to start and win two playoff games.

Was I surprised that we were one win away from the Super Bowl? No way. We believed the whole time, the whole year, even when probably it wasn't the popular choice or the popular opinion. We didn't have to apologize to anybody. The win over San Diego was just old-fashioned ground-and-pound football, throw completions, and great defense.

Up one week, down the next. That's football sometimes. Our dream season ended against the Colts and that son-of-a-gun Manning on January 24. We were held to only 86 yards rushing after averaging 170 yards on the ground in our first two playoff games. Manning threw for 377 yards to help the Colts advance to the Super Bowl, where they fell to New Orleans, for the second time in four seasons. Despite winning the Super Bowl back in 1969, we still have never won three playoff games in one year (back in 1969, there was only the AFL title game and then the Super Bowl). I can guarantee you, though, that we won't stop trying.

So many players contributed in 2009. Sanchez finished with 2,444 passing yards, 12 touchdowns, and 20 interceptions. Offensive guard Alan Faneca, center Nick Mangold, offensive tackle D'Brickashaw Ferguson, cornerback Darrelle Revis, and defensive end Shaun Ellis made the Pro Bowl. One who really stood out to me, however, was receiver Braylon Edwards. In 2007, Edwards had his first big year, making the Pro Bowl with Cleveland after catching 80 passes for 1,289 yards and 16 scores. The next season, as the Browns went through turmoil and ended up firing coach Romeo Crennel, Edwards's numbers fell to 55 receptions, 877 yards, and three touchdowns. In 2009, he continued to go backward as the Browns' offense struggled, catching only 10 passes for 139 yards in four games before we traded for him.

The third overall pick by the Browns out of the University of Michigan, Edwards was an incredible talent. But many questioned his work ethic and his legal troubles. I knew he had a bad rap coming out of Cleveland. They said he wouldn't play hard; they said he was selfish. That was funny to me, because the Braylon Edwards I knew was one of the top receivers in the league and I hated to go against him. I am telling you, this guy is good. I let him know that, too. "Hey, that's why we traded for you," I said after a big play in October 2009. "You are my guy now." And he kept on performing.

Each Monday, we have a "Play Like a Jet" film showing highlights of players who play like a Jet. And Edwards was highlighted nearly every week. He blocked, he knocked defenders on their ass 20 yards downfield, he made great catches. I told him heading into the 2010 season that I wanted him to be the best receiver in football. I didn't say of all time, just the best receiver this year. He looked at me like "What the . . . ?" I told him he had more ability than any receiver in the league. And the very next day in practice, he went out there and caught balls off the heads of defenders and did some of the damndest things I had ever seen from a receiver. I know it can happen and I believe it can happen. Sometimes if you say it enough, with conviction, they start believing it.

All I want is the very best you have; and if you don't give it to us, you don't give it to me, then you'll probably see a different side of me than that. I want guys to play loose. I want them to have fun and enjoy playing this game. It is a game, yet you have to be accountable—not just to me, but to your teammates. Whoever we bring in in the future has to play and practice and study to a certain standard, or they'll be an outcast and be gone quickly. It's as simple as that. I'm not ever going to beg somebody to do anything. If you don't belong and you don't see it that way, then you won't be here.

People ask me all the time what I learned about myself in 2009. That is easy to answer: I believe in myself. My confidence has always been there, but during that season I saw how valuable my confidence was to the entire organization. I believe in our systems and I believe in the people in our building. We lost six of seven games in 2009, and it would have been easy to say, "Oh shit" and give up. It would have been easy, too, to point fingers. As a first-year coach, you can get away with it. People like to shrug off that responsibility and undersell their product by not putting any pressure on themselves. My ass. I believed in who we were, and I knew if we just stayed the course we would get through it. And we did.

We put ourselves one game away from the Super Bowl.

17. Coach-Speak: Getting Up in Front of the Players and Coaches

As much as the game is about what happens on the field, from those blunt-force trauma hits to executing a good play, you also have to set the tone for your team in meetings. You have to express to them the plan and the emotion that goes into executing that plan. The other thing is, you have to get the message across in just the right way. If you talk too much, you lose guys. If you talk too goofy, you lose guys. If you get too emotional, you lose guys. If you start saying the same thing, you lose guys.

In other words, you had better have a sharp, focused message that works at that moment the right way. That means that sometimes you have to be serious and sometimes you have to be funny—but you had better always be on the mark and speaking from the heart.

First, there's the serious message. One of the most important ones I ever had was when I was still the defensive coordinator of the Baltimore Ravens. It was in 2008 and it was the last regular-season game ever played in Texas Stadium, where the Cowboys had played for 38 years. When they finished that place back in 1971, it was considered

a palace. As a kid, I remember watching games from there, listening to Pat Summerall call the game, watching Tom Landry on the
sideline, and cheering on all the great Cowboys players. Well, now
I was going to be one of the last people to ever coach in the place.
It was pretty cool, even if by that time the place was sort of a dump.
You put that place next to what the league has now and it's no comparison. Now, here's the messed-up part: The Ravens were supposed
to be the sacrificial lambs. This was some serious BS and everybody
made a big deal about this one. During the previous off-season,
when the league was putting together the schedule, Cowboys owner
Jerry Jones asked the league to make us the team they played to close
down Texas Stadium in the regular season. Jones saw that we were
5-11 in 2007, we fired Brian Billick, hired John Harbaugh, changed
the quarterback, and all the rest of our shake-ups—and he figured
we were the weakest ones on his schedule. We were the team he
wanted for the homecoming game, the automatic win. Well, you
can only imagine what I and almost everyone else with the Ravens
was thinking. Actually, it doesn't take much imagination if you know
me, but I'll just give you a couple of hints with the words "duck" and
"few."

The other thing about this game is that Jones wanted it on Saturday night to play for the NFL Network crowd, because he figured
it was also going to be like a coronation. That was the only NFL
game played that day. It was us and the Cowboys on center stage,
although Dallas wasn't really looking to share the spotlight. The season before, the Cowboys were 13-3 and won the NFC East, which
was the best division in football that season. They had a stud squad
with everybody playing great—guys like Tony Romo, Terrell Owens,
Jason Witten, DeMarcus Ware, and a bunch of others. It was a total
stud operation, but they lost in the playoffs to the New York Giants,
who then went on to win the whole thing, beating New England
in the Super Bowl. The loss to the Giants was really close, so the
Cowboys thought they were *this* close to winning the whole thing
themselves.

Finally, the whole plan after the game to close Texas Stadium was that all those great former Cowboys were supposed to show up and they were going to have a big party to say good-bye to the stadium. Put it all together and you can only imagine how amped up our team was to play that game. By itself, it was going to be a big challenge, because both teams were 9-5. I think the Cowboys were expecting to be a lot better, and they had lost a couple of games early in the month, so they were kind of teetering. Still, they were really good. We were kind of a surprise, especially since we were playing with a rookie quarterback in Joe Flacco, and we had just come off our second frustrating loss to Pittsburgh. Anyway, coming into the game, both teams were thinking of the playoffs, since whichever team won would be in. Obviously, both the Cowboys and Ravens were pretty excited.

Like I said, we'd been talking about all the stuff all week about how the Cowboys viewed us as their homecoming team and all they are planning for is the big dance after the game, and so on. But you can't just keep repeating the same message all the time, so I felt like I had to come up with something new for my speech the night before the game.

Hello, Jason Garrett.

Jason Garrett was the Dallas offensive coordinator at the time and had been during the previous season. He's a smart guy, went to Princeton, was the son of a terrific coach, and had a brother who worked for Dallas as well. He's a good football man and I've got nothing personal against the guy, but during the previous off-season, while the Ravens were going through their coaching search, he was offered the Baltimore job. Well, he went back to Jones and Jones gave him a monster raise to around $3 million a year on a three-year contract. That's the kind of money that a lot of head coaches get when they're starting out. Garrett was still the offensive coordinator, but it's pretty obvious to everybody in the league that he was going to take over for Wade Phillips. (Sure enough, Garrett did replace Phillips in 2010, but it's because the Cowboys were 1-7 halfway through that season—not exactly what Jones had planned, I think.) So, as you already know, Garrett turned down the Ravens job. That was the job I was begging for at the time, the job I dreamed of having back then—and that guy turns it down. Now, it was basically my defense and me against him and his offense that week, with all the other BS going on.

There aren't many times in your career that you get better material than that to work with for a pregame pep talk. Bart Scott, who was playing for Baltimore that year, really understood how deep it got for me in that meeting with the defense:

> Rex is not afraid to show his emotion. The day before that game, he came in our meeting and he couldn't hold it in. He always looks like Droopy, that real old cartoon character, when he starts crying and all that stuff. He was really upset; it wasn't even about the playoff implications. He said: "I have never wanted to beat a team so bad. That guy over there, man, he didn't want to coach you. Are you serious? Who wouldn't want to coach the men in this room?" He was talking about Jason Garrett. Rex is like: "He didn't believe in the character of the Baltimore Ravens. Are you serious, he would turn down an opportunity to coach you guys? This team?" It wasn't like we were a team that had sucked forever. We were the Baltimore Ravens, a great team. He knew at the end of the day it was his defense against Jason Garrett's offense and that could be the difference in us going to the play-offs. He didn't want to give that guy the satisfaction of knowing that he outfoxed him.

The other thing Scott and the players will tell you is that these messages are delivered in a pretty coarse fashion. Some of the guys even have under-over bets on how many times I'll drop the f-bomb during a speech. One guy is in charge of counting. I've heard that I'll get to 40 or 50 in a 10-minute speech. Well, that's me talking from the heart, and Scott and a lot of those guys will tell you it gets them fired up. Trust me, not all coaches swear like me. They just don't. I'm not just doing it for show, though. Scott will tell me, "If you hear a coach talking that way, saying he wants to f— up the other team, that gets you thinking as a player, 'Damn right! Let's go beat the hell out of them!'"

I can't tell you exactly how great my speech before the Dallas game was, but I probably had more f-bombs than the Cowboys had yards for the first 54 minutes. We kicked the crap out of the Cowboys. On their first eight possessions, they punted five times, we intercepted two passes, and they scored one gimp touchdown after we fumbled at our own 4-yard line when Flacco got sacked. They gained a total of 113 yards on those possessions. This is an ass-kicking, total domination. Finally, they got a field-goal drive to open the fourth quarter, driving 51 yards on 12 plays (still not exactly awesome stuff for a team with that kind of talent). After we got a field goal, it was 19-10 with 6:30 remaining, when the game got a little wild. They had good drives, but we answered with a 77-yard run by Willis McGahee and an 82-yard run by Le'Ron McClain. Damn, McClain is almost built like me, and he went 82 yards—that's how much the Cowboys gave up by the end. We won 33-24 and we were just laughing all the way home to Baltimore. We won the next game to close the season and ended up going to the AFC Championship Game.

The Cowboys? After that game, they lost the final game of the season at Philadelphia 44-6 and the Eagles got the last spot in the playoffs over the Cowboys. How funny is that? Call it coincidence if you want, but that loss to the Eagles was the most lopsided for Dallas since that famous 44-0 game they lost to my dad when he was in Chicago in 1985. Thank you, Jason Garrett. All it took was a little extra motivation.

Of course, meetings can't all be about emotion. Trust me, you can go to that George Patton speech only so many times before guys get tired of hearing it. Plus, you're draining guys if you do that too much. Football is a sport where you have to get amped up to a controlled frenzy (how about that for an oxymoron?) at just the right time. Do that too early or too late and you blow it. Do it too often and it gets harder and harder to get there. This isn't like baseball or basketball, where you play so many games that you have to control your emotion. Football is that rush like being shot out of a cannon after gulping 20 energy drinks.

Sometimes when you're coaching, you have to bring it down just a little, cut the mood. Trust me, I'm always talking about winning the next game, dominating, doing whatever it takes—but you have to have some fun along the way, too.

Even if that fun isn't exactly the stuff from an after-school special.

Now, before I go too much further, you have to understand some things. First off, not everything I do completely translates to the corporate world. Not that I've ever been a part of that world, but I can't imagine you can always do these things in front of a mixed crowd. In football, there are 53 young, testosterone-laced men who aren't exactly training to wear a suit and tie for their career. As I said before, we have rough guys from rough backgrounds . . . and that's just some of the coaches.

Anyway, it was Week 14 of the 2009 season and we were playing at Tampa Bay. By this time in the season, the Bucs had Josh Freeman playing. He was a rookie and he was also the other guy we thought about taking if we didn't get Mark Sanchez. Freeman is a great kid and a big, strong athlete. We just liked Sanchez a little better; we had a conviction about him. Freeman didn't start the year, but the Bucs had Byron Leftwich get hurt and then another backup named Josh Johnson played awhile until Freeman was ready, which was about midseason. By that time, though, none of those guys would have been ready for us. We just crushed them. Through the first half, the Bucs gained zero yards once you throw in their penalties. That's not a typo. I mean zero yards. They didn't get a first down and they didn't have a drive of longer than three plays. One interception, six punts, and a kneel-down at the end of the half is all they got against us.

In the second half, it was more of the same. On their first possession, they went three and out after gaining five yards. The second possession was the same thing: three and out after we fumbled to give them the ball at their own 45-yard line. On third-and-9, Scott sacked Freeman but got called for unnecessary roughness. They got 15 yards and another first down. They finally cobbled together a first down on their own (it only took them 38 minutes of game time to do it) after going for it on fourth down, and then settled for a field goal after they got to our 25. They gained all of 15 yards on their own after Scott gave them 15 yards. With all of that, we blew the shutout. We ended up winning 26-3 and gave up a total of six first downs for the whole game.

Well, Scott is my guy, but I have to give him hell. That is part of breaking the ice with your players and keeping things loose. So I have to come up with something special for him and finally settled on the Dumb Dick Award. Now, with awards like this, it's not enough to just say he's earned it—it has to be like the Oscars. You have to do the presentation, the whole award performance. I even thought about having an orchestra come in and play that music you hear when they announce the winners. It was going to be a real special event.

The trophy was . . . how should I put this . . . a seriously impressive phallic statue. It was the biggest one I could possibly find. I called a meeting with my coordinators, Mike Pettine and Brian Schotten-heimer, plus a couple of other coaches and our special-teams coach, Mike Westhoff. Laura Young, my great assistant who loves a practical joke, was in there too, taking notes with me for my presentation to the team. I told them all about the statue and my idea, but made sure to do it before Westhoff arrived.

Westhoff came in and then, after a couple of minutes, Laura said, "Mike, can you throw me that towel?" He didn't know what was there and he damn near had a heart attack. It was hysterical, and was a good warm-up for what I wanted to do when I awarded it to Scott. Again, I know this stuff wouldn't go over in some boardrooms, but that's not who I am. If you heard me on *Hard Knocks*, this isn't exactly news to you.

Now, the other thing I did is I gave Scott the heads-up before I gave this thing to him. That is part of the deal—that I wanted him in on it. You can't just embarrass a great athlete like him with a surprise like that, and it is never my goal to humiliate someone. Scott is an important guy on this team. He has to be part of the joke. So after I cleared it with him, I stood up in front of the team and said, "Guys, we had a great game, but I got an award to give. It's a bad one to get. It's the Dumb Dick Award." The "trophy" had a wrapper on it, but everybody knew what it was. They were all laughing and having a great time as Scott came up and grabbed the thing, then he used it to hit people and we were all cracking up—but let me tell you, that's one award you don't want to win. We don't give that out every week, and you only give it to guys who can handle it. You have to do something really dumb to win it.

That's one example of keeping it light but also getting your point across. Not everything can be a lecture or a punishment. Now, that one is hugging the line on being negative and I make sure I do more things that are positive, but you have to have fun.

———————

There are all sorts of stories about things that coaches have done to motivate their players. Bill Parcells was an expert at those kinds of messages. He had done the one with the mousetraps a bunch of times. You put the traps on your players' stools in front of their lockers on weeks when you're playing a team with a bad record. That's called a trap game, one of those times when your team can start looking ahead and get beat. On the other side, Jimmy Johnson one time went into a meeting before a game against Cleveland when the Browns were bad and told his coaches, "We should be able to beat the Browns without having to even prepare." You get all different approaches. Parcells once put a gas can in front of a player's locker. Parcells left a note on there telling the player he was performing like he was running out of gas. Parcells used to get Lawrence Taylor, who's probably the greatest linebacker of all time, amped up with all sorts of challenges about how Taylor couldn't outplay the other team's offensive linemen.

You're always looking for little things like that that will motivate in an unconventional way. In Baltimore, I did a lot of stuff on the field. Once a week, I'd line up against the defensive linemen like Tony Siragusa, Sam Adams, and Rob Burnett and let them go against me. Yeah, it bruised the hell out of me, but they really looked forward to it. I'm not saying I could handle those guys, but it gave them a way to take their frustrations out and gave us a way to bond a little. I wasn't afraid of them. That said, I don't advise a lot of coaches to do that. It's not the easiest thing.

The better way is to find something in a meeting that really gets guys going. The best way, in my viewpoint, is highlighting a specific guy on a specific play. There are going to be one or two times in a game where I'm really going to try to highlight somebody, give that guy a chance to be a star. Not every guy can be Ray Lewis or Bart Scott or Tony Siragusa all the time. It doesn't work. But if you give that guy a chance, maybe design a blitz for him or a coverage where you're trying to force the ball to the guy he's covering, something like that, that gets that guy pumped up. That's what all those guys are looking for, because really that's what they've been all their lives. These guys were stars when they were kids, when they were in high school, most likely when they were in college, and now you want to make them feel like that again.

Even if it's only for a play or two.

18. *Hard Knocks*

One of my biggest goals for this franchise is for every coach to want to coach here and for every player to want to play here. We had already changed the culture of the Jets on the inside. We were a whole new team and we knew exactly how great we were. Our next step was to find a way to make sure outsiders knew it, too. In order for that to happen, we had to sell ourselves, and it turned out that *Hard Knocks* was our platform.

Mr. Johnson was actually approached by NFL Films last year with the proposal to do *Hard Knocks* during the 2009 season. He ended up saying no, because it was my first year as head coach and clearly we were going through changes. I think he knew that I needed a year to get settled, and truthfully, I'm sure he needed a year to get settled with me. When NFL Films came back in 2010, it was really Ross Greenburg, president of HBO Sports, who was pushing hard for us to do it. Mr. Greenburg is a great guy. He's very smart and is highly respected by everyone in the league, so when Mr. Johnson knew he was behind it, he agreed. Over the years we had been deemed "the same old Jets" and Mr. Johnson was sick of it. Like any NFL team owner, he has a lot of pride in his franchise, and to him "the same old Jets" was a derogatory term that he wanted to get away from. There was a new head coach, a new practice facility, a new stadium, and most important, a whole new culture to the Jets. *Hard Knocks* was the way to show all that and to let everyone see firsthand that the New York Jets were not the same old team.

I would be lying if I said that I was sold on doing the show right off the bat. I had experienced the *Hard Knocks* cameras before when they followed the Baltimore Ravens through training camp back in 2001. Needless to say, when I was first approached with the idea of doing it this year, my initial reaction was to pass. It wasn't until I realized how important it was to Mr. Johnson that I was 100 percent on board. Mr. Johnson knew the kind of potential *Hard Knocks* had for us. He knew it would be a great vehicle to show the American public exactly what this franchise stands for. He was sure of the good it would bring to the Jets, and, honestly, the more I thought about it, the more I realized he was right. When I looked at it that way, there was no reason not to do it.

Before we signed on the dotted line, though, we needed to make sure that we were all on the same page about a couple things. We had to agree on the goals. In other words, what were we hoping to gain from doing the show? It was simple: When *Hard Knocks* was said and done, every coach and player should want to be a part of this franchise. It was agreed upon by Mr. Johnson, Mike Tannenbaum, and me that the only way that was going to happen was if we stayed true to who we are. I wasn't going to change the way I coached, and they never expected any different from me. The way we looked at it, *Hard Knocks* was a reality television show and reality was exactly what we were going to give them.

In itself, *Hard Knocks* was a commercial for the Jets. It was a five-hour commercial that followed our team through two weeks of training camp. It cut two weeks of footage down to a one-hour episode that aired Wednesday nights for five weeks. And what can I say? We were a hit. We gave *Hard Knocks* the highest ratings in history and provided sports broadcasters with enough color commentary to last them the entire regular season. People loved the show; they may not have loved us, but they sure as hell loved watching us.

Training camp is one of the most critical times during the whole season. Those are the weeks that you're building the team—not only from a roster standpoint, but the foundation and ideals of the team, too. As a coach, it's the time when you are developing a relationship with your players. You're learning them and they're learning you. It's a constant roller coaster from beginning to end. You have players who have dreamed their entire lives of playing in the NFL. They're out there fighting harder than hell for a spot on that roster, giving you everything they've got—and then you have to be the one to tell them that their best just isn't good enough. You have to cut guys you love and guys who are damn good athletes, because in the end it's about getting down to the 53-man roster. It's emotional for the players and it's tough for the coaches; there's no question about it. *Hard Knocks* followed us through the entire process and showed everything from players getting cut to the coaching staff's private meetings. A lot of people were shocked by how much the cameras revealed during episodes. Apparently, they showed the depth chart in one episode and it immediately sparked some talk. A lot of people felt like that was crossing the line (those were our fans). Others looked at us like we were stupid for just leaving our depth chart lying around (those probably weren't our fans). It makes me laugh when I think about what a big deal they made out of stuff like that. There were teams that truly thought they were going to get some sort of an advantage out of watching *Hard Knocks*. Obviously, they were wrong.

First of all, let me tell you that there is a board in every office with one of those charts. The names are not set in stone and the order has no significance. Secondly, I will tell you that there was a trust level between the *Hard Knocks* producers and our staff. There had to be because of situations like that. Sure, I guess they potentially could have revealed our entire season's game plan, but nothing that important was even decided by then and they knew that. If it had been, I can promise you the producers never would have aired it. The names on those charts were not set in stone, clearly, given how the 53-man roster turned out.

"Distracted" was just one of the many opinions about our team that spun from us doing the show. But I will tell you this right now: During those five weeks of filming, there was never a moment that this project became a distraction to me or to the players. *Hard Knocks* did such a good job of really being invisible. The producers had cameras all over the place. They also put these microphones the size of a pen cap all around the facility. I didn't realize there was one on my desk for a while. The producers wanted to get a realistic perspective of us, and that was made very clear to the players. Before they started shooting footage they said, "If you act like an idiot or if you ham it up for the camera in any way, we will stop filming." They were serious about that. The minute the players or staff stopped acting like themselves, the cameras stopped. Knowing this, it's funny to listen to people say that *Hard Knocks* was a distraction for us. It wasn't a distraction for us while the cameras were in our faces during games, so I have never understood why they think it would have been a distraction for us during the start of the season.

When we agreed to allow the public to see the ins and outs of this franchise, we knew exactly what was going to come our way. No one ever gets to see the way coaches interact with their players; whether it's in practice, a pregame meeting, or training camp, most of those interactions are behind closed doors. Well, not with us; we opened the doors to them. In fact, we opened the doors and rolled out the carpet. I mean, why wouldn't we? We have nothing to hide. No two coaches are going to lead their team the exact same way, so it's expected that everyone is going to have a different opinion of what's the right and wrong way to lead a team. With *Hard Knocks* filming every aspect of my leadership strategies, it was a given that my method was going to be criticized. Honestly, I didn't care.

When Mr. Johnson hired me as the head coach of the Jets, he

hired me knowing damn well the type of person I am, and he has never once asked me to be someone different. Mr. Johnson does this job for one reason: the fans. He has always wanted a way to reach the fans, but before hiring me he couldn't reach them exactly the way he wanted to. When I came on board, it became easier to speak to the fans. I feel the same way as Mr. Johnson; both of us work every day for the fans and we know that the media is how we get to them. The media is our voice, and with me being as open as I am, Mr. Johnson knows that the fans are going to get a lot; they're going to get the good, the bad, and the ugly.

When *Hard Knocks* aired, I knew that it would get some press. One of the things that people were the most critical about was my language. Right after that first episode aired, all hell broke loose. Aside from Roger Goodell and Woody Johnson, who have never said one word to me about it, I really don't think anyone is in a position to tell me the way I should or should not be doing something. Yet for some reason other coaches and players, such as Tony Dungy, Tom Brady, and Terry Bradshaw, felt that they had a right to judge me based off something they saw on TV. People were so quick to judge me because I dropped an f-bomb here and there, yet they fail to take into account the context I said it in. In a team meeting, at a team function, that's how I talk—but do I talk like that in interviews? I never curse when I'm speaking to the press, but when I am talking to my team I can't help but get carried away. I feel passionate and intense about what I am trying to say and it honestly slips out without me even knowing it. I am not intentionally trying to offend anyone. That's who I am, though, and that's who I've always been. Whether it is the right way to coach is not for anyone to decide but me. A lot of people don't stop to think about the fact that I allowed cameras to come in and film me in situations that are usually private. Apparently, people thought that because the cameras were there I was going to censor myself. I'm sorry for the misunderstanding, but that's not how I operate. I don't think it would be fair to have given you this false picture of myself, not on *Hard Knocks* and not now.

I was asked a lot during the filming if I regretted anything I said on camera, and my answer was always "Absolutely not." I think everyone knows me well enough by now to know the answer to that. I sat down on Wednesday nights just like every other fan and flipped to HBO. I had no clue what was going to make it on the air and what was going to be left on the cutting-room floor. That's a risk Mr. Johnson, the league, and I all took when we signed on to do it. I honestly didn't care what people's opinions were about me or my coaching style. I think I am a good coach and I think my players would agree. With the exception of my mom, I really couldn't care less who is disappointed by my choice of language.

There were a couple things that were just expected by doing *Hard Knocks*. I mean, the feedback was given, the compliments were welcomed, and the criticisms (for the most part) were brushed off. Of everything that arose from *Hard Knocks*, the issue that grabbed the most media attention happened to be one that I just couldn't seem to brush off. Of course, I'm talking about the comments made by Tony Dungy. I'm not going to lie—it really upset me. I was incredibly disappointed that he judged me the way he did. I just kept thinking to myself: I had never met Tony. He has built his reputation on being this honorable, Christian man, yet he was judging me without even knowing me? I didn't understand it. I don't judge him even though I know he's not perfect—although he might be a lot closer to perfect than I will ever be. I was shocked by it. I really was, and I think the part that upset me the most was that he wasn't just attacking me; he was attacking my father. To say comments like "He grew up with that" and "He gets it from his father"—well, you know what? You're darn right I do, and I'm awful proud of that. I will follow my dad any day.

I thought for a long time about all this, and in the end I felt the right thing to do was to call him and talk it out with him. I called and left a message on his machine inviting him to come out to New Jersey. He was the one who had brought it all into the media, so I knew that he had to call me back eventually. I had nothing to hide, and I wanted him to know that. When someone wrongs you, the best solution is to open all your doors and invite them in, so I did just that. It was about a week before I got a call back from him. We talked man-to-man and basically just made it a point to make our positions clear to each other. He took me up on my offer and on Saturday, September 25, he came out to my office at the Jets' facility.

Surprisingly, it was great. I think we both left with a very different understanding of each other. We sat down and talked, and he proceeded to tell me about some players he had coached who had also played for me. They told him that he didn't know me and that he was dead wrong in his opinion of me. He went on to tell me that his whole issue with me on *Hard Knocks* was that he had a dear friend who wanted to watch the show with his son and had to turn it off because of my language. I understand that completely, and I made sure I told him that. On the other hand, it was important for me to let him know, too, that I am not a monster. I'm just a person who maybe doesn't use appropriate language all the time, but I'm going to be who I am. I told our team to be true to themselves and I would do the same, cameras rolling or not. I wasn't going to change anything about myself just because I was on *Hard Knocks*. I never felt it was my responsibility to clean up my language. It's my responsibility to coach a football team and lead it any way that I choose to. Tony Dungy is not going to lead my team and he's not going to lead me. Now, do I have things to work on? Absolutely. I have an enormous amount of respect for Tony Dungy. I'm just a different person than he is, a completely different person.

Aside from Tony, the rest of the feedback from *Hard Knocks* was humorous. Tom Brady spoke out and said he hated us as well as the show. Well, guess what? We hate the Patriots. What's your point? It's about competition. There is nothing better than to get the juices going. You want to hate an opponent. When you get fired up over one team, you go out there playing harder than you've ever played before because that hatred is inside you; it's what's driving you. I call your attention to our recent AFC Divisional Game against them . . .

a real highlight win for us. Do I really hate Tom Brady? I really don't know Tom Brady, but who wouldn't hate him? Look at his life. Actually, look at his wife. Every man in America hates Tom Brady, and he should be proud of that.

As I said earlier, I didn't know what was going to air on *Hard Knocks* until Wednesday night at 10 P.M. I was just like any other fan. And while I think it did a great job of highlighting positive aspects of the franchise, there were a couple things that aired that really bothered me.

One philosophy we have is that we want it to be fun for the guys. We make no bones about saying that in the press. We want them to enjoy being here. We try to not take ourselves too seriously, but when it's time to be professional we are going to play with everything we've got. We love to have fun and that's our mentality, but I don't necessarily think *Hard Knocks* showed enough of us working. This team works their asses off, but I felt like it didn't portray them as these dedicated NFL players as much as it showed some of their other sides. There were situations when the show had the opportunity to go left and film them in one way, and it went right and made them look like this rowdy, undisciplined group of kids. That's just not true, and that's not the picture I wanted to paint to the public. For example, the episode with the whole cheeseburger incident was blown out of proportion. What really happened was that I moved the practice up 50 minutes early because we went to Long Island. There was a storm coming in, so I said let's just move this thing up. The guys hadn't had anything to eat on the bus trip and they saw a McDonald's. It was literally their only option at the time. We were starting the practice off and they were bringing those orders in. It wasn't like that happens all the time, but it just showed our guys in a bad light. Next thing I know, we are being referred to as the *"Animal House"* team and people are saying that I can't control my team. What people forget, though, is that I chewed their asses for eating those cheeseburgers and *Hard Knocks* showed that, but people don't remember the positives; they only remember the negatives. I know that, and I know that's what makes good TV. I just don't like seeing something panned out on TV that isn't completely true or that just doesn't need to be mentioned.

Antonio Cromartie is a good example; that is another situation that really bothered me. See, *Hard Knocks* producers would choose a couple guys from each practice and mic them up so viewers could listen to them during drills and stuff. Once the practices were over, they would interview them. A lot of times they would ask them personal questions, but mostly it was just about the practice, how camp was going, and so on. Anyway, I think it was the first or second episode they had a microphone on Cro and, during the interview portion, they asked him what the names of his kids are. I guess you would have to see the episode to know what I'm talking about, but I was not happy with how they filmed it. I was unhappy they even asked him that question and brought his personal situation into the show. Cro is an awesome guy and an unbelievable athlete. Unfortunately, he has had some personal struggles, but who hasn't? Watching the show later on TV, I wanted to shout, "Everyone knows the story. Why do you have to set him up like that?" It wasn't necessary. It had nothing to do with what we were trying to accomplish from *Hard Knocks*, nor did it have anything to do with who we are as a team. It was stuff like that I didn't like. I think it placed negative ideas in some people's heads about who we were before we played the first regular-season game.

Despite that, when I look back on the *Hard Knocks* experience I can honestly say that I am really glad we did it. We went into it with one goal, which was to show people who the Jets are and what we are all about, in the truest form. For the most part, I think we accomplished that. I think the show did a great job of highlighting all that we have to offer and the extent we will go to for each and every one of our players, how we will get them anything they need— whether it's a masseuse, a chiropractor, or a yoga instructor, we will find a way to get it for them. It was really important to Mr. Johnson, Mike Tannenbaum, and me that people see how we take care of our players. We treat them like men, not children, and I personally make sure each of them is aware of how important their role is to making this team whole. We treat them right, and we take pride in that.

Aside from making sure the public saw the relationship between the franchise staff and the players, making sure they saw our facilities was just as important. We have the number-one facility in the league. Mr. Johnson is amazing at providing the absolute best for us in every situation. *Hard Knocks* did a great job of showing all of that. People were able to see where we held training camp; we were fortunate enough to spend two weeks at an unbelievable campus at SUNY Cortland in upstate New York. We had fields unlike any I have ever seen before, dorm rooms, meeting rooms, and a kick-ass cafeteria. As a player and as a coach, you literally could not ask for anything better. I mean, after seeing that on TV, who wouldn't want to be a Jet? That's exactly what we wanted to get out of *Hard Knocks*.

Not everyone was left with the same impression of us from *Hard Knocks*, but one thing's for sure: We were entertaining as hell. Mr. Johnson says he knew people who would leave dinner parties early just to be home in time to watch it. I remember after watching the first episode that I thought it was great. I was entertained, and whether you know us or not, you can't help but laugh. We have so many stories to tell, and *Hard Knocks* was kind of a five-hour preview into the environment that we play in. We hooked people just by being us; that's the coolest thing in the world to me. I think everyone, whether they admit it or not, thought to themselves, "I bet it would be awesome to be a part of the Jets."

We are building a reputation in the league that is making people want to play our way of football, and that feels so damn good. Thanks to *Hard Knocks*, people were able to see firsthand that "the same old Jets" are gone. It was a great experience and one that I am truly glad we were given the opportunity to do. Would I do it again? Well, I think it's probably someone else's turn.

19. Revis: The Art of the Deal

This is the story of how I got my autographed Satchel Paige baseball for free, sort of. Trust me, I would have rather just bought one.

Let me set the scene: It's 2 A.M. on September 3, a Friday, and it's time to get serious. I finally get home early in the morning after our last preseason game in Philadelphia, and I am hoping to get a couple of hours of sleep, but I can't. The only thing on my mind is that we're 10 days from opening the season and we're pretty much screwed. Why? My best defensive player, cornerback Darrelle Revis, is still holding out.

The whole thing with Revis was driving me nuts. I couldn't say much for most of training camp after we put the gag order on the whole thing, but this was getting ridiculous. Revis was probably on the back page of the New York tabloids more than any athlete in the city during training camp, and he wasn't even doing anything. Distraction? What do you think?

By now, I've got the point he's not showing up. I don't think this is right. The kid had three years left on his contract. I know the negotiations hadn't worked out, and I know he has hard feelings, but we've been talking about this deal all off-season. Literally, our first big meeting was way back in February at the scouting combine in Indianapolis. That went on forever. It was the first time I ever met Revis's agents. They are these two guys from New York, Jonathan Feinsod and Neil Schwartz. Feinsod, it turns out, is a big Jets fan (not that it's helping get the deal done), but he's talking and talking about how much he loves the Jets. At one point, he says, "Rex, I'm really pulling for you, because Jets coaches just don't last. I think Weeb Ewbank was the longest-tenured coach in Jets history."

I know Weeb because of my dad, and of course this has me thinking, "How long was Weeb here?" I mean, how long do Jets coaches last, really? But the bottom line is that Weeb isn't here — I am — and we have to work something out. The time for playing around is done. I've been pissed at Revis's agents and I got upset with him, but that doesn't mean anything anymore. The only thing that matters is that we've got to have Revis, because he's special. He changes the game.

Trust me, I know. I was there in 2000 in Baltimore when we had a great defense and won the Super Bowl. Actually, it wasn't just a great defense, it was a *historic* defense. You can put that group up against the 1985 Bears, the great defense my dad coordinated. There's no question in my mind. I have total respect for the Bears, what those players did and what my dad did. The Bears changed the way people viewed defense with the 46. That changed everything. From Ray Lewis to Chris McAlister to Duane Starks to Peter Boulware to Rob Burnett to Mike McCrary, they were off the charts. The two guys who really set everything apart, though, were Sam Adams and Tony Siragusa, the two defensive tackles. Those were my guys. I was in charge of getting them to play hard, and that's the hardest those sons of bitches ever played.

Those guys were rough and tough, not just on the field, but in everything they did. In the meeting room, at practice, during games, you had to handle those guys a certain way if you wanted to get them going. When I got to Baltimore in 1999, Goose was already there. We brought in Sam in 2000. Trust me when I say that those guys made the whole thing go, because both of them played the best they'd ever played that year. We're talking about one of the best bull rushers in the history of the game with Siragusa, and Sam could do anything he wanted whenever he felt like it.

This is where I'm coming from with Revis. He's not a defensive tackle, so people don't really understand the comparison, but what Revis does is change the X's and O's for the opposing teams. He can play any system. You want to play man-to-man, up-in-your-face defense? He can do it. You want to play zone? He can do it. You want to put him on the other team's best guy all the time? He can do it. You want to put him on a receiving tight end, the kind of player who normally overpowers a cornerback? Revis can do it. We did that in the playoffs against San Diego sometimes.

What I know is that if we're going to back up all our talk from this off-season, our defense has to be extraordinary. Like in 2000, our defense was phenomenal. Last year, my first year with the Jets, we led the league in defense, but we weren't historic on defense. We will be if Revis comes back. There's no question; I know we will be.

But I also know, at this very moment at 2 A.M. on Friday, September 3, that Revis isn't showing up. I've felt pretty strongly about this for a few weeks now, since shortly after we got to training camp. I guess the biggest thing I noticed was that he wasn't talking. He wasn't around anywhere; he was barely talking to his teammates. You know that serious silent treatment people give you when they are trying to show you they mean business? Anybody who has been married knows what I'm talking about. Heck, Revis's agents weren't even talking much. I just had that feeling he was resolved. As most people know, his uncle is Sean Gilbert, a former first-round pick who was a pretty good defensive tackle in his day. Gilbert was resolved enough to sit out a whole year one time when he was playing for Washington. And it paid off, because when the Redskins finally traded him to

Carolina, the Panthers paid him twice as much as Washington was offering him, so he actually made more money sitting out. That is the kind of resolve we're up against, because Gilbert is the guy Revis talks to and trusts the most.

You see, getting involved directly in a contract situation isn't a good idea for a coach. I know some coaches are part of that deal, like Bill Belichick. He knows what's going on with the money up in New England, because he really runs the football operations. To me, that's our general manager's job. Mike's a sharp guy. He knows the salary cap backward and forward, and he knows what Mr. Johnson wants. My job is to tell those guys what I think of the players, who we have to keep and who we can probably get by without. That's tough, because you want everybody, but that's not how the system works. We may not have had a salary cap in the NFL in 2010 because of all the collective bargaining stuff (again, that's way above my pay grade), but that doesn't mean you get to keep everybody.

See, that's where it's a real problem for a coach. You want every good player you can get. In this sport you can't have enough. You get too many injuries or a guy just loses it at some point. As coaches, we're not thinking about the money part of it when it comes time to playing the season—we're just greedy to get a good player.

If you lose one guy, it can ruin the chemistry of a whole group. Here's a primary example: After the 2009 season, we had to make a tough decision on left guard Alan Faneca. Faneca is a veteran guy, a former Pro Bowler, and won a Super Bowl with Pittsburgh before the Jets signed him as a free agent in 2008. This guy is a true pro, knows the game, and is a great anchor to have between our younger combination of center Nick Mangold and left tackle D'Brickashaw Ferguson. In a perfect world, I would have kept Faneca, but we had to make a judgment about him. I knew Faneca could still play, but I also knew he probably was not worth the kind of money he was slotted to make. Spending that much on a guard would be tough to justify, especially since we were looking at signing some young guys in the off-season to long-term contracts.

In this situation, we were talking about redoing Revis's contract and we also did new deals with Ferguson and Mangold. That meant we had to make a tough call and let Faneca go. We wanted to keep him for less, but that wasn't going to work out. He signed with Arizona, which has Russ Grimm as the offensive line coach. Faneca knew Grimm from when they were in Pittsburgh together, Grimm coaching Faneca on the Steelers' line. That made sense; it was a pretty smart move for Faneca to go work with somebody he knew. That's what all vets should do. Familiarity and comfort go a long way in this game.

Anyway, like I said, I wanted to keep Faneca but we just couldn't do it. If you watched HBO's *Hard Knocks*, you know we had problems at left guard, which is where Faneca played. We had two young guys competing to take the job. The guy who ended up starting was Matt Slauson. He's 24 years old and he's a sixth-round pick out of Nebraska. He's big, strong, tough, and smart, but he's obviously a little limited athletically. That's just reality, but he's played great for us. Our offensive line coach, Bill Callahan, knew him from when Callahan coached at Nebraska, so we knew it would be a good fit that would hopefully develop with time. Again, that's the familiarity thing that I talked about with Faneca. Football players are really smart when they work with coaches who know them and know how to use them properly.

The other guy we had over there was Vladimir Ducasse, a rookie—a good rookie, don't get me wrong. Ducasse is big and strong and he has great athletic ability. That's why we drafted him in the second round. He played left tackle at the University of Massachusetts. But he was a rookie, and if you noticed what college he went to, it wasn't one that had him competing against teams in the toughest conference every week. I was afraid it would be like going from the JV to starting for the varsity in one week. Ducasse grew up in Haiti and didn't move to the United States until 2002, when he was in high school. I don't know what kind of football they play in Haiti, if they even play it at all. He didn't start playing until he got to high school, didn't get recruited by any schools, and then ended up playing at UMass in the Colonial Athletic Association.

So he was jumping from the CAA to the NFL. Even if the guy had played football from the time he was in his mom's belly, he just wasn't ready for what he was about to see. There's nothing like Vince Wilfork or Haloti Ngata in the CAA. I'm sure there are probably some great coaches there doing some interesting things, but any coach will tell you that you're a little bit limited on what you can do when you don't have that kind of talent. You can be a defensive guru like Bill Belichick or Dom Capers, but your talent limits what you draw up. No offense to the CAA, but that's the truth.

Now, I bet what you're thinking right now is, so what does this have to do with Revis? Good point. Here's what it means and why I was still stuck at my desk at that ungodly hour: I know we're going to have to be a defensive team again this season. I'm confident our quarterback, Mark Sanchez, is going to be better, but we're not going from averaging 22 points a game (which is what we did in 2009) to putting up 30 points a game this season. That's great if we do, but I'm not expecting that because we shouldn't have to. We should be getting a lead, playing defense, and then grinding the shit out of our opponents. We don't need to be throwing the ball a ton. If we do, we're going to expose Slauson or Ducasse, which will expose Sanchez to getting pounded.

This means we better have Revis. I know it. Tannenbaum knows it. The owner knows it. Anybody with an ounce of common sense knows it. My brother Rob—even *he* called me. He knows as well as anyone: You've got to have the players. He just reminded me, in his own way, don't believe your own BS. I have to say to our guys: We're going to win no matter who lines up. That's my job and it's up to me to find answers, but guys like Revis make the answers a lot easier.

Now, I spent the entire end of last season building Revis up, because he truly deserved it. He played great in 2009. Green Bay cornerback Charles Woodson had a terrific season and I know he was named the Defensive Player of the Year, but I wouldn't take anybody ahead of Revis. You can't tell me that Woodson was better than Revis. You just can't. Nobody was better than Revis. I honestly believe that, and I said it. Hey, who pumped Darrelle Revis more than me? I put him on the map, basically because I had a platform to do so. There's no way he can doubt my sincerity on that, because I put it out there for everybody to hear. Now, in hindsight, should I have done that? Some people tell me no, that it came back to haunt us in the negotiations. I don't buy that crap. I believe in telling it like it is with the players so everybody knows what's going on. My players are never going to accuse me of being dishonest about them with the media or trying to play games with the media. Sometimes the players may not like what they hear, but they know what I say out there is exactly the same thing I tell them to their face. Sometimes they come in and I tell them what they don't want to hear, but at least I tell them the truth. That's why I have credibility; I speak from the heart. I may not always be right, but I'll speak from the heart. I'll tell you what I believe to be the truth.

It's like what I went through with Revis at the end of the off-season program. On one of the last days of the off-season program (June 14, to be specific), the whole thing came to a head. We were at practice and Revis came out of a drill saying he felt "light-headed." It was four plays of an off-season program drill and he'd been out there almost the entire time, so I wasn't going to squawk about it. He said he didn't eat, so I wasn't going to question him, even if some people thought that he was faking an injury to make a point about his contract. Like I said, the kid is great and I love him. I was not getting into it.

Then, after practice, he joked about how he might get a hamstring injury the next day, like he was planning to sit out practice and make up some excuse. So the next day, Revis said in an interview: "I did feel a little light-headed, [but] I didn't have a hamstring [injury] . . . The hamstring, I kind of exaggerated that." Later on in the conversation, he said he didn't regret doing that.

"I spoke from the heart," Revis said. (I think he stole my line.) "Some people might not like it. Some people might not care. Some people might not know who Darrelle Revis is. . . . But it doesn't matter. I spoke from the heart. . . . When you get to a frustrating point, other things start happening." Then he added, "I want to be a Jet forever. I don't want to get cut, get released, or get traded."

Then he said he was going to talk to me about it later on. He said: "We're going to try to see eye to eye and make sure this thing doesn't get out of hand. I don't want this to go negative. But negotiations do get crazy sometimes. We're trying to stop it before it gets to that point."

Unfortunately, I got asked about all that stuff before I got a chance to talk to him and I said: "It's so not him. It's uncharacteristic of him to get out of anything. I got to hear it from the horse's mouth. I know what he told [the media]. . . . It might just be that this is a thing that he wanted to do. And that's fine. But he knows that's not right . . . My door's always open. He knows that. He'll probably just get me for a couple minutes."

Now things were getting sticky, because he knew where I was coming from. He knew I'd been totally supportive of him, telling everybody who would listen how great he was. But then he pulled the injury stunt, and I didn't even hear about it from him but from the media. Well, he came into my office afterward and must have apologized 50 times. I told him, "You put me in a bad way. I love you but you understand I'm not going to have this. I'd rather that you just stay home instead of us going through this. You've got to understand something: We're going to plan on winning either way."

That was earlier in the preseason, and now, when he hasn't shown up, I kind of figure he is taking me up on what I said he should do. I don't like that it turned out that way, but I'm glad he isn't around the team acting like a jerk. What he did in June, he knows the way he was acting. So if he's going to continue like that in training camp, I figure he is doing me a favor by not coming to camp. We're in the middle of trying to build a team, and if everybody isn't pulling in the same direction it can destroy everything you're trying to do.

Still, it has gotten to a point where we have to fix this thing. We play in our final preseason game and I get home to my house in New Jersey after the game. I invited Neil Schwartz, one of Revis's agents, over to the house. Schwartz lives in Montebello, New York, about 40 minutes from my house, and arrives there before I get home. My wife lets him in and they talk for about 20 minutes or so. At one point, she says to him, "Are you the agent who told Rex that Weeb was the longest-tenured coach in team history?" You've got to give her credit; she pays attention. Finally, I get there and Schwartz and I go to the kitchen to talk. I have to give Schwartz credit; he's pretty funny. There are four chairs around the table, so he sits in one, I sit in another, and he drapes a Revis jersey over one of the other chairs. It makes me chuckle.

Over the next two hours, we talk a lot. At times, it is pretty hard for me to not want to reach across the table and just grab that skinny Schwartz and scream, "Get me my player!" But I resist. He explains his concerns over our offer and explains their proposal. Every time Schwartz talks about Darrelle, he points at the jersey. "Yeah, yeah, I get it," I think. "Now, get me the player." Again, I'm not negotiating anything here. That's not my job. I'm just trying to get the communication going, because we're not even really talking at this point. I've got to make something happen so we can get this done.

What I've always heard from people is that big deals like this are as much about relationships as anything else, and right now we've got no relationship. Revis is sitting in his house down in South Florida, outside of Fort Lauderdale, doing nothing but working out a little and hiding from the media. No matter how much he's working out, I know he's not in football shape and I know it's getting down to the wire to get him ready. So I'm sitting here at some crazy hour of the morning talking to Schwartz. We talk baseball for a while. He collects autographed baseballs just like I do, and we go downstairs and look at my collection. At that point, I tell him I've always wanted to get a Satchel Paige ball and he tells me he has one. Then he tells me, "Rex, if we get a long-term deal done, I'll give you the Satchel Paige ball." I laugh and think nothing of it. It's a good conversation, but I know this is just the start. We've got to get to Revis. It will have to be owner Woody Johnson and me. It has to be Woody because he has to be comfortable with this. No disrespect to Mike Tannenbaum, but he doesn't make the final decision any more than I do.

Schwartz leaves my house probably sometime around 4 A.M. We're both exhausted, and he offers me the jersey. I tell him, "I don't want the jersey, I want the player." I know what Schwartz is trying to do, but I can go get the jersey for free.

Later that morning, I am on the phone with Tannenbaum and Mr. Johnson, explaining what's going on. We agree that we need to meet with Revis. So Mr. Johnson and I fly down to Florida later in the day and sit down with Revis and his whole family. I give Mr. Johnson a lot of credit. I have been so focused on the immediate, this season, trying like hell to win our first game against Baltimore. But Mr. Johnson changes the whole deal and talks to Revis about the Hall of Fame. That is smart, because it gets Revis thinking about the big picture, what this all means, his image. Mr. Johnson sits there explaining how much he admires Revis, how highly he thinks of him, and I think that really is when Revis starts to realize that this isn't some short-term relationship. Mr. Johnson is thinking about the big picture. We end up leaving on better terms. There's still no deal, but we're making progress. We fly back to New Jersey, and now it's up to Tannenbaum and Schwartz. We know from talking to Schwartz that there's a way to get a short-term deal done. There's a compromise.

Saturday night comes and goes and we get into Sunday, and I'm getting edgy—and now I'm going to let those guys know what this really means. The time for trying to get this done peacefully is over and I drop into Rex the Wrecking Crew. It's tantrum time for me. I let everybody have a piece of my mind. Both sides get a taste of it. He wanted to play, I wanted him to play, but it wasn't happening, so I was letting everybody have it. These guys are talking about the right amount, and it has to be on a four-year deal versus the long-term deal and all kinds of technical, minutiae crap, and I'm trying to tell them, "I don't care about any of that, because if we don't win, *I'm not going to be here in four years."*

Now, don't get me wrong, there are no excuses. If Revis doesn't play for us this season, we still have to win—and we still can win. But let's be realistic: Revis is a bigger piece of the puzzle than a lot of other guys. He makes me a better coach. He makes our secondary coach, Dennis Thurman, a better coach. Heck, he makes our offensive coordinator, Brian Schottenheimer, a better coach. That's reality. That's what star players do in this league. They make the job of the coaches easier, and they make us better. But if you don't have them, you better find a way—that's the job of the coach. Again, there are no excuses.

So I make my point, and by around midnight, they finally get the thing agreed to. Both sides ended up happy. Tannenbaum put in some clauses to keep another holdout from happening, which I'm glad to hear, because I can't take this shit again.

Anyway, after the deal is done, everybody gets together on Monday, September 6, in Tannenbaum's office. It's Mike, Mr. Johnson, the two agents (Schwartz and Feinsod), and me. After it all gets done, Schwartz pulls out this baseball with the Satchel Paige autograph and gives it to me. I blink. "But we didn't get the long-term deal done."

"That's okay, Rex, you deserve it," he says.

I guess you could say that was my commission for helping get the deal done. I guess that's not bad, all told. But all I really want is for Revis to be good and for us to win. If that happens, I can buy all the baseballs I want myself.

20. Bring It On: Putting Pressure on Yourself

Let me start this off by saying that I love our general manager, Mike Tannenbaum. He is awesome for me because he is everything I'm not. You need that in an organization. You need people who complement you. Whatever I don't do well, I need somebody to cover for me. When it comes to putting together a team, running the contracts and the salary cap, that's where Tannenbaum comes in. He will kill you with paper. He has volumes and volumes of information right at his fingertips. I'm the guy who says, "Can you give me the *Reader's Digest* version or just give me something in color? Laminate it and I'll read it. Just make sure it's on one page." I'm not going to read a 500-page report. I can't. Literally, I can't. It would take me forever. Mike will go through everything, every word. He's always saying, "Did you see that?" or "Oh yeah, I read that on page X."

Trust me, I know I scare Tannenbaum sometimes. He's very careful about what he says or what he does. Me, well, you have the picture by now. The difference is that sometimes when you know everything, when you have read every possibility, it's easy to get overwhelmed by the information. That happens in football a lot. We do all these printouts and readouts and tendency charts, and this and that. Sometimes we forget to just look at the situation and say, "Okay, I know what they're going to do and here's the play to run against it."

Here's a great example. In the third game of the 2009 season, we were playing Tennessee at home. We were 2-0 already; they were 0-2—and this is after they made the playoffs the year before and I was still in Baltimore. We beat their ass then, and we were about to beat their ass again now that I was with the Jets. The Titans had Kerry Collins at quarterback and he is a wily vet, but he's also an old guy—and an old guy who doesn't want to be hit. He's strictly a pocket passer at this point in his career; not that he was ever all that mobile, but I knew in that game he was not taking off for a 40-yard run unless all 11 of our guys broke their legs simultaneously.

Anyway, we were leading 24-17 and it was fourth down. They needed 23 yards after a penalty and a sack moved them back. Fourth-and-23 is an eternity. You convert that play about once a decade. I can play just about any defense, and we had a good chance to stop that play no matter what. In that type of situation, most coaches play it safe. They might call some three-man pass rush and have eight guys sitting back, making sure nothing goes over their heads.

Me? I figured it was time to all-out blitz. Upstairs, Tannenbaum was watching this and he was looking at all the risk, how a big play could tie the game, and all of those factors. Tannenbaum is a smart football guy. He's been around the game long enough to know what most people would do. To me, those coaches play it safe because that's what everybody does. If they get beat, they can look at the GM and the owner and say, "How can I help that? I did what everybody else did." They're scared to do what they think might really be right, because they think they'll be second-guessed and lose their jobs. That's why all those people who second-guessed New England coach Bill Belichick later in the year for going on fourth-and-2 in his own territory against Indianapolis didn't have a clue. Yeah, it didn't work, but are you seriously telling me that anybody could know his team better than Belichick? He's the best out there. I have total respect for him. As I said before, I'm not kissing his rings and I'm not afraid of him, but I respect him.

Anyway, I knew what the best call was for my team in that situation, and that was an all-out blitz. Why? Here's how I looked at it: If I left Collins back there, he was going to recognize the coverage and I knew he had a strong enough arm to stick a pass against a good secondary. He may be old, but he can throw the damn ball. The other part about it was that I knew the Titans' protection schemes. I knew what they were doing the previous season and I knew what they were doing in the present one. So I knew that if I dialed up a certain blitz, we were going to get to Collins before he had a chance to let one of his receivers get far enough downfield to hurt us.

The other part of this was that I knew our chances of being called for a pass interference call were pretty high if I just let Collins throw the ball. In other words, I'd analyzed the entire situation and I knew it was time to call the blitz. Just as I expected, they can't handle the blitz, Collins has to get rid of it too fast, and the ball falls incomplete. In fact, we did the same thing this year against Minnesota in Brett Favre's first game (and one of his few games) playing with Randy Moss. I wasn't afraid to blitz that guy, either, and he's had a much better career than Collins. Favre's one of the greatest of all time.

Anyway, we walked into the locker room, I talked to the team and the media, and I headed back to my office. Tannenbaum came in and looked at me for a minute, then said, "Rex, I just have to ask you: What were you thinking with that blitz at the end of the game?"

I just looked back at Tannenbaum, smiled, and said, "Oh, I figured out their protections."

Tannenbaum didn't quite get it. "What if they made an adjustment?"

"They wouldn't."

Tannenbaum was still curious. That's his nature—he's always thinking about what if this and what if that. That's who he is and that's his job. So he pondered that a second and then asked, "What if we didn't get there on time?"

Hey, I understand, some people get scared at those critical moments, wondering about the downside, about what happens if you fail. I get it. Me, I'm not worried. Like I told him the first two times, I had it down. So all I said was, "Mike, I knew what they were going to do." I think that's when Tannenbaum really started to understand my sense of confidence, that all my bravado wasn't based on BS. I'm not just talk; I know what I'm doing.

That's why when I say, "We're going to win a Super Bowl," it's not just bluster. I really believe it. That's why back in August 2010, when the ESPN guys came rolling through training camp up in Cortland, New York, I wrote on the side of their tour bus, "Soon To Be Champs." I know we have the team and the right mix of talent and I still believe that firmly. I knew it in 2000 with Baltimore and I said it before that season. It's just that I was a defensive line coach in his second year with the team back then and nobody really gave a damn what I had to say. I said the same thing in 2006 with the Ravens. We didn't win it, but we lost to the team that did win it (Indianapolis) and we would have beat their ass if we had caught one of the two interceptions we had in our hands. It's a shame, too, because that defense might have gone down as one of the greatest of all time if we had won it all. Instead, nobody will ever remember it.

In 2008, 2009, and 2010 I was with teams that lost in the AFC Championship Game. Does that bother me? In some ways, yes. But am I damn proud of that run? Hell yes. I don't see it as a cluster of seasons where we failed to bring home the title. I see it as a terrific accomplishment, a springboard to a big run of success with the Jets. And eventually we're going to win this thing.

I've always believed we could win every game. If you really believe it, then you shouldn't be afraid to say it. I remember in 2009 sitting in the coaches' meetings and talking about how the game was going to go. I'd say something like, "Oh, we're going to kick their ass here and pound the crap out of them there" and Cam Cameron, our offensive coordinator, would just look up with this big smile and say, "Rex, you're beautiful." Cameron is different from me. He's a good guy and very smart, kind of like a professor, kind of proper—and a great play caller. I think I just got the juices flowing for him, saying stuff he'd probably never think of saying aloud to a big group, even if he thought it. I don't know why, but I believe not just in myself but in everybody.

Some people think that's putting undue pressure on yourself and all that jazz, that a coach should be some civil, polite guy in public who downplays expectations to keep everybody on an even keel. Well, here's my thinking on that strategy: To hell with it.

I didn't become a coach so that we could do our darndest to try to win a few ballgames and try to just be competitive every year so that we could have a chance because you know this is a tough league and all. I became a coach because I wanted to be great at this. I wanted to win championships. I wanted to help other people win championships. I wanted to be part of a group that could do something special. I get so freaking tired of coaches who try to downplay expectations. You know what they're really trying to do? They're trying to cover their ass in case what they say the first time doesn't work out so that they have excuses. I came here to win titles, not just come in second place and feel like that was good enough.

It's like when I say, "We're going to kick their ass," I mean we're going to kick their ass. My best one last year was when we were playing Houston in the season opener. Everybody thought we weren't ready, that we had no chance because they had such a great offense with Matt Schaub and Andre Johnson and all that crew. Everybody doubted us, but they didn't have a clue. They didn't realize we had saved a bunch of stuff in preseason, we hadn't shown anything, and the Texans had no idea what was coming. On top of not showing anything, we were without two of our best players, Calvin Pace and Shaun Ellis, who were suspended at the time. But I knew what was going to happen. I knew what the Texans would do and what we were going to do to it.

We were getting ready to beat the shit out of one of the top two or three offenses in the NFL, so I told our team how it was going to go, how we were going to pummel the crap out of the team. "We're going to show the whole NFL, the whole league is going to know after today what we're going to be" was running through my head. "That secret is going to be out." That was my first game as a head coach, my first opportunity, and I told the players how special this was going to be for all of us. I can't even remember the exact words, but I said something along the lines of "Go to sleep tonight knowing we're getting ready to kick the shit out of this team." Guess what? We beat the crap out of the Texans on their home field. Right in the middle of their pretty Reliant Stadium with the cool retractable roof, we beat their ass. They didn't score until the fourth quarter. Heck, they didn't really score so much as we gave them one, a fumble their defense returned for a score. Their offense? Guano, nada, zip, not a point. Oh, it was beautiful, and the best part is how much that helped the players and their confidence. That's one of the big reasons why we started 3-0: We were confident. We believed we really could do everything I talked about.

Look, I'm that way all the time; I have that confidence and I want the players to get a good night's rest, going to bed with that same confidence, thinking that way. Really, I think you can will your way to victory sometimes if you have the right mind-set. I've told our guys, if the only people we have left in the building are me, the cook, Mike Tannenbaum, Woody Johnson, and maybe the janitor, I believe that we can go out and get it done. I want to hit that field with that mentality. I smile at the other coaches and the officials and I tell them all the time: "If you let us play, we will beat the crap out of this team, and I mean it. I absolutely mean it. I know I've got tough guys. I know my guys are better than your guys."

Now, I'm not so dumb as to think we'll never lose. You're going to lose some games. But you have to be confident about what you're doing and you have to believe. That's what I think. I don't think about failure. I believe the pressure you put on yourself is what drives you to be better. That stuff drives you when everything else is going bad. Hey, we hit our rough spots last year—there was a reason we finished 9-7. But when you start to lose, you can't sit around looking for excuses and trying to explain why you're losing. Again, that's that same old crap I hear from coaches who are trying to couch everything in noncommittal terms by saying, "We're going to make progress, we're on the right track, we're not looking too far ahead." Don't give me that. I'm looking to win the Super Bowl, and I'll tell you that's what I expect. I want my guys thinking that, too. I want them amped up, pushing themselves as hard as they can. Are they going to do that if I'm saying stuff like "I think we have a chance, maybe, perhaps, if everything goes right"? No way.

Of course, when I'm saying what I say, it doesn't come out pretty and polished. As Bart Scott mentioned, I get pretty f-bomb happy on occasion. That's who I am, love it or leave it. If you notice, though, I'm not swearing *at* my players. Well, at least not in some "You stupid mother . . ." way of doing it. I swear in front of them, like I'm making a point. People can say what they want about me or the way I choose to talk to my players. I honestly could not care less. There are players and coaches in this league who have done far worse things than throw a few f-bombs here and there. It's like I told *The New York Times Magazine*: "I never tortured or killed animals. I'm an animal lover! I used a few cusswords! At the end of the day, no matter what, I'll walk out the door and say I always was who I am."

Really, all this stuff just motivates me, and I think it motivates the players because they know how behind them I am. If the newspapers want to make fun of me, go ahead. Now, be funny. That "Fatman and Robin" headline with me and Sanchez was pretty good. There are guys dressed up in the stands like Batman and Robin now. That's hilarious, but you go ahead and make your jokes now. I'm going to be on the cover of GQ by next year. At least, that's what I'm telling myself.

My point is that pressure doesn't bother me. That stuff is just joking around. I love to watch special moments in sports, like when

Buster Douglas beat Mike Tyson. That was an awesome fight. I'll watch the whole thing when it's on, because you see what kind of heart Douglas had during that fight. Or there's the story about the heart of Secretariat. Secretariat was the greatest racehorse ever, totally dominant. He was a big, strong horse—a real monster. When they did the autopsy on Secretariat, they found out his heart was twice as big as other horses'. You hear talk about the heart of a champion, and that's a literal example. You have to have that strength. I've watched the Boston Celtics with Kevin Garnett, Paul Pierce, and Ray Allen, and you see that heart. You look at Derek Jeter with the Yankees. He talked one time about how they were going to make every single out matter, every single at bat matter, for all 162 games—and then they did it. That's how much one guy can influence a whole team, getting everybody to lay it on the line for each other. A real coach knows the value of that kind of heart, that kind of charisma, that kind of leader.

It's like our decision to take a quarterback with our first-round pick in 2009 while I was talking about winning right away. If you want to win now, you don't take a rookie quarterback because now the odds are stacked against you, but I knew we needed a young guy to build with, so I said we should do it. I wasn't afraid to do that. I also wasn't afraid to say we were going to win anyway. We had one game in 2010 where we lost in overtime to Buffalo even though we ran for 318 yards. Why? Sanchez threw five interceptions. That's going to happen when you have a young quarterback. Was I happy? No, but was it right to take him? Absolutely, yes. Look, if you want to be a champion, you have to have a quarterback, and I said we were going to be champions so we had to have a quarterback. Yeah, he's young and I took a big chance, but I have never wanted to be like every other coach. I'm going to do what I believe is right, what is right in my heart. If that means more pressure, fine, I'll take it. The pressure just pushes me to be great, and that's really what it's all about.

21. Let's Go Snack

Here's the ironic part about the whole weight thing: I was never this heavy until I devoted myself to coaching. I guess this is the price I pay for having such devotion to the game. When I was in college, I was an undersized defensive lineman. I couldn't even put on weight when I tried. I would eat all the time, even six peanut-butter-and-jelly sandwiches for lunch. Literally, it was like we had an assembly line: I'd do the peanut butter, Rob would do the jelly, then we'd put them in a bag and off to work we'd go. That's just how we did things. But I didn't really grow much.

The problem was that even when I was playing, I was always going and going and going. We'd practice and I'd go for a run. I remember one of the assistant coaches when we were in college would always joke that if they could bottle up my energy and Rob's energy, we could all make millions. Seriously, I would practice and then go run six miles a day. I just loved to move. Even early in my coaching career, when my dad brought me to Arizona to work with him, we used to run all the time. If we were done at midnight or even 3 A.M., we'd run three miles or whatever, just get the body moving. Now, that's the frustrating part: People see me now and they have no idea what I looked like before. My only help is Jeff Weeks, our defensive assistant, who went to college with Rob and me. He knows, he's my witness. He saw me when I was skinny.

That's when I had it goin' on. Oh yeah, I had the guts to ask some serious women out, which is the only way I ended up with my wife. Some of the other women were way out of my league. Back in high school, I went out with this 20-year-old Playboy Bunny named Roz. I'm serious—my brother will verify. We met at some couples skate event at the roller rink. You were supposed to ask a girl to skate with you, so I went for it. Back then and all through college, I was a good-looking guy and very confident about those situations. Now my looks are all distorted, which bothers me, but I'm still comfortable with who I am when you get right down to it.

Anyway, back then I was thinking, "Hey, you only live once, so you might as well take your shot." She was smokin' hot. Rob said she was the best-looking girl in history. So I hit her with "Where are you from, heaven? You look like an angel to me." She bought it, and I was shocked. I'm serious as a heart attack—she not only bought the line, she agreed to go out with me. I have no idea where she is now, but it happened. That night, Rob and I took her and her friend out for pancakes, some stupid kid thing. Remember, I was in high school. As Rob likes to say now, it was one of those Ripley's Believe It or Not moments.

Of course, where I really got lucky was with Michelle. She is gorgeous, smart, skinny, and unbelievably strong, reliable, and supportive. I still can't believe that I got lucky enough to find someone that amazing . . . and that willing to put up with me.

I know plenty of women in this job—and being a coach's wife is a job—who get resentful and jealous, jealous of the game and how much guys like me love it, jealous of the competition that we eat up. Trust me that my wife could also be resentful of everything I eat up, literally, after I took this job. I was 200 pounds when we got married.

I've gained about 150 pounds at my heaviest. It's not right, but she never really says a word to me. Yeah, she might say, "Honey, you're looking a little husky, you should drop some weight." Husky? I look like the refrigerator. I have lost the weight before. I got down to 235 one time, then bounced right back to 310. I was 310 when I took this job, and all of a sudden it was 340. Is it the stress? Is it that I'm so happy? I don't know exactly why, but I know that I'm loving what I'm doing so much right now, I don't want my health to get in the way of this time in my life.

I hear people say that you should just make time to work out, that's the answer. Right—when am I going to do that in this job the way it needs to be done? As it is, I don't see my family enough, and now I'm supposed to get up an hour or hour and a half earlier so I can hit the treadmill? Look, I've done that and I know it's the best way, but it's not realistic. I'm 48 years old and I'm the head coach of this team. I love doing my job and I love my family. If I have to sacrifice somewhere, I'll do it another way.

That's why lap-band surgery was important for me. I dropped 40 pounds almost right away and I felt so much better. The inspiration for me was Tony Siragusa. He told me he got to be over 400 pounds at one time and then decided to do the procedure and got back down to 325 right away. Jamie Dukes, the old offensive lineman who is with the NFL Network now, he had it, too. We also had a woman in our office who did it, and it really worked. The only drawback for her was that she would throw up if she ate too much. I hate throwing up. I'll just fight through it rather than throw up. When people look at me they say, "Just get rid of it if you're feeling bad," but I just can't.

I had to do the surgery, even when my brother was telling me not to. I had to get off that roller coaster of dieting, then ballooning back up. And it's been the greatest thing I ever did. I studied it beforehand to make sure it was the right choice for me. So did our owner, Woody Johnson. In fact, the band is one that's made by his company, Johnson & Johnson. He got involved and he said, "If you're going to do this, we're going to find the best person." The other thing I did was look at the gastric bypass option. I wasn't going to do that. I found out that 3 percent of the people who do that die, and I know that Charlie Weis had real problems with it. Plus, I've heard that people eventually gain some of the weight back. Probably not so bad that it's not a good idea, but eventually your stomach stretches out again even with the gastric bypass. I know there are ways around the lap band. People who eat a lot of ice cream don't have as much success with the lap band. Still, it just seemed like a better option for me. Look, either way that people do it, I understand. Once you get on the eating roller coaster, it's so hard to get off it. It's brutal.

The funny thing is that I didn't do it because my health was awful. I'd go to the doctor and all the tests would come back looking fine. My cholesterol, my blood pressure, liver function, and kidney function—all that stuff was just fine. Back in Baltimore, the doctor used to bust my balls all the time. He looked at me and said, "You look great . . . on paper." I'm huge. I love to eat. Like I said, my favorite is Mexican food. I just love tacos. Then there's pizza and lasagna. Yeah, just pour on the carbs. I don't even know how many I'd eat when we went out—probably more after a loss, but you just eat because you love it. You start and all of a sudden you forget how much you have pounded down because you're having such a good time. It's like at Thanksgiving—I love all that food. You get turkey, stuffing, green bean casserole, the cranberry sauce, the corn, then pecan pie, pumpkin pie, apple pie.

Yeah, just line up the pies and keep them coming.

The lap band has been great for me, because now I still eat a lot of that stuff; I just can't eat as much. Now when I'm full, I stop or it gets uncomfortable, or if I try to have something like a cheeseburger, I feel awful. The bread just expands in my stomach and I'm miserable. With pizza, now all I can do is eat the toppings, not the bread. I get pissed about it, but that works for me. I have to watch what I eat, because physically I'm not going to feel good. We still go out after games, but I get uncomfortable very quickly and I just stop eating. It's perfect. I will tell anybody who needs this that they should do it. I feel great now and I don't have to constantly think, "Hey, how much did I eat earlier today? What can I eat now?" When you're going and going and going the way we do in this job, it's like you're always looking for something to fuel you.

Maybe that's why I always end every team meeting with the line "Let's go snack." Now, I know people who were watching that stuff on *Hard Knocks* were thinking, "Yeah, there goes the fat guy. He can't wait to eat." But that's not how I'm thinking about it. Yes, I love to eat, but I also want guys to finish on a positive note after a meeting. It's one thing to talk about being great, but you have to follow through on it. That's the point of putting pressure on yourself, to keep you working at it. Now, I want the guys to have fun when we're doing our job, but I make sure they know we're here for a purpose, even if we may not all be here forever.

That's one of the things that had been brought up about the 2010 season. They said that we were just going for it this year, which is why we brought in Jason Taylor, LaDainian Tomlinson, Braylon Edwards, Santonio Holmes, and Antonio Cromartie. All those guys are either at an age where they could retire soon or they had one-year contracts and would be free agents at the end of the season. I hear people say that those guys are "rentals."

Well, for many of these players this may be a rent-to-own situation. You don't know what's going to happen with certain guys and we're open on a lot of fronts. Some players are best off when they have that one-year deal, where the pressure is on them all the time to make good decisions, work as hard as they can. That's a tough decision, and that's where you have to be a business manager in this job as well. Obviously, that's where Mike Tannenbaum gets the brunt of it. The key thing is we'll never keep a player I don't want just because of salary. We have to do what's best for the football team. Sometimes it's a tough decision, like letting Thomas Jones and Alan Faneca go. Sometimes it's an easy one, like letting Eric Barton and Chris Baker go. With Faneca, it was really hard, but I was able to lean on coaches like Bill Callahan and Director of Player

Development Dave Szott. It was the same type of situation we had with our kicker, Jay Feely. I didn't want him to go. Mike Westhoff, our special-teams coach, loved him and Feely was a guy who was emotionally tough. He could handle the pressure in New York, but we let him go and got Nick Folk, and Folk has been great for us. I wanted to keep Marques Douglas, but I couldn't. I've been around that guy for like 10 years. He's one of my guys, but these are the decisions you make because of the rules.

Coming into the 2010 season we were in a tough spot. Because we finished in the top four of the league in 2009—meaning, we were one of the four teams to make the conference championship games—we were really limited about what we could do. It'll be the same thing preparing for 2011. If we lost a player in free agency, we could sign somebody. Otherwise, we had to wait until June to sign some guys, like we did last year with backup quarterback Mark Brunell and Jason Taylor. Now, some teams might complain about those rules because it was all based on the fact that the collective bargaining agreement went into the last year and there was no salary cap. What I did was use it as motivation for our guys. I told them that we were going to lose some players and not be able to replace them because of the rules. That meant they were going to have to find ways to get better on their own. They were going to have to find solutions. All we had to do was get a little bit better across the board and we could get to the top of the game, because we were already a conference finalist. We were that close—it wasn't going to take much more to get to the Super Bowl. So coming into last year each guy worked his butt off. Physically, we got better in the weight room. We are the only team in the league that had 100 percent participation in the off-season program. I knew that as a coach I was going to have to get better, too, if we were going to stay with teams like Indianapolis and New England. That's how it is every year.

So when people say we're just going for it one given year, I tell them that's complete bull. We're going for it every year. I'm trying to win every year with the best collection of players I can get for that given season or set of circumstances. Did it hurt us in 2010 that we brought in Taylor or Tomlinson? Hell, no. They weren't taking some guy's job away or keeping some young guy on the bench. Those young guys that we had to have play, like Matt Slauson, they're out there. They're getting their chance. With Taylor and Tomlinson, we knew they'd help us and we knew we'd have to fill that position somewhere down the line.

When you get desperate, you're bringing in guys you don't care about. You're bringing in guys to just be mercenaries. I never do that. That's why with Edwards, Holmes, and Cromartie, I'm not hoping they leave. I'm hoping our mutual experience has been so great that they want to stay and that we can find a way to make it work. The thing I'm going to make sure they understand is I'm 100 percent behind them. However long they're here, they're my guys and I'm supporting them. Yeah, there are going to be some rough times along the way. Guys are going to get in trouble here and there. I don't like it and I don't want them to like it, but it happens and we're going to fix it. Maybe that means that I'm going to rip somebody's ass once in a while, but when I'm done I trust it won't happen again and I'm letting that moment go.

My guys are professionals and I respect them. I also support them, and I do whatever I can to have their backs. That's why I try to end everything on a positive note and keep us all together as a group.

That's why I always say, "Let's go snack."

22. We'll Be Back

O kay, time to get back to the rest of our 2010 season . . . and the *Monday Night Football* game in New England. We were flying high at 9-2—as were the Patriots—but let's remember that no matter how well things seem to be going, in the NFL the whole mood of a team can change in a snap. It's just like I was talking about in the beginning with blunt-force trauma. You get that first big hit, the one that can set the tone, and that moment can change everything right away.

The same thing can happen in a snap. The snap of a bone, in this case. It happened on the Friday before we were scheduled to play at New England on Monday, December 6. All week leading up to this game, I'm talking about how big this game is, how it's the clash of the titans, the whole deal. The AFC East title is resting on this game. Both teams are 9-2. We've won four in a row and nine of 10. Yeah, we've been a little lucky, but we're playing good football overall and, most important, we're winning.

Likewise, New England is rolling along now. They've dealt with all the distraction from trading Randy Moss earlier in the season. They bring back Deion Branch just after trading Moss and Branch is getting on a roll. They've won three straight coming into this game and put up 39, 31, and 45 points in those games. Tom Brady is really starting to crank it up.

Still, we had beaten them earlier in the season and we're feeling very confident this whole week. Really, really confident. I'm putting myself out there, as usual, but that's all part of the plan. The important part is that the players are feeling loose, prepared, really on top of what they need to do. Nobody plays the Patriots better than we do, as we showed in the playoffs, and we just felt like this was going to be the same thing. We were going to play them hard.

Then, late in practice Friday, free safety Jim Leonhard breaks his leg. When I say he broke his leg, let me tell you, you knew it right away. You could hear it. It was a compound fracture and you knew just from the sound that it was bad. It was a crazy thing. It was the end of a defensive team period. The receiver is going up to get the ball and Jim is going to challenge it, trying to make a play on the football. Well, Jim does make a great play to get the ball, and he comes down and looks like he's landing and turning all at once. He wasn't even hit, but his leg snaps right there.

What made it seem stranger is that in the two years I've been head coach of the Jets, we haven't had an injury like that on the practice field. We've had them in games, but we've been good in practice. Nothing. We've had pulled hamstrings, but nothing major, so the players aren't really expecting it in any way. Well, as soon as it happens, it's like we're completely deflated. It was a killer moment. All the great energy from the week was gone, and you can't have that when you're playing New England. You have to be all in against the Patriots, both physically and mentally, or you're not going to beat them.

I know what some people are going to say: "Coach, you're talking about Jim Leonhard, not Darrelle Revis or Bart Scott or David Harris or Antonio Cromartie." People don't understand what Leonhard means to our team. Look, I talked about him earlier in the book.

He was one of the guys I brought with me from Baltimore. He's a scrappy, tough, smart guy who has worked hard to make himself into a terrific player. Leonhard is all of 5-foot-8 and about 190 pounds after a big dinner. But he's going to hit you and he's going to be smart.

When I mean smart, I mean quarterback smart. He was the guy who was the quarterback of our defense, the guy who made the calls and got people into the right spots all the time. So put it this way: How do you think most teams would do if they had their quarterback break his leg and had to play a game three days later? I'm not trying to say we would have won the game. We got killed 45-3. That's the worst beatdown of my career. That was the Monday Night Massacre, the Monday Night Meltdown, the Monday Night Beatdown, whatever you want to call it. We got outplayed and outcoached in every phase of the game.

And I mean every single phase. The only thing we did right in this game was hold them to a field goal on their first drive. We didn't tackle, we didn't cover, we played horrible on offense, we had a punt go 12 yards, it was everything. Even the weather seemed to affect us. We were cold and couldn't get anything going. You looked at their sideline and their guys are into it, really pumped up. That's why I said Belichick outcoached me that night. He did, he had his guys ready to play. I didn't. That's why I took the heat.

But let me say this, if we'd had Leonhard, there's no way we would have been beaten that bad. I'm telling you, we were having the best week of practice we've ever had. We had put in a very complicated scheme for that week against New England and Leonhard was on top of it. He had it down. As soon as he got hurt, it was total deflation. It was horrible. I could feel it with the players and I think they sensed it coming from me. As soon as Leonhard got hurt, I still thought we could win, but I know that I was confused for a little while about how we were going to do that. I think the players picked up on that confusion. It doesn't take a lot of mental gymnastics for guys to pick up on what I'm feeling, because I'm not a phony. I didn't know how we were going to scale back the defense and make things work.

Remember, after Friday, you really only have one more walk-through practice for the week, so we didn't have time to work with Dwight Lowery, Leonhard's backup, on much more than the base calls.

And, trust me, you're not beating the Patriots with base calls and formations. You run base formation against Tom Brady and he's going to kill you. They took it right to us. They ran up the score and they talked trash to us. Their fans were complete assholes to us. They let us have it. I've never had my butt kicked like that in my life, and I admitted it at the postgame press conference. But I also said I'd play them again, right now. I would have gone right back out on the field and played again. If I get decked in a fight and a guy gets the best of me, I'm fighting again. If it takes 50 times to win the fight, then I'm fighting 50 times. The other thing is—and I'm not saying it's physically possible for a team to have gone out there and played another game right away—but I believe if I had walked in and said, "Men, let's go out there again," I think I have the kind of guys who would have followed me back out there.

Of course, when it got to playoff time, all of us who got our butts kicked that day were able to settle up the score. But trust me when I say that it took some rough weeks to get there. We weren't done playing poorly that day and we still had a lot to overcome and a lot to deal with, on and off the field. The next week, we played Miami at home and we end up losing 10-6. We handed Miami 10 stupid points in the first quarter on two turnovers. Their two scoring drives go for a combined 39 yards and we hand them 10 points. The Dolphins didn't do anything to us on offense the entire game. Nothing. They finished with 131 yards of total offense and only 55 yards passing.

Then, on top of the fact that we lost to Miami, we have our latest bit of news to follow us when the league discovers that Sal Alosi, our strength and conditioning coach, had tripped one of the Dolphins players. I'm telling you right now, I had no idea about it. Mike Westhoff, our special-teams coach, had no idea about it. I promise you that. I'd happily take a lie-detector test to prove it. I didn't see

Alosi forming that wall with the other players and I didn't see Alosi trip the Dolphins guy. I saw the kid on the sideline, hurt, and I'm trying to get the Miami trainers to come over and look at him. That trip was wrong, it was stupid, and it's really a shame because Alosi is a heck of a coach. He was doing good work here.

It's funny, he really didn't want to be here at first. When I came to the Jets after the 2008 season, and I met him to see if he wanted to stay on staff, he acted kind of aloof. He was tight with Eric Mangini and I felt that he wanted to get let go from his contract so he could go to Cleveland. That's fine, if you want to leave, you can go. It's always a little awkward for the assistant coaches who were part of an old regime when a new head coach arrives. But before Sal walked out of the room, I said: "Let me tell you something. Whoever gets this job is going to have the best strength and conditioning job in the NFL, because I'm going to let you do what you want. I don't know anything about strength and conditioning, so I'm going to trust you to do the job the way you want to do it. I'm not going to interfere." So as we're talking, he's coming around and by the end of the conversation, he's telling me he wants to stay and he ends up being great for us. He really worked hard. He had great ideas. He had motivational stuff, too. It's a shame this all happened. The guy made a stupid mistake. Everybody makes mistakes. But I think he's a hell of a coach.

Anyway, that story goes on in the news for a while. We had to suspend Alosi (later on, after the season, he eventually resigned) and fine him, and the league fined us. We got all these questions from the league and from the media. But the other issue that's going on, the one that's really more important to the whole team at this point, is that our quarterback was struggling. When I say that Mark Sanchez was struggling, I mean he was shitty. For the past two games, we couldn't move the ball at all.

Now remember, as I said before, Sanchez has done some amazing things so far in his young career. He has four road playoff victories in his first two seasons—which actually ties him for the NFL record. You have no idea how great an accomplishment that is in this league. But that doesn't mean he's a finished product. He has his ups and his downs. In 2010, he reduced the ups and downs significantly, so that was great progress. But he still had them, and this two-game stretch was a prime example of what the downs can look like. We go two games and all we scored were three field goals. It was terrible.

The worst part is that when you struggle so much like that, it can tug at guys in the locker room. In this case, we had some defensive guys complaining about the offense. Never mind that we got torched by New England the game before, the defense started grousing about the offense. That happens and you have to deal with it.

The way I had to deal with it was first talking to Sanchez, because you have to be honest about it. I called him into my office and I told him. Also, that week, I started giving our backup quarterback, Mark Brunell, more snaps in practice just to let Sanchez know I wasn't kidding around. Now, it got Sanchez's ass going sideways a little bit. He wasn't happy at all. When he was in my office, he was pouting a little about it, but I could give less than two shits about that. I'm in the win business. The rest of that week, Sanchez is still getting killed in the papers, so I just let him deal with it. Now we have to get ready to play at Pittsburgh and I need to have him on top of his game, keyed up.

But by the end of the week, on Saturday night, I shifted it. The night before we play the Steelers, I put the burden on everyone BUT Sanchez. I called out our defense. I called out our offensive line. Sanchez had already taken his heat. Those guys had to hear it now. Those are the two groups that I know can handle it. Why, the night before a big game after a week where he's been taking heat from everybody, would I put it on the quarterback now? The kid is 24 years old. At that point, it was up to the veterans on the defense and the offensive line to set the tone.

To begin with, I was pissed at the offensive line. We're a well-coached, tough offensive line. There's a reason that we have the highest-paid offensive line in the league. They're good. But I'm watching the tape against Miami and it's like, we're doing okay. The guys they're blocking aren't making tackles, the guys are in the right spots, it's all technically right. But nobody is knocking anybody off the football. Nobody is really kicking ass. That's why I challenged them.

The other thing I said the night before we played Pittsburgh? I told the whole team that everything I said before the season, I truly believed. I said I thought we had the best team in football and I still believed it. I said I thought we'd be the champs and I still believed it. I thought we had the talent and the men to do it, to rally in any situation. But I told them I didn't think they believed it. I challenged them to be the team I believed we could be, but I wasn't seeing. I was emotional about it and we came out and bullied the Pittsburgh Steelers. We beat them up at their place.

Here's the other thing about that game. The Steelers went to a five-wide-receiver set to get going, and we have no defensive backs. We don't have enough. We're pulling guys out of the game and I'm down to like three calls on defense. That's a pretty helpless feeling. I'm watching them drive and it comes down to the wire. They had two plays from the 8-yard line and instinctively I want to blitz. I'm fighting myself not to call a blitz because we just didn't have the guys to do it. So on third down, we play coverage and hold them. After that play, I call all the guys over and say, "What do you think?" Remember, I believe that you don't go down without throwing a punch. That's just me and what I believe. But I know in my head the right call is to drop eight and play coverage. I got our secondary coach Dennis Thurman to the side of me. He said drop eight. Revis and all those guys, they are ready to do anything I ask them to do. They don't fight me. With Baltimore, you'd have Ray Lewis saying, "Let's do this, Rex." Sometimes I'd say, "Yeah, okay, Ray" and sometimes I'd say, "Just do what I'm saying, here's the call." I don't have that with these guys. But in my head I'm thinking, "Let's make Roethlisberger make the play to beat us. Make him read the coverage and make the throw." Let's not force the issue. So we drop eight and, sure as heck, we stop them again and it's like, "Oh my God, thank you."

After that game, I told Pittsburgh coach Mike Tomlin, "We're coming back." I told the team, make your mark on the schedule, we're coming back here. We felt that way about Pittsburgh.

We have two games left, the first one at Chicago and then the last game at Buffalo. But before we play Chicago, it wouldn't be the Jets' 2010 season without some weird thing happening, so this is the week that the story about me and my wife comes. Like I said at the time, this is a personal issue, so I'm not going to talk a lot about it. Unfortunately, this thing got out and it's everywhere. All I'll say is my wife and I have a great marriage and we love each other very much. No apologies for that.

So back to the season. We go to Chicago and we're ready to play, but a strange thing happens. We lose the game in exactly the opposite way that we lost to Miami two weeks earlier. Our offense was great. Sanchez was terrific, and we're scoring against a pretty good Bears defense. But our defense was just awful. I mean, we can't stop them and it is just a joke. We're losing jump balls in the end zone. It was just absurd. But, in a way, it was good for us, because all those defensive guys who were grousing about the offense after the Miami game really got the overall message I was selling. You win and lose as a team. It doesn't matter what the stats look like. If it was just about stats, I could tell you that I was really satisfied with how we played all those years I was in Baltimore. Statistically, we were good enough on defense to win the Super Bowl five times. I could sit back and say that I did what I was supposed to do, but that's not how you win. You win as a team, all the units, the coaches, everybody together, and you can't lose sight of that or it all falls apart.

Anyway, we finish out the season with a big 38-7 win against Buffalo and we're 11-5 on the season. And after a little sweating over how the other teams were going to finish, it's on to the playoffs for our second straight year. And all we end up facing along the way are three quarterbacks with a combined six Super Bowl titles and nine appearances. No big deal, right? Well, to make it more interesting, we also have to go on the road for each game.

The first stop is Indianapolis to face my old friend Peyton Manning, the guy who has twice kept me from getting to the Super Bowl, in my first year with the Jets and in 2006 with Baltimore. Again, the first thing I do this week is tell everybody that this matchup is personal between me and Peyton. Really, this guy has broken my heart. The first time we faced him with the Jets, we had a lead at halftime. In 2006, Baltimore had the best team in football. It wasn't even close, but the guy came up with all the crucial plays to beat us. So when I say it's personal between me and Peyton, I mean that. But the other reason I do it that way is it takes the focus off my players and allows them to relax and just get prepared. Think about it; there's 50 million people who are going to watch this game. There's all sorts of pressure on the guys in this situation. So I'm doing what I can to deflect the attention away from my players until we get to game day. If you can be loose and confident when you're preparing to play, you're going to play better. If you're nervous, you won't do well. It's like the guy standing over the five-foot putt. If he's uptight and nervous, he's going to miss it. If he's relaxed and loose, he's going to make it.

Everybody says I put too much pressure on myself by speaking brashly and making predictions. Look, I already know what's going to happen. If we lose, the papers are going to kill me, absolutely murder me for taking it on myself this way. But that's okay, because they're going to kill me if we lose anyway. I get paid the big bucks because this is what I do. I know if I can take it off my team and not get the guys caught up in all of it, they don't have to worry about all this other stuff. It's like in the week before the Pittsburgh game, none of us talked that much. When we lost, the media was still coming down hard on me, not the players. That's fine. I'm the guy who wrote "Soon To Be Champs." I'm the one who said we would win the Super Bowl.

As for Manning, we came up with a plan that we just weren't going to blitz him very much. We were going to sit in coverage and take away as much as we could. Look, if you blitz Manning a lot, eventually he's going to kill you. He's going to come up with an open receiver. You're not going to fool him. Plus, their receiving corps was banged up by then. No Dallas Clark, no Austin Collie, and Reggie Wayne was hurting. We felt like we could cover their guys. Now, they hit us on a couple of big plays to Pierre Garçon, but we basically did a great job of keeping everything in front of us. Of course, as the fourth quarter is ticking away, they end up getting the ball and driving for a go-ahead field goal with 57 seconds left. Along the way, we had to change up a little, because I didn't want him to be able to run the clock out and then just let their kicker, the great Adam Vinatieri, send us home.

So let's back up a few plays. We get to a second-and-9 situation with 1:10 remaining. The Colts are at our 35-yard line and we have all three time-outs remaining. I have to make sure they don't get another first down or we're really stuck for time. So this is when I decide it's time to blitz. We're going with a zero coverage (just man-to-man in the backfield, no one hanging back) and we're going to make Manning get the ball out of his hand as fast as possible, because we know he's not going to risk a sack at this spot of the field. He throws a short pass for a three-yard gain to the 32. The situation is pretty much the same on third-and-6, so we blitz again and force an incomplete. Perfect. Vinatieri hits the 50-yard field goal like it's a 20-yard attempt, straight down the middle. But that's okay, because we know we have enough time and time-outs to get a field goal. You've got to be confident you can do it in this situation, and I was confident in my guys. This was the money time.

On the kickoff, Cromartie does a great job to get out to our 46-yard line. Now, this is the time when Sanchez really steps up. For most of the game, he's been a little wild, but he really started to settle down in the second half. By this point, he's in a groove. He hits Braylon Edwards for nine and Santonio Holmes for 11. We run a dive play to catch the Colts off balance, but only get two yards and now we're at the Indianapolis 32 with 29 seconds left. We're in field-goal range, but we're right on the edge of it. I'm confident Nick Folk can make it, but the offensive guys come huddle with me on the sideline and they want to take a shot.

Braylon Edwards, who has been telling me all game that he's getting man coverage and can take his guy anytime, says he wants a long sideline route—and Sanchez is totally on page with him. So our offensive coordinator, Brian Schottenheimer, goes with the call. The guys run back in and Mark takes the snap, makes a beautiful pass down the right sideline and boom, Braylon pulls it in. We pick up 18 yards and we're on the 14-yard line. Folk ends up nailing the field goal to win it 17-16. Man, I finally got Manning, the guy who had been my kryptonite. I give him a lot of credit—he was really classy after the game. He came over to our team bus and talked to me for about 15 minutes, congratulating our team and the job we did. My son Seth came over and Manning invited Seth to his football camp. Total class act.

Believe me, in the NFL—and particularly in the playoffs—there's not much time to celebrate a huge win like this. We know we're going to New England for the next game. And I promise you, we laid it on the line against Indy—offensively, defensively, special teams, every phase of the game—just so we could go back to New England where we got our ass kicked. We did that for a reason. We knew we could beat the Patriots, even though they destroyed us that last game. Nobody on the outside thought we could beat that team, and nobody wanted to acknowledge that we had beaten them in Week 2. This is the one our entire team wanted.

Going into the New England game, just like our lead-up to Indianapolis, I had to find a way to distract our players, get their minds off the last game as much as possible. So, just like with Manning, I issue the challenge against Belichick. It's me vs. Belichick and it's personal again. Look, we were the only team out there that could beat the Patriots. So that was why I put it on me to challenge Belichick. Everybody was saying, "Oh, you don't challenge Belichick. You don't mess around with Jim," like the song goes. Well, I was his Slim that day. I respect him more than any coach in the league. He's completely dedicated, a great coach. But I was going to get him back.

During the week, we modified some of the things we did against

Indianapolis. Our plan was pretty much the same in terms of philosophy. We were going to play mostly coverage. We were going to mix in a few more blitzes, but it was really going to be a lot of loaded zones. We were going to make Tom Brady work his ass off. We were going to make him have to be perfect. And we were going to make him make mistakes. Without Randy Moss, the Patriots didn't have the same vertical threat in their offense, and we planned to show them how much that hurt their offense by constantly challenging the short stuff.

A couple of other things happened during the week. Of course, there was the stuff that New England wide receiver Wes Welker said about me and my wife. Look, it didn't bother me, I'm not going to let that affect me. But it did get Welker benched for the first series by Belichick, so I was fine with that. With Welker, there's a lot of good-natured talk that goes back and forth. I know that. He talks to us, and we talk to him about how we're going to knock him around all game. When I went to Hawaii, the kid came up and apologized to me and my wife. No hard feelings.

The other thing that happens is that, out of the blue, we get a jersey delivered to our offices. It's from former Jet defensive lineman Dennis Byrd, along with a letter from him. I get it on Friday and I read the letter and it's amazing. Turns out this is the jersey he was paralyzed in. I'm thinking to myself, "Why me? Why'd he pick me for this?" But it was amazing, about how proud he was of our team. Here's a guy who was paralyzed and taught himself to walk again. What a spirit that guy has. As soon as I see this stuff, I say, we gotta bring him to see the team. It's late Friday afternoon and he's in Oklahoma, but we have to get him here. His message was so humbling and so emotional. I had no idea how good he was going to be, but I had to have him.

So we get him to the team hotel on Saturday and I meet him like an hour before he's going to talk to the team. He looks at me and says, "Rex, what do you want me to say?" I said, "I want you to say what's in your heart, nothing else. I'm not telling you what to say." So he got up there and he talked about how much he'd like to play just one more play and how he had never gotten a chance to speak to a group of men who could be world champions before, but we had that kind of ability. He was apologizing because he couldn't walk so well. I'm like, please, this guy shouldn't even be walking, but his faith and determination got him back on his feet.

We played a little clip of Dennis from when he was a Jet. The room was dead quiet, totally silent. His message got through so strong. The next day, we wanted him to lead us out onto the field, but the league wouldn't go along with it. So instead we had a special Byrd jersey made up—an authentic game jersey exactly like the ones our guys were wearing that day—and our captains carried it out to midfield for the coin toss. It was deep, really emotional.

Then, of course, the battle begins, and we played great. We were so jacked to play that game. Our defensive game plan was so strong. I wasn't going to get outcoached again. I owed Belichick on this one. We got embarrassed the last time. We got humiliated. Don't think for a second that wasn't what they were trying to do before. I'm the wrong guy to do that to. That's why I challenged Belichick. Nobody does that. He's the greatest coach ever, and people don't normally call him out. You slip at all, he'll beat you. It's true. But I said from day one, I came here to kick his ass, not to kiss it, and that's what I'm going to do.

———

I knew the Patriots were concerned about me and this football team. I'm the guy and we're the team they didn't want to face. As I said, we were the only ones who could beat them. Trust me, Pittsburgh was the happiest team in the world when we beat New England, because the Patriots would have spread them out and beat the crap out of the Steelers. Of course, everybody saw how happy I was after that touchdown by Shonn Greene. He scored and I took off after him into the end zone, showing off the speed that turned me into a coach. I'd like to call that running, but whatever. Actually, I had slipped on the ice earlier that week and banged up my leg, which is why I was limping so much. But the speed? No, I have none of that.

After the game, Belichick was great. He came up to me and said, "That was an unbelievable coaching job; you deserve it and I hope you win the whole thing." He really said that, and I could tell he was sincere. People get the wrong message sometimes when I talk about Belichick. I really do respect him. I admire the guy. He has his way of doing things and he stays true to it every single week. I do the same thing, although we're different types of people in a lot of ways. I may be loud and over-the-top, but we do have similarities. You're not going to find two more competitive people.

Finally, it's on to Pittsburgh, just like I predicted after we beat them in December. Now, a lot of people say that we were flat in that game because we didn't have any swagger during the week. We didn't talk much. Really, what was I going to say? We had already spent everything we had those first two weeks and the Steelers are different. Yeah, I lost to them a few years ago in the AFC Championship Game when I was in Baltimore and that sucked, but my players didn't have anything to do with that. At least not most of them. There was no real connection like there was with Indy and New England.

People have made a lot out of us deferring after winning the coin toss and allowing Pittsburgh to have the ball first, like we somehow challenged the Steelers and got them psyched up. Look, with our defense, we're going to defer all the time. And it wasn't that we were flat. What really happened is that we didn't execute. Defensively, we get a penalty on the first third down of the game. If they go three and out, it's going to be a different game, but they don't. They go right down the field with a long drive and that sets the tone for the first half. We couldn't get anything going on offense — in fact, that sack-strip for a touchdown by Pittsburgh to make it 24-0 really hurt at the end of the first half — and they keep pounding away because we can't tackle. There was one play where we have them stopped for a two-yard loss in the backfield and they break free for a nine-yard gain. Just sloppy.

At halftime, we're down 24-3 and I just ripped the defense, tore into them. I said, "How about this for a halftime adjustment—how about tackling some motherfucker, because there's nothing wrong with the scheme!" I put in one or two different calls, but really it was like, "Let's go play like Jets and tackle someone. How about we do that?" Then, I said, we can still win this game. This isn't the first time we've been down. Let's go win this. So we go out there and we started coming back. The Steelers are going to be tight as hell over on the other side, and that's what happened, and the game really started to flip. We had 50 yards of offense in the first half and 239 in the second half. Same goes for them. They had 231 in the first half and only 56 in the second. Roethlisberger's quarterback rating for the game was 35, and Sanchez's was 102. Everybody talks about the great game Ben had, but the facts are way different.

Of course, Roethlisberger did hit that huge pass on third down that allowed them to run out the clock on us. Funny thing is, we had a guy come off coverage and let that happen. Ben couldn't have found black in a field of white mice at the time. He was throwing passes up all over the place at that time. Again, I was thinking about blitzing, but then I thought no. They came out in five wide and he wanted to throw it to the open side. Sure as shit, he threw it to the open side, and we should have had two guys there, but one guy came off coverage. If he stays in coverage, it's either intercepted or Ben has to throw it away. I don't know why our guy came off coverage, but he did. Maybe he thought Ben was going to scramble because he did earlier in the game, but the rule is that you stay in coverage until the quarterback crosses the line. Our guy just came up too quick. That allowed Ben to make the throw, and that's what I have to live with. For the third year in a row, I lost in the AFC Championship Game.

After that, I just watched the Super Bowl at home. I'm only going to the Super Bowl if my dad or my brother is in it. It's too painful. We don't even do a party at the house. I thought Green Bay was going to have the upper hand on Pittsburgh. Their passing attack was giving everyone problems. But I truly believe we would have beaten Green

Bay. We only lost to them 9-0 during the season, and we gave them two of the field goals because of mistakes.

The bottom line for me and the Jets is, we'll get there. We're right there now, and everybody knows it. That's why I don't back down when people ask if we're going to win the Super Bowl. The answer is yes. We're going to do it. I don't think we need anything. I said when I took the job that I want every player in the National Football League to want to play for the Jets, and I want every coach in the league to want to coach for the Jets, and we're well on our way. There's not a player in the league who wouldn't be happy to play for us in New York. I think that's going to give us some opportunities.

I'll go into next season with the same mind-set I've had since I got here: We plan to win. I'll underline it. I go into every game thinking that. There's no way, as a competitor, that you go in thinking that you can't win. In fact, the day I stop wanting to compete—to be the very best—I'll know it and I'll get out.

Until then, you can count on my teams to play like they mean it. And to have a lot of fun doing it. I look at my career so far and I feel tremendous pride. A lot has been accomplished. I also feel like one hell of a lucky guy. I've loved football since I was a kid, and here I am, the head coach of a great NFL franchise with a fantastic future. I'm grateful for the players I've been able to coach, the coaches I get to work with every day, and the unbelievable fans who energize the Jets in ways they probably don't realize. I'm grateful that I have guys like Woody Johnson and Mike Tannenbaum next to me.

I'm ready to start a new season right now . . . today. I know the New York Jets are an elite team—a team to beat—and I know I'll have a hard time sitting still until we can get out there and start bringing some huge hits and making big plays. Certainly, there will be more changes and more challenges as we get ready for next season. There will be roster moves, tough decisions. There will be coaching staff changes. Over these first two amazing years as head coach, I've learned that change is a guarantee. How we handle those changes will define us.

But if you're a Jets fan, there's one thing I will promise you: Everything we do, everything I do, will be to make sure that we bring the Lombardi Trophy home. I said it the week after we lost to the Steelers and I'll say it every time I'm asked. . . . This team is soon to be Champs!

Acknowledgments

This book would not have been possible without the time, talents, and patience of a lot of people.

First and foremost, I've got to thank everyone at the Jets organization for supporting me and this project, and for making themselves available to meet with my writing crew as we crafted this book.

Woody Johnson, the greatest owner in the NFL, made time in his busy schedule to talk with us and offer some great glimpses into the inner workings of the team. He also trusted me enough to write this book, and I respect that.

Mike Tannenbaum, our general manager, was also great about giving his time and sharing his insights, and I'm very grateful to him for that.

Bruce Speight, the public relations director for the Jets, was a huge help as well. I really need to thank everyone in his department; they do a phenomenal job for us every day and they don't always get the credit they deserve.

Laura Young, my right hand, has got to be one of the most long-suffering and accommodating people on earth. The work she put into lining up all the interviews and meetings is really what allowed this book to get off the ground.

My assistant coaches and players were wonderful, too, and I know I'm the luckiest SOB in all of professional football for the people I work with every day. I am so proud to be a Jet, and I hope that each one of my guys knows how happy I am to have him on my team.

I need to thank the folks at HBO for all their work on *Hard Knocks*, which really helped our season start off with a bang. The show gives fans a great look into the inner workings of a team, and I'm so glad they decided to profile the Jets this year.

Ian Kleinert, the agent for the book and a hell of a nice guy, did a bang-up job matching me with Doubleday, the best and bravest publishing house out there.

Jason Kaufman at Doubleday is the best editor ever, and I want to send out a huge thanks to his crew: his able assistant Rob Bloom, and the talented legal and copyediting team. I know this wasn't the easiest project you've ever had to work on, and I just wanted to let you know how deeply I appreciate everything you did. This book would not have happened without you, and I really can't begin to tell you how much I appreciate your patience and dedication. You went above and beyond. From the bottom of my heart, thank you.

There are some great writers who cover the Jets for the New York–area media, and their good work served as quite an amazing foundation for several portions of this project.

The writing team Don Yaeger put together of Jason Cole, Kalil Conway, Tiffany Brooks, and Jim Henry really attacked this project with all their energy, and it shows. Their help was instrumental in bringing together all the different parts needed to make this book work.

To my family: Michelle, Payton, and Seth—thank you all for your love, patience, and support. You're the greatest family anyone could ask for, and you're a hell of a lot better than I deserve. I love you all more than I can put into words.

To my brother Rob, who is now with the Cowboys—I am so proud to be your twin (and I'm sorry, again, about that press conference). To my brother Jim, thanks for putting up with all my antics and for being such a strong figure and someone I was always able to look up to. To my mom, Doris, you are the single most patient mother I know, and I am so thankful for everything you did to help me get to this point. To my step-mother, Joanie, for taking us in and treating us like your own. And to the one and only Buddy Ryan, you have been not only an amazing father but an amazing mentor. Thank you for teaching me all you know about coaching and for opening so many doors through your brilliant mind and unique leadership.

And, finally, to all the Jets fans out there: Thank you for your tireless support and enthusiasm. You are the greatest fans in the NFL, and without you, I don't have a job. Thanks for believing in your Jets. We've got a championship coming, and I can't wait to celebrate it with you!

Index